The last Yugoslav generation

MANCHESTER
1824

Manchester University Press

The last Yugoslav generation

The rethinking of youth politics and cultures in late socialism

Ljubica Spaskovska

Manchester University Press

Published by Manchester University Press
Altrincham Street, Manchester M1 7JA, UK
www.manchesteruniversitypress.co.uk

British Library Cataloguing-in-Publication Data is available

ISBN 978 1 5261 0631 5 *hardback*
ISBN 978 1 5261 0632 2 *paperback*

First published by Manchester University Press in hardback 2019

This edition published 2020

Typeset by Out of House Publishing

For my parents

Contents

Figures

Tables

Acknowledgements

At the children's summer camp on Prespa Lake in 1991, the Yugoslav flag was still high up on the mast. The hostel bore the name of a young Macedonian revolutionary and poet Mite Bogoevski, a 'People's Hero' who died in 1942 at the age of twenty-three. We were kept entertained during the long summer evenings by singing competitions, fancy dress parties, disco nights, and although my close friend Jelena and I held a grudge for being sent 'to the lake' that year (a mere three hours away on the bus, whilst the previous summer the two of us had spent three weeks at a children's summer camp in northern Croatia and a whole day on an adventurous train journey to get there), we had a lot of fun and were oblivious to what was going on elsewhere in Yugoslavia. In fact, we were quite eager to wear our red pioneer scarves, while the teachers seemed not to care much and kept repeating that parading our socialist rite-of-passage tokens was 'optional'. One evening, our teacher asked me if I could read out 'YUTEL's Appeal for Peace' at the evening stage, before the start of the scheduled entertainment programme. I still remember the page-long, old-fashioned blue typescript and the sheer disbelief at the prospect of war the text talked about. The following year my girl friends and I were the first to join 'The First Children's Embassy in the World – Megjashi (FCEWM)' which aided and provided shelter for children refugees from the Bosnian war. After 1992, although it still seemed that the past was not a wholly foreign country, it nonetheless became a distant place where things were indeed done differently. Yet, music remained a binding thread and my generation grew up with the Yugoslav punk/rock bands which had risen to fame during the 1980s. We had a secret admiration for the older punks who used to congregate at an outdoor concrete stage in Skopje downtown and although we did everything to emulate their style – to the horror of our parents – we only admired them from afar. So, when I first visited London in 1998, I went straight to Piccadilly to see what I had hoped would be the authentic children of punk. It did come as a surprise when they asked me for a fiver if I wanted to take a photo of them. Although we ridiculed 1980s fashion, the music and some of the cultural icons that had marked the decade stayed with my generation, while the political turmoil of the 1980s and some of the protagonists continue to haunt the post-Yugoslav region in different ways.

This book has been inspired by the numerous conversations I had both with my interviewees and my friends, acquaintances, relatives and colleagues who had the experience of having studied or lived in Yugoslavia. I am deeply grateful for my interviewees' kindness, time and willingness to share their thoughts and memories. This project would not have been possible without a generous fellowship I was awarded by the History Department at the University of Exeter and in particular without the invaluable support and guidance of Professor James Mark. Professor Florian Bieber of the University of Graz, Professor Sabina Mihelj of Loughborough University and Dr Jasna Dragovic-Soso of Goldsmiths, University of London also provided invaluable insight and advice at various stages. My former colleagues and friends from the University of Edinburgh-based project on the 'Europeanisation of citizenship in the successor states of the former Yugoslavia' (CITSEE) have been very supportive. I am grateful to Professor Jo Shaw and Dr Igor Štiks, as well as to Jelena Đankić, Dejan Stjepanović, Julija Sardelić, Nataša Pantić and Yorgos Karagiannakis, who have been great, good-humoured colleagues and friends in Edinburgh. I am also grateful to Professor Dejan Jović from Zagreb for kindly allowing me access to material from his personal archive.

The employees at the National Library in Belgrade, the Central Military Library in Skopje, the Peace Institute in Ljubljana and at the Archives in Belgrade, Skopje, Sarajevo and Ljubljana have been extremely kind and helpful. Friends and colleagues from across the post-Yugoslav region have been kind to help me in terms of logistics or host me during my field research. I am indebted to Vladimir Mandičevski-Mande, Tanja Petrović, Jelena Vasiljević, Vesna Vasiljević, Elmina Hadžić, Viktor Koska, Vladimir Rajtar and Tomo Pavlovski. I am particularly delighted that the photographs in the book are by photographers from 'the last Yugoslav generation' who began their careers in the 1980s – I am deeply grateful to Milomir Kovačević – Strašni, Jože Suhadolnik and Šahin Šišić. Robert Botteri, Zemira Alajbegović, Milan Lišanin, Dr Risto Ivanov and Simo Spaskovski were also kind to contribute their own photographs.

My partner Gëzim Krasniqi has been by my side in the best and the worst of times. I am grateful for his moral support, academic insight and our passionate debates on the labyrinths of Yugoslav history. Finally, it was my parents' generation that I wanted to understand and dissect. They have been a constant source of both inspiration and unconditional support. Our numerous conversations about the past, their courage and determination not to compromise their moral principles and values in turbulent times were crucial in instilling a fascination with the (post-)Yugoslav region and its diversity.

Abbreviations

GDR	German Democratic Republic
HDZ	Hrvatska demokratska zajednica [Croatian Democratic Union]
HOSI	Homosexuelle Initiative
ILGA	International Lesbian, Gay, Bisexual, Trans and Intersex Association
ILIS	International Lesbian Information Service
IUS	International Union of Students
JNA	Jugoslovenska Narodna Armija [Yugoslav People's Army]
JUPIO	Jugoslovenski program za istraživanje omladine [Yugoslav program for research of the youth]
LL	Lesbian Lilith
MKC	Младински културен центар [Youth Cultural Centre – Skopje]
ONO & DS	Opštenarodna odbrana i društvena samozaštita [General People's Defence and Social Self-Protection]
OOUR	Osnovna organizacija udruženog rada [Basic organisation of associated labour]
RK	Republička Konferencija [Republic's Conference]
SAP	Socijalistička autonomna pokrajina [Socialist Autonomous Province]
SDA	Stranka demokratske akcije [Party for Democratic Action]
SFRY	Socialist Federative Republic of Yugoslavia
SKC	Studentski kulturni centar [Student Cultural Centre – Belgrade]
SKJ	Savez komunista Jugoslavije [League of Communists of Yugoslavia]
ŠKUC	Študentski kulturni center [Ljubljana Student Cultural Centre]
SSMM	Сојуз на социјалистичка младина на Македонија [League of Socialist Youth of Macedonia]

SSO	Savez Socijalističke omladine [League of Socialist Youth]
SSOJ	Savez Socijalističke omladine Jugoslavije [League of Socialist Youth of Yugoslavia]
SSRNJ	Socijalistički Savez radnog naroda Jugoslavije [Socialist Alliance of the Working People of Yugoslavia]
UJDI	Udruženje za jugoslovensku demokratsku inicijativu [Association for Yugoslav Democratic Initiative]
ZSMS	Zveza socialistične mladine Slovenije [League of Socialist Youth of Slovenia]

Introduction: revisiting the 1980s through a generation lens

Education and schooling stand on the basis of achievements of modern science, and particularly on the basis of Marxism, as the foundation of scientific socialism, which serves to train workers for the working process, self-government and their education in the light of the victories of the socialist revolution, socialist ethics, self-management democracy, socialist patriotism, brotherhood and unity and equality of nations and nationalities and socialist internationalism.

The Constitution of the Socialist Federal
Republic of Yugoslavia, 1974

Post-Yugoslav culture has been fascinated by the generational story of those who left their mark on the last Yugoslav decade. An impressive number of documentary films, books, exhibitions and plays have been produced since the early 2000s which in one way or the other deal with the popular youth culture of the last Yugoslav decade and with the generation which experienced the violent dissolution of the state in their late twenties and early- to mid-thirties.[1] Authored by the protagonists themselves or by individuals who witnessed the events, this explosion of interest in a particular generational story and subsequently in Yugoslav late socialist culture, demonstrate a need for self-reflexivity that could be interpreted as an urge to reflect back on the last Yugoslav decade and its legacies and make sense of the social rupture caused by the break-up of socialist Yugoslavia.[2]

The last Yugoslav decade saw a challenge to established norms and practices in late Yugoslav politics, media and culture unfolding within the institutional youth sphere. This book addresses the experiences and work of the activists and the more prominent representatives of the last Yugoslav generation within the broad framework of the League of Socialist Youth of Yugoslavia [SSOJ; *Savez socijalističke omladine Jugoslavije/Сојуз на социјалистичката младина на Југославија/Zveza socialistične mladine Jugoslavije/Lidhja e rinisë socialiste të Jugosllavisë*]

	- SSO of Bosnia- Herzegovina - SSO of Croatia - SSO of Kosovo - SSO of Macedonia - SSO of Montenegro - SSO of Serbia - SSO of Slovenia - SSO of Vojvodina - SSO in the Yugoslav People's Army (re-introduced in1974)	Republic conference
The League of Socialist Youth of Yugoslavia		Basic organisation Municipal/city organisation University organisation
	Collective/interest- based members	- Youth Hostelling League - Music Youth - People's Engineering - Red Cross - Scouts' League - League of Organisations for Physical Education - Pioneers' League - Esperanto League

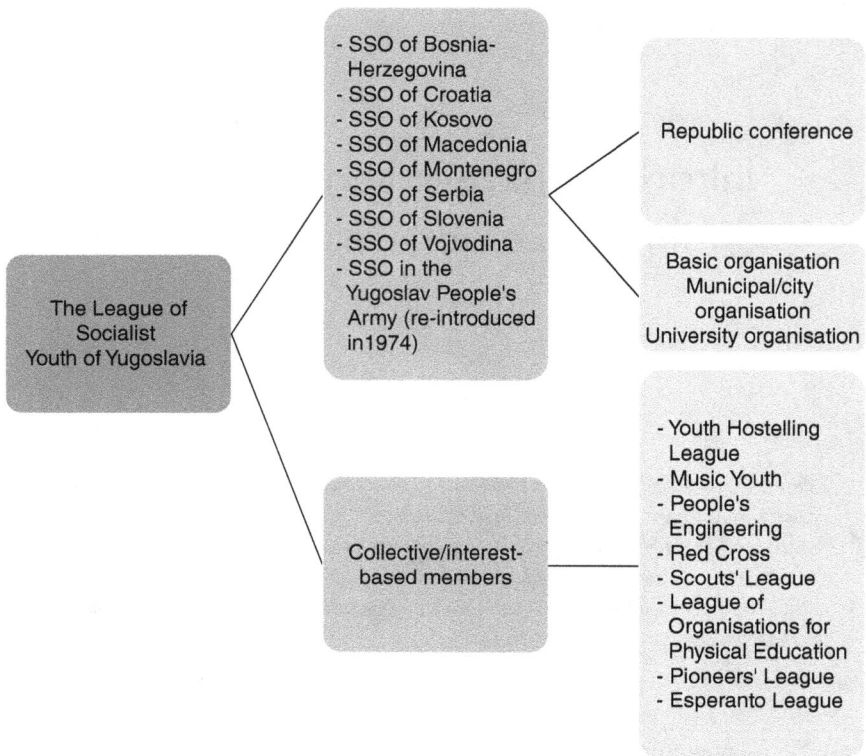

Figure 1 Structure of the SSOJ

(see Figure 1). By combining oral history interviews and archival and other primary material the book seeks to map both the institutional youth sphere and the lived histories of the last Yugoslav generation. The generational lens is used to provide new insights into the decline of socialism and the collapse of socialist Yugoslavia. It shows that the youth's challenge to the socialism of the older generation was an important feature of 1980s Yugoslavia and that there was a deep commitment to the reforming (and not the dismantling) of the federation, based both on leftist and liberal principles.

The book contributes to the literature on late Cold War challenges to state socialism, in that it examines a case in which nearly all of the dissenting political and cultural projects were contained within institutional structures. Amidst a rich body of literature dealing with late socialist Yugoslavia and its eventual demise, few depart from the realm of high politics and even fewer scrutinise the ways the multi-level crisis affected a particular group – in this case the youth and young adults – and how it shaped the group's understanding of the state and of its role in it. The book attempts to blur the line between what is considered 'alternative', 'oppositional' versus 'institutional' or 'official', by shedding light on the intricacies in the youth's interaction with the state and on the inner dynamics of the wide youth infrastructure, which was a product of the particular Yugoslav institutional arrangements and the doctrine of self-management. Hence, it maintains that the League of Socialist Youth still represented a location for real meaningful politics. Consequently, research focusing less on dissidence and resistance and more on adaptation within existing institutional structures could provide new insights and open up new venues within the field of socialist studies. Furthermore, the book seeks to deconstruct labels such as 'anti-Yugoslav' and contextualise particular acts, demands and initiatives.

Scholarly literature on Yugoslavia views the 1980s primarily as the prelude to the violent dissolution of the country and has generally dealt with the end of Yugoslavia as a *fait accompli*. The political trajectories of the major actors in the break-up, as well as the major political events, are well mapped and have been subject of a range of studies and approaches,[3] as scholars were initially interested in uncovering the roots of the demise of the country. However, few academic works have shifted the focus away from the institutional/political sphere and attempted to explore the inner dynamics of parts of 1980s Yugoslav society on its own terms without necessarily framing it within the dissolution narrative.[4] Indeed, the existence of alternatives and other attempts at rethinking the Yugoslav framework have been overshadowed by an imperative to explain the violent break-up and establish the major reasons behind it. However, more recently the field has begun to expand beyond the dissolution/ethno-nationalism paradigm, although many authors still choose to analyse only one of the former Yugoslav republics or regions.[5]

This is one of the first attempts to explore this alternative world of 1980s Yugoslavia through a generational lens, taking the variety of political and cultural projects that sought to redefine – but not destroy – the Yugoslav project. Focusing on the politically and culturally prominent amongst this younger generation, the book addresses how the Yugoslav youth in the 1980s attempted to rearticulate, question and rethink Yugoslav socialism and the very notion of Yugoslavism. Contestation and negotiation were intricately mixed, as the Yugoslav youth elite of the 1980s essentially strove to decouple Yugoslavism and dogmatic socialism. They framed their artistic, media or political activism as targeting certain prescribed norms, particular malfunctions of the system, or the older elite – rather than as strictly anti-institutional or anti-Yugoslav.

While acknowledging the essential fact that there were prominent differences in social status, education, ethnic/religious belonging, gender and/or profession, the book departs from the idea that this generation was marked in different ways by the 'historical trauma' of the Yugoslav collapse and the subsequent wars, while in their earlier or later formative years they were all exposed to the omnipresent discourse and reality of a multi-level crisis. Broadly, the book explores the last Yugoslav generation during the last Yugoslav decade 1981–91 within the broad framework of the institutional youth realm – the extended network of the League of Socialist Youth of Yugoslavia (SSOJ). It focuses on individuals born between 1954 and 1969, who belonged in the category of youth (16–28) at some point during the 1980s, born to parents who belonged to the 'first Yugoslav generation'. Although the last Yugoslav generation is approached as a socio-political generation that spans several biological generations, the members of which experienced the 1991–92 historical juncture as young adults, it is evident that there are two distinct cohorts within it: the older born in the mid- to late-1950s and the younger born after 1960.

The individuals who in the 1980s were involved at different levels in the youth organisation constitute an undeniably heterogeneous group. Yet, two more or less clearly delineated groups emerge: one constituted by the youth functionaries, which at that time were openly criticised for the numerous privileges they enjoyed, and the other camp of more non-conformist, intellectually oriented youngsters who were part of the wide range of related youth organisations and bodies (magazines, newspapers, cultural clubs and centres, publishing and research centres, etc.). Many of those who held important positions within the youth organisation would pursue political careers after 1991. Although the principal carrier of the dissolution and the post-socialist transition was the 'post-war generation' of older socialist elites, there were some of the younger youth functionaries who joined the reformed communists (in Macedonia, Serbia and Montenegro) or entered politics through newly-established parties (such as in Slovenia, Macedonia and Bosnia-Herzegovina). The 'progressive' stream, which both within the youth organisation and in culture embraced different liberal, civic ideas or articulated apolitical voices of rebelliousness and anti-war activism, generally remained marginal and sidelined during and after the dissolution. Nevertheless, they were visible in the political youth sphere at the end of the 1980s and especially prominent in the realm of 1980s youth media and culture.

The book also seeks to provide a pan-Yugoslav perspective. Most work which has dealt with late socialist culture has done so through case studies of particular republics – an approach which has often been the product of a post-socialist and post-Yugoslav retrospective determinism, or, indeed, 'methodological nationalism'.[6] The observation that 'The social sciences have become obsessed with describing processes within nation-state boundaries as contrasted with those outside, and have correspondingly lost sight of the connections between such nationally defined territories' might not ring true for all area studies, but it is a valid observation in the context of Yugoslav studies. Research which has focused on youth politics and culture in late socialist Yugoslavia has tended to concentrate on Slovenia,[7] generally internalising the narrative of the developed, democratic North and the under-developed, conservative South and the peculiarity of the Slovenian case in comparison to the other parts of Yugoslavia. As it has been argued, 'Not only a gap was widening in Yugoslavia between the north, which was slowly entering the post-industrial age, and the south, which was remaining or drifting back into premodern times, but a similar gap was emerging between the urbanites and the peasants, workers, and petty bureaucrats'.[8] By taking a broader frame, the book engages with important questions about the evolution of Yugoslav youth culture and politics as a whole in the 1980s. It addresses, for instance, the extent to which there was a fragmentation of the institutional youth realm at the end of the decade along national/republican lines. Did political and cultural divides within republics, or links across republican borders, remain equally important? Did the *de facto* confederal institutional set-up of socialist Yugoslavia, which meant that most of the youth did not for the most part engage with the federal level, imply that republican centres remained heavily bounded spaces for activism, and that attempts at rethinking Yugoslav politics, culture and identity were always limited by the reality of the particular republic? Or, did trans-republican reformist or liberal networks, which cut across these ethno-national divisions, remain important? Acts of 'trans-national cross-fertilisation'[9] have generally been overlooked or over-shadowed by an emphasis on growing friction and inability to reach any type of consensus in the 1980s. The same is valid for the various articulations of Yugoslavism in a context where the Yugoslav identification was politically and practically discouraged. Hence, the book explores the idea that comparisons across republican lines and a pan-Yugoslav approach enables us to trace the mutual influences, interactions and debates in the youth sphere seen through its wide institutional network of the SSOJ, especially in the light of the various attempts at youth reform across the different federal units.

Adopting a generational lens gives fresh perspectives on the decline of state socialism, as in the realm of post-socialist studies there has been an increased interest in examining the rise and fall of socialism in Eastern Europe in generational terms.[10] By analysing a particular social group, it is possible to view the exit from socialism in other ways and challenge the teleological accounts of socialism's decline and Yugoslavia's collapse. More specifically, it enables us to examine the experience of crisis. This book embeds the 'last Yugoslav generation' within the discourse of crisis that marked Yugoslav late socialism. It designates three prominent generational markers of the 'crisis generation' (*generacija krize*) – the multi-level economic and political crisis, internationalism/Europeanism, and a new understanding of Yugoslavism as citizenship in its dimensions of rights and identity.[11] A 1986 federal research survey on Yugoslav youth noted that Yugoslav society was witnessing the proliferation of a 'non-classical political generation' [*neklasična politička generacija*], 'a generation which desires and brings along *changes*',[12] while a 1988 study referred to it as a 'new political generation'.[13] This underpins the notion that a generation which rose to prominence as the new decade and the post-Tito era were dawning had been socialised differently and was bound to bring change in advance of that actually materialising. I map the first level – the generation of the crisis – as something that occurred as a process of external labeling, the second level – Europeanism/internationalism – as a generational consciousness, a dominant way of self-narration and self-perception within European/global frameworks, and finally the third level – layered Yugoslavism – intricately related to the second as a form of self-definition, i.e. what I observe as this generation's new 'sense of citizenship'[14] and differently conceptualised activism which sought to rearticulate socialism and Yugoslavism. Hence, the first generational pillar as identified here, which revolves around the notion of 'crisis', reflects the dominant scholarly/sociological observations with regard to the Yugoslav youth dating from the period under scrutiny, i.e. the 1980s; the second generational pillar relates to this generation's own sense of Europeanism/cosmopolitanism/internationalism as conveyed at the time by its representatives and as construed by its members *a posteriori* in the post-socialist period; the third generational pillar complements the previous two with my own reading of this generation's new forms of youth activism and engagement with/perception of the state.

The citizenship lens is employed because it is useful for accounting for social and political activism and its relation to space in late socialism, as it elucidates one significant dimension of the youth's engagement with the state in the 1980s – negotiation, pragmatism and challenge from within. The debates concerning the reform and future of Yugoslav socialism which unfolded in the political realm in the 1980s have been mapped by numerous scholars who chose to engage with the political history of late socialist Yugoslavia. The book seeks to elucidate both the similarities and the differences between the debates on the future of Yugoslavia and Yugoslav socialism in the youth and the political realms. Essentially, it addresses the specificities of what was seen as a generational challenge to an 'ageing' socialist system embodied by an older elite.

As I explore below, the idea that this challenge to established notions of the Yugoslav project was generational was noted at the time both by youth and external observers. For instance, the idea of a new generation that would bring forward significant changes was current in contemporary international and domestic political/scholarly discourse. As the 1980 UNESCO report on youth noted:

Finally, it should be recalled that the youth of the 1980s are the children of the youth of the 1960s … The new generation faces a considerable challenge in carrying their parents' hopes and dreams into an economically inhospitable future. Many argue that the new generation is more realistic and less utopian than the generation that came before it. It may be suggested, however, that the sobering tasks and even the defeats that confronted their parents never eclipsed a belief in real progress towards justice, equality and peace.[15]

New ideas about the socialist project, about the extent of media freedoms, and notions of Yugoslavism were for the most part concentrated in critiques advanced by a younger age cohort who had been socialised in the 1960s and 1970s, and within an institutional space devoted to socialisation of the young – the SSOJ. The book maintains that a generational approach provides new insights into the processes of remaking/rethinking and decline in late socialism. The younger generation was not central to negotiating the dissolution, yet some of its representatives were at the forefront of trying to rethink Yugoslav socialist federalism. The stretching of the boundaries of media freedom – a phenomenon led by the youth press – is one among many examples of the inner dynamics of transformation of late socialist Yugoslav society led by a younger cohort. Furthermore, a generational lens provides insight into new forms of political expression in the 1980s, some of which found shelter within the different parts of the youth organisation and (re)shaped youth journalism and the youth press as a space for debate and contention.

In this sense, this book draws upon the work by Karl Mannheim, who advanced new understandings of how generational cohorts form. His seminal essay posits generation as 'nothing more than a particular kind of identity of location, embracing related "age groups" embedded in a historical-social process'.[16] Later studies, however, proposed that the problem of generations could be summarised as one of the 'linkage of personal time (the life cycle) and social time (history)',[17] i.e. that one sociological (or what one may call historical) generation may in fact encompass many biological generations, since age groups[18] are not to be identified with generations. Given that 'generation' is a subject of study in history, sociology, anthropology and politics, it is often an elusive, slippery concept that requires more precise definition depending on the context of analysis.

Few scholars have drawn on Mannheim's insights – whether explicitly or implicitly – in framing Yugoslav history in generational terms. From this outlook, socialist Yugoslavia becomes a generational project of a combined revolutionary and partisan generation – the older cohort (born at the end of the nineteenth and the first decade of the twentieth century) which led the underground communist movement in the interwar period and the revolutionary liberation struggle during the Second World War and drafted the socio-political contours of the new federation; and the younger cohort of revolutionaries who joined the partisan guerillas led by Tito as youths. Although few of them were still active in the late Yugoslav political scene in the 1980s (such as Minister of Defence and first general of the army Veljko Kadijević, born 1925), the positions of power were in general held by the 'post-war generation', that is the first Yugoslav generation of individuals who did not have any conscious personal experience of the Second World War. Indeed, what has been referred to as 'a generational shift within the regional party leaderships'[19] took place gradually in the second half of the 1980s in different federal units as well as at the level of federal leadership. Beside Slovenian Milan Kučan (born 1941), Azem Vllasi (born 1948) also took the helm of the League of Communists of Kosovo in 1986, and Slobodan Milošević (born 1941) took over the Serbian Party branch in 1987. A number of scholars have attempted to build these generational frames into their understanding of politics in the 1980s. As Lenard Cohen observed, for example:

> The ascendancy of the post-partisan elite generation to the highest level of the political hierarchy received striking recognition at the 13th Congress of the Yugoslav League of Communists in June 1986. Thus, while 58 percent of the former Central Committee elected in 1982 had participated in the National Liberation War, this was true of only 24 percent of the 1986 Committee … Forty years after founding the communist regime, Tito's 'younger' comrades-in-arms were relinquishing the country's highest positions to a new political generation.[20]

In addition, Cohen underlined 'the juxtaposition of different generational cohorts, with different formative experiences and different levels and types of skills'.[21] Nebojša Vladisavljević also used these generational frames to make sense of political change in the 1980s:

> Members of the younger generation had very different formative experiences, values and skills from the old guard, which inevitably affected the general direction of policy, relations within the political class and state-society relations. Unlike members of the old guard, most were well educated, with a background in administration, business or local politics … priorities gradually shifted toward economic reform, more open intra-party debates, the relaxation of repression and more autonomy for low- and middle-ranking party and state officials.[22]

Nevertheless, in the Yugoslav political and public/media scene in the second half of the 1980s, three different political generations were present, more often than not with different and conflicting visions. Although there was a shared consensus that the Yugoslav socialist framework needed reform, consensus on the way it should be achieved, the scope of reform and the particulars of it could not be reached. This study seeks to offer insight into the most junior of the three generations, which was at the forefront of trying to rethink the Yugoslav project, attempted to reform certain aspects of the system and believed in its reformability much longer than members of a young cohort in other parts of Eastern Europe. By ushering in new grievances, envisaging new solutions and a new understanding of the polity the previous two generations had built, it searched for both liberal and leftist models to do so. Thus, the book seeks to reinforce the idea that alternatives did exist in the 1980s.

The book does not overlook the diversity of outlooks within a particular generation, i.e. what Mannheim referred to as 'generational units'.[23] The ensuing chapters look both at the divisive and the cohesive points among the youth functionaries, the young journalists, the youth in the alternative culture circles, or the army youth. In this sense, the idea of generation does not simply describe an age cohort shaped by similar life experiences, but also the emergence of a consciousness of belonging to an age-determined group, even amongst groups with seemingly different political or social views. Here the book draws on more recent constructivist work in generation studies, which explores the construction of the feeling of belonging to a generation within groups over time to a far greater degree than Mannheim attempted.[24]

Second, a generational lens is important because *generational discourse* was a central feature of public and political understandings of youth, as well as of the Yugoslav research on youth in general. In the 1980s, this was constructed by academic and public discourse as a 'crisis generation', or, indeed, as a generation that will bring changes.[25] It is important to note that the generational lens was appropriated by many, if not all, scholarly studies on the youth in socialist Yugoslavia – the terms used were *(mlada) generacija* or *pokoljenje*. It has been observed that the generation concept was one of the preferred analytical lenses among Yugoslav scholars because it was understood as oppositional to the Marxist class paradigm.[26] Even the 1986 all-Yugoslav youth research clearly referred to Mannheim's terminology and stated as one of its goals the description of the 'characteristics of the different *generation units* which might exist within this generation'.[27] Nevertheless, few have taken up this conceptual apparatus to analyse the story of post-Second World War Yugoslavia. Many studies which have dealt with youth and generation originate from the socialist period. Yugoslav sociologist Djordjije Uskoković,[28] for instance, argued that one can observe the existence of three dominant generations in socialist Yugoslavia: the war generation – which took part in the anti-fascist revolution and began the rebuilding of the state; the post-war generation, which mainly came of age in the 1950s and was modelling self-management according to its own interests – which is also the generation that, because of the general lack of educated professional cadres after the Second World War, managed to establish itself in all of the key positions in the spheres of politics, economy and culture. Finally, according to Uskoković, there is the 'young' generation – coming of age in the 1970s and at the beginning of the 1980s, facing the contradictions between the proclaimed values and norms and the day-to-day reality they faced.

Third, this generational discourse has also continued in popular memory, and continues to shape the way in which people from this generation understand the 1980s and the (post-)socialist decline.[29] This is largely due to the impressive cultural production and creative output from young Yugoslavs in their late teens or in their twenties throughout the 1980s. This generational self-identification has persisted mainly because the majority of those cultural products have preserved their prominence in the post-socialist context (in particular in music/popular culture, sport and cinematography) and the actors continued their careers within the same spheres after the Yugoslav dissolution. Hence, a generational lens is chosen to deconstruct a generation which has featured prominently in post-Yugoslav music and culture, as well as in order to demonstrate the effect of the systemic crisis of the 1980s on a particular group which contributed to many of the debates, but did not have a real stake in the resolution of the Yugoslav crisis. Post-Yugoslav works have sought to find 'our generation' within late Yugoslav literature, music, media, sport, politics or theatre.[30] This was a generational consciousness solidified for some by the experience of war, the break-up of Yugoslavia and the loss of geopolitical and international status. The violent break-up of Yugoslavia also had a lot to do with the veneration and even the mythologisation of the Yugoslav 'new wave' music scene, for example. It should be noted that some are reluctant to use or appropriate the generational mould, or are prone to refuse it outright. The scepticism towards identifying as a part of a generation is generally a result of a deep sense of disappointment and bitterness towards the eruption of violence and the subsequent destruction of the state, often related to the political or even personal splits between former colleagues and friends. The concept of 'generation' has been also rejected by many of those who became successful nationalist or anti-communist figures, and who did not wish to define themselves according to their cultural or political projects of the 1980s.

Finally, embarking on a generational study makes a pan-Yugoslav approach both inevitable and viable. Work conducted in the post-Yugoslav period has tended to focus on the experience of particular republics or groups: using the generational frame enables us to tell a pan-Yugoslav story. This does not necessarily mean a homogenisation of a diverse set of experiences – rather, the concept of 'generation' can be used to address how far activists worked across national boundaries as young people, or how they interacted within the institutional youth sphere, noting both the divides and connections that emerged. The youth, of course, was a vast heterogeneous category that the system identified as a potential guarantee for its future preservation and, consequently, invested a lot in shaping it into a progressive force and a unique front that carried the labels of 'socialist' and 'Yugoslav'. Hence, a generational lens also provides insight into the very making (and unmaking) of Yugoslav supranationalism. Although the sense of supra-ethnic/Yugoslav belonging was conceived of, acted out, internalised, passed on, propagated in different ways by different groups and individuals, it essentially embodied an additional layer of identification, as well as an additional sphere of interaction and convergence, which this research aims to dissect and illuminate, in particular with regard to those who experienced the 'crisis decade' as youngsters or young adults.

Rethinking dissidence, civil society and space

As it has been observed in the context of the youth 'alternative scene' in Slovenia, 'it was free from the figure that played a central role in other socialist countries: the dissident. The alternative understood its own action as the production of the social sphere, the creation of social spaces of otherness, and would refuse to be characterized as dissent or opposition'.[31] Indeed, even press reports intended for a non-Yugoslav audience at the time did not fail to stress that petitioners were in no way seeking to topple the regime or the state: 'These dissidents can certainly not be described as hostile to the post-Tito regime. On the contrary, their loyalty to "self-management socialism" is beyond doubt. They do differ from the ruling "professional politicians", however, in their interpretation of what "self-management socialism" should be.'[32] This resonates with Anna Saunders' observation in the context of the German Democratic Republic (GDR) that 'Ironically, many who demonstrated against the regime revealed surprising patriotic potential, for they were engaged in the public debate and often believed in the basic principles of socialism; their aim was to improve the GDR rather than to overthrow the state'.[33]

Hence, the book critically engages with the actors themselves to establish how they saw their relationship with the state and the envisioned reform. While many authors situate such actors within the framework of dissidence and civil society, this study, by contrast, questions the utility of the uncritical application of both notions, by arguing that the opposition to the political elite and the malfunctions of Yugoslav socialism within the youth realm did not transform into an outright opposition to the system as such, i.e. into demands for 'an exit from socialism', until very late in the decade. Rather, it explores why there was a genuine belief amongst many of the critical actors that they could still work within the system to reform it in such a way that it would preserve its progressive and Yugoslav dimensions. They neither withdrew nor opted out of the institutional/public space and culture; rather, they met the state in its own 'official' territory and challenged it there. In this sense, this particular case study of youth

politics, culture and reinvention of space in late socialist Yugoslavia could offer
an excellent platform from which to approach the complexity of the period and
transcend some of the established approaches in the field of state–society relations in both socialist Yugoslavia and the socialist world.

Some scholars used the term 'socialist civil society' to make sense of this relationship between state and society. A 1986 publication dedicated to 'socialist civil
society' argued that there were three fundamental conditions for the existence
of civil society: political pluralism, an independent public sphere and rule of
law. However, they underlined that by political pluralism they do not necessarily
understand a multi-party system, but 'the possibility of political expression and
activism within the framework of an independent Socialist Alliance'.[34] The term
does capture aspects of the progressive liberalisation of the public sphere after
1980 that allowed the young to utilise the youth infrastructure for channelling
novel demands and to act as one of the 'main promoters of the spontaneous
modernisation',[35] i.e. of the process of progressive democratisation from within.
Arguably, 'the society looked at itself on a big, pluralist screen, covered with different images, icons and discourses'.[36] Yet, for others, this term remained problematic because, in the literature, the very notion of civil society is conceived as
a force that inevitably undermines socialism.[37] 'Civil society' was indeed being
used at the time both in the Yugoslav and in other Eastern European contexts.
The Polish dissident movement in the late 1970s, for example, was hailed as 'the
rebirth of civil society'.[38] Yet, 'the elevation of civil society meant not so much
a new relationship between state and society as their virtual uncoupling'.[39] In
the Yugoslav context, this relationship was much more dynamic and the public/
private or state/society dichotomies were not as apparent and straightforward.
Considering propositions that different concepts could meaningfully address the
same phenomena as civil society does (namely curtailing state power, promoting
and upholding pluralism, and securing the right for contesting the status quo
and political action), it seems plausible that 'the concept therefore needs to be
broadened, relativized and adapted to local conditions'.[40]

In order to address the issue of (youth) activism, I borrow the notion of
'acts of citizenship'.[41] Particularly useful for addressing the subtle and pragmatic
ways of dialoguing, interacting with and navigating the youth institutions and
the institutions of the state, i.e. for addressing the fact that the activist core of
this generation was essentially working to reshape the idea of participation in
the system, acts of citizenship are those that 'rupture or break the given orders,
practices and habitus. Creative ruptures and breaks take different forms that are
irreducible. They can, for example, take forms of resistance or subservience'.[42]
Beside political – 'in so far as these acts constitute constituents (beings with
claims)' – acts could also be ethical, cultural ('carnivalesque'), sexual or social.
They are 'those acts that transform forms (orientations, strategies, technologies)

and modes (citizens, strangers, outsiders, aliens) of being political by bringing into being new actors as activist citizens (claimants of rights and responsibilities) through creating new sites and scales of struggle'.[43]

The book also brings together the concepts of generation and space. It focuses for the most part on the institutional youth sphere, i.e. the one contained within the spaces of the SSOJ, both at federal and republican level. Unlike studies on other Eastern European countries, this work focuses on how a new generational challenge came from within the institutions of the system. Accounting for youth activism and its relation to space in late socialism does not only help transcend the prism of 'binary socialism',[44] but it also provides us with a valuable secondary framework through which to study the inner dynamics of socio-political change in late socialist Yugoslavia. In this context, Francesca Polletta's argument that 'Counterhegemonic ideas and identities come neither from outside the system, nor from some free-floating oppositional consciousness, but from long-standing community institutions'[45] seems particularly relevant. The book addresses space through the notion of a youth sphere/youth realm. In particular, it focuses on the range of spaces – from the ones associated with the 'liminoid'[46] settings relevant for youth politics and culture in the 1980s – the youth media, the student cultural centres, etc., to the political arenas of the SSOJ and its role as a 'socio-political organisation'.

The book does not aspire to tell an exhaustive story of the last Yugoslav generation. It engages with its 'public face', i.e. with a progressive, predominantly urban elite which was socially, politically or culturally engaged and publicly present in the youth realm. The majority of these individuals came from the big urban Yugoslav centres and appropriated urbanity as a prominent trait of their image and self-perception. The 1986 federal youth research revealed some striking differences along the lines of urban/rural residency and social origin. It showed, for instance, that those whose parents were functionaries, highly educated and well positioned within society displayed a higher extent of discontent with the socio-political reality when compared to the rural or less educated youth.[47]

One cannot help but consider the question of how legitimate it is to treat these particular individuals as representatives of a generation and what the possibilities and limits are of such an approach. It should be emphasised that venturing outside of the realm of political history of late Yugoslav socialism is a step into largely uncharted territory. There has not been a study of the youth in Yugoslavia comparable to those quoted above dealing with generations and youth in the Soviet Union or East Germany. Not all archives are accessible because of the thirty-year rule and events have to be reconstructed through other types of material (interviews, media accounts, etc.) Departing from the institutional youth framework and tracing the 'official' youth representatives and those who claimed to speak on behalf of a new generation of youth, is, simply put, a more viable goal for a research topic which has not been studied in any depth. However, taking the SSOJ as a framework – because of its decentralised and flexible network which accommodated many non-political and non-mainstream initiatives, individuals and groups – allows us to incorporate wider segments of the youth population. What it does not offer is an insight into other more marginal groups which began to gain prominence at the very end of the decade, such as various groups of religious youth, football fans and those who converged around the newly formed political parties after 1990. Also, the book does not specifically reflect on what could be considered separate generation units: the last Yugoslav sports generation, or the last Yugoslav literary generation, for instance. Last but not least, it is almost impossible to acknowledge and take into account the entire set-up of the institutional youth network, as almost every factory, army barrack, secondary school, municipality, town and every faculty and university had their own SSO branch and some sort of a youth bulletin or newspaper. Rather, the book reflects on a carefully selected range of youth 'case studies' through which we gain access to a range of generational experiences and challenges.

Recovering the voices of the shadow elite

In order to capture the multiple debates that occurred in these official and semi-official spaces across the different republics that demonstrate the experiences of this Yugoslav generation, the book combines oral history and archival research, supplementing it with survey data from larger quantitative research projects conducted in the 1980s on a pan-Yugoslav sample. Although the official records of the SSOJ and their trans-republican nature allows for a comparative approach, institutional histories can elucidate only a certain aspect of the political and cultural activism of the youth in the 1980s. Rather, drawing both on published material and on oral history testimonies provides a sense of a range of responses in different parts of the youth sphere and acknowledges the voices of multiple actors. Throughout the book this is supplemented with the many studies of youth attitudes by state-supported institutions – surveys that reveal how youth and generational challenge were conceptualised at the time and thus provide important material to contextualise that challenge. Oral history testimonies shed light on this critical generation in its own words and provide insight into patterns of meaning making.

The oral history interviews are used in combination with archival and other primary material (such as newspaper/magazine articles, visual material) in order to fuse what I have referred to elsewhere as 'the Yugoslav project', i.e. the political and institutional framework which has so far dominated scholarly works, with 'the Yugoslav experience'.[48] The latter relates to the socio-cultural fabric, but more importantly to the lived experiences, perceptions and narratives within the framework of the Yugoslav project, i.e. the flash, the 'thickened' time that Bakhtin refers to in his definition of the chronotope.[49] A turn towards the life stories/lived histories of the defunct federation provides the field with a venue not only for the *normalisation* of Yugoslav history, but also for a departure from the 'dissolution' paradigm, towards more substantial engagement with different social groups, periods, events or places in Yugoslav history, without the inclination to retrospectively detect anomalies and reasons which led to the violence and the break-up. While official sources offer only a limited perspective concerning the functioning of socialist institutions, oral history provides insight into the ways in which people negotiated with power from below and into the complexities of that interaction. Although the oral history approach to research essentially tries to 'give back to the people who made and experienced history, through their own words, a central place',[50] this book seeks to emphasise the diversity of voices and include those that have been left out of historical accounts. Above all, this approach, which departs from a conventional choice of either archival research or oral history, allows access to the subtleties of interaction between the individual activists and the state, or, to the different interactions taking place within the framework of the SSOJ.

One of the challenges of putting together oral history testimonies and archival sources lies in the fact that they represent two very different genres of material fulfilling different functions. Yet, these different source genres provide important and different perspectives on the problem, as they are often embedded within a range of discourses and agendas. Furthermore, matching archival/ primary sources with corresponding oral history material was not always possible as some archives were not accessible, but it was possible to supplement it with media reports from the time, for instance. Also, the fact that many of the interviewees were publishing their own texts in the media or were interviewed as holding positions within the youth organisation made it easier to compare their past and present views and locate any distortions in the narrative or 'selective' remembering. Indeed, 'rather than replacing previous truths with alternative ones ... oral history has made us uncomfortably aware of the elusive quality of historical truth itself'.[51]

It is not surprising that the testimonies often bridged the Yugoslav dissolution and reflect on the present or through the present upon the past. Considering the profound changes which occurred after the Yugoslav dissolution, the oral history interviews reveal a very prominent 'relationship between self-concept and cultural norms'.[52] Acknowledging that oral history is 'a living record of the complex interaction between past and present within each individual and in society',[53] the book does not take the oral history testimony at face value. When using interviewees' words as 'history' and trying to build 'memory' into 'history', it is essential to have in mind the dialectical relationship of past and present. In that sense, it is important for the oral historian to strive to understand why individuals are inclined to talk about particular issues and what motivates their narratives. Comprehensive knowledge of the context and of the contemporary socio-political situation and the debates that surround the interviewee might help in understanding the insistence on certain comparisons or aspects of the past and the present. Where possible, the book relies on primary material to provide the framework for the testimonies and maintains that both bodies of source material are mutually illuminating. However, this is not done in order to shed light on the patterns of remembrance, but rather because the book seeks to account for a greater range of voices as a way of being sensitive to individual perspectives and lived experiences. Undeniably, 'Oral history is a *dialogic* process; it is a conversation in real time between the interviewer and the narrator, and then between the narrator and what we might call external discourses or culture'.[54] Although this work is predominantly concerned with reconstructing a historical era, rather than exploring the dynamics of memory, remembering is addressed where it appears to shape testimony profoundly – albeit mainly with the view of reflecting on how an account of the period can be best obtained.

A range of materials produced at the various levels of the SSOJ – from meeting minutes, internal reports on various issues (voluntary work, Youth Day, participation in the delegate system, finances, reports on the work of the different commissions – such as, for example, the commissions for political system), programmatic documents, congress materials, speech transcriptions, to domestic and foreign correspondence – not only help to gain a sense of the different debates at republican and at federal level, they proved crucial in analysing the language and the different ways in which contention and negotiation with the state were framed. However, being sensitive to the limitations of any archival material remains of paramount importance. After all, documents were drafted by individual authors, or by smaller groups of individuals within the various commissions of the SSOJ; hence, in no way could they be taken as absolutely reflective of the multitude of attitudes and voices within the SSOJ, or of the respective SSO branch as a whole. Therefore, supplementing this material with a range of contemporary sociological data and with the oral history testimonies bridges certain gaps and illuminates the subject of the book from different angles.

The book draws upon a wealth of sociological and statistical material produced throughout the 1980s. The questions posed in the surveys and the themes and subjects around which they were conceptualised clearly convey a sense of the major social and political concerns of the time: 'anti-system' activism and attitudes, decline in membership in the Party and in the self-management bodies, sentiments of Yugoslav/European/national/regional belonging, attitudes towards religion, support for the constitutional changes and the programmes of political/economic reform, etc. The research studies also shed light on the scholarly elite in this field in late socialist Yugoslavia, which was apparently sympathetic with the youth. More often than not it was the SSOJ, its branches and/or the respective publishing/research centres, which initiated or published the various youth studies. While all-Yugoslav comprehensive youth research projects were rare, if not nonexistent until the 1980s, studies whose primary focus was the youth in the separate federal units or even cities (such as Belgrade) were more abundant.[55] The spectrum of scholarly studies dealing with the Yugoslav youth in late socialism convey a belief on the part of the authorities and intellectuals that this generation was, or had the potential to be, unique because it had come of age and lived its youthful years at a time of profound crisis. At the same time, their importance could be also located in that this scholarly (as well as media and political) discourse dealing with the youth produced the very idea of a generational experience. The studies detect the diversification and the social differentiation of the young generation. It is from the beginning of the 1980s that empirical sociological studies really began to engage with the reality of the crisis. Indeed, the very expansion of sociology in the 1980s in Yugoslavia reflected this broader sense of crisis in the socialisation of youth. As Nebojša Popov, a leading Yugoslav sociologist and activist noted in 1988: 'The new upswing of sociology happens in the 1980s, above all with the awareness of the scope and the depth of the roots of the crisis; which led to an immediate conflict with the dogmatic ideologues and politicians, who at the time even refused to admit that it was possible to talk about a crisis, but very soon accepted it.'[56]

In 1983 the first Yugoslav-wide youth research was launched under the name *JUPIO – Jugoslovenski program za istraživanje omladine* [Yugoslav programme for research of the youth]. It was initiated by the presidency of the League of Socialist Youth of Yugoslavia in 1983 as a 'long-term continuous program for scholarly research on the contemporary questions and problems experienced by Yugoslavia's young generation', offering a framework for 'interdisciplinary empirical and theoretical research on Yugoslav youth'.[57] The *JUPIO* study, beside certain flaws (it was meant to be a long-term project which was in its early stages in 1986), provided a valuable overview of the Yugoslav youth in the mid-1980s, recalling the findings of other empirical studies dealing with the youth which showed that 'it is a profile of youngsters who by no means consent to formal participation, to being disciplined participants in the conventional forms of political life'.[58]

This becomes even more visible in the last all-Yugoslav youth research conducted in 1989 and published in 1990. Curiously, the publication bears an introductory note that the research was commissioned by the SSOJ (as in the case of *JUPIO*), but, 'preoccupied with its own disappearence',[59] the SSOJ eventually renounced the project and declined to publish the findings. The editors under-lined that the research was illustrative only of 'one slice of time' and that if it was to be repeated again, it was likely that different results would be obtained – considering the incongruous developments on a political level and in everyday life. Illustratively entitled *Deca krize: omladina Jugoslavije krajem osamdesetih* [The children of crisis: the Yugoslav youth at the end of the 1980s], the study reflects the change in socio-political discourse which occurred between 1985 and 1990 (most notably the hopes for accession to the European Community) and in addition examines additional aspects of the young generation: discontent with regard to democracy in Yugoslavia, attitudes towards the new social move-ments, views on the Kosovo issue, as well as a rather frequent comparison with recent Eurobarometer findings or with different Western European surveys on youth.

While it is important to bear in mind that official sources on youth reflect a particular understanding of the role and position of youth within a given society and that they operate with categories which might be no longer relevant, they, nevertheless, do detect certain important trends among the young, as well as important perceptions on the part of the state and the intellectual elite which produced them. Studies that originate from international organisations such as the United Nations Educational, Scientific and Cultural Organisation (UNE-SCO) also might be said to reflect the particular views of the number of states whose representatives were involved in the creation of the report. The idea that the youth was going through a crisis and that this would reshape the expecta-tions of a new generation was a worldwide phenomenon of the early 1980s. UNESCO published a report entitled *Youth Prospects in the 1980s*, prepared 'on the basis of a survey carried out in every region of the world'.[60] Beside indicat-ing some core issues which have persisted well beyond the 1980s, such as youth unemployment ('the most serious issue for the coming years'[61]) and the fact that 'young people are taking on growing importance as a social group',[62] the report, among other things, helps situate socialist Yugoslavia in a wider, global con-text and offers a solid basis for transcending Yugoslav particularity. As has been argued, 'a concept of generation that locates young people within specific set of economic, social, cultural and political conditions offers a way beyond seeing generations as a series of birth cohorts because age alone is no longer the defin-ing feature'.[63] Hence, here, this group of sources is used to outline a broader setting for the study of the last Yugoslav generation. True to its nature as a policy paper, the report also made certain predictions for the upcoming decade which indeed proved to be true:

> The key words in the experience of young people in the coming decade are going to be: 'scarcity', 'unemployment', 'under-employment', 'ill-employment', 'anxiety', 'defensiveness', 'pragmatism'; and even subsistence and survival

itself. If the 1960s challenged certain categories of youth in certain parts of the world with a crisis of culture, ideas and institutions, the 1980s will confront a new generation with a concrete, structural crisis of chronic economic uncertainty and even deprivation.[64]

The third corpus of primary material consists of the oral history testimonies. I conducted forty-one semi-structured oral history interviews, which lasted from forty minutes to four hours. My informants were young journalists, musicians, artists or those professionally involved with the SSOJ in the 1980s. My goal was to achieve a relatively balanced representation of the different federal units and the different sub-groups, although the research was principally structured according to a preliminary list of historiographical data in terms of better known events and places from the 1980s. The interviews revolved around a pre-drafted set of questions, although the format adopted was in general 'semi-structured'. The questions differed among different activists in order to address the specificities of their particular public engagement. Some of the questions I most often posed related to some of the major themes of the research, such as, for instance, becoming an activist; the relation to the institutional youth space(s); the understanding/ self-perception or critique of Yugoslavism; the perception of and participation in official youth rituals, such as the Youth Relay or the voluntary work camps; perceptions and experiences of the Yugoslav People's Army and military service; the break-up of Yugoslavia. The interviews were conducted in Skopje (Macedonia), Prishtina (Kosovo), Belgrade (Serbia), Sarajevo (Bosnia-Herzegovina), Zagreb (Croatia) and Ljubljana (Slovenia), initially through referral-sampling and later through direct contacts. The sample was selected from a range of groups who were active in the youth realm and/or contested the system from a variety of positions and from across the different republics. Few interviews were conducted with individuals who did not belong to this generation, but were closely following the events or worked in the youth realm in more senior positions. It also seemed important that the interviewees demonstrate a range of post-socialist trajectories and that they belong to groups that have been left out of mainstream accounts. I decided to focus on five groups: young musicians/artists, young journalists, young peace/feminist/gay activists, young army officers and young political functionaries. The apparent gender imbalance partially reflects the under-representation of women in the federal and federal-unit level youth leaderships. Although the number of women in general and young women below the age of twenty-seven in the youth organisation, in the workforce (for instance, the number of female delegates in the workers' councils rose from 13,401 in 1952 to 151,289 in 1983[65]), in the political institutions and in the League of Communists was steadily rising (see Table 1), they were under-represented in the top echelons of government and in the highest ranks of the 'socio-political' organisations. In 1982, for example, out of the 308 delegates in the federal assembly, only fifty-four

Table 1 Party membership according to gender and age 1969–80, in percentages

Year	Total Party member-ship	Women	% of total Party member-ship	Youth (under 27)	% of total Party member-ship	Women under 27	% of Youth (under 27) member-ship
1969	1,111,682	212,877	19.1	295,115	26.5	66,994	22.7
1970	1,049,184	201,946	19.2	218,967	20.8	58,227	26.6
1971	1,025,476	200,022	19.5	212,434	20.7	58,595	27.6
1972	1,009,947	196,937	19.5	212,686	21.0	58,596	22.5
1973	1,076,711	214,503	19.9	258,124	24.0	72,095	27.9
1974	1,192,466	248,182	20.8	323,787	27.1	94,173	29.1
1975	1,302,843	281,319	21.6	371,434	28.5	111,560	30.0
1976	1,460,267	328,577	22.5	451,653	30.1	139,499	30.8
1977	1,623,612	378,507	23.3	529,648	32.6	166,028	31.3
1978	1,774,624	426,286	24.0	597,768	33.7	185,904	31.1
1979	1,884,475	464,950	24.6	614,106	32.6	198,902	32.4
1980	2,041,299	521,808	25.6	675,484	33.0	223,774	34.6

Source: Dušan Davidović (ed.), *Mladi Jugoslavije: opšti pregled* (Beograd: Centar za istraživačku i dokumentaciono-izdavačku delatnost Predsedništva Konferencije SSOJ, 1982), pp. 78–9.

were women[66] and the League of Socialist Youth of Yugoslavia had only one female president during the 1980s. However, despite the fact that female political, cultural and media activism was less visible, young women were actively involved at all other levels/domains of the youth realm, not least because 44 per cent of all university graduates in 1981 were female.[67]

From the 'crisis decade' to a 'crisis generation'

President Josip Broz Tito was admitted to hospital shortly after the Soviet troops invaded Afghanistan in December 1979. The Soviet occupation of Afghanistan sparked a wave of reactions in the Yugoslav press and among the political elite and caused a sharp divide within the Non-Aligned Movement, leaving Yugoslavia rather isolated and opposed to the pro-Soviet camp led by Cuba. A sense of looming uncertainty and impending change was present from the moment he was admitted to hospital, when 'the panegyrics have expressed in lofty and often poetic language not only the sincere love Yugoslav Communists cherished for their great leader but also their unconcealed fear about changes after his death'.[68] With the death of its supreme leader, the country lost not only a symbolic, but also a very crucial centre of gravity, a 'generally respected arbiter'.[69] Curiously, the 'syndrome' of the absent leader was echoed in many public debates where intellectuals, politicians and ordinary people reflected upon the contemporary crisis through the lens of the question 'How would have Tito solved this crisis?', or 'What would Tito say to you today?', as a 1988 issue of the Vojvodinian youth magazine *Stav* asked.[70] Moreover, the fact that the Soviet military engagement in Afghanistan somewhat overlapped with the passing away of Tito in 1980 and the Polish events of 1980–81 around 'Solidarity' and the introduction of the martial law, helped resurrect the old Yugoslav fears of a Soviet intervention or interference in Yugoslav internal affairs. The Yugoslav press vigorously followed the Polish events and generally upheld Polish anti-Sovietism and the struggle led by Solidarity. In November 1981 the Student Cultural Centre in Belgrade hosted a weeklong 'Young Polish culture' event and the renowned rock band Azra included in their 1981 album *Sunčana strana ulice* [The sunny side of the street] a song entitled 'Poljska u mom srcu' [Poland in my heart], one of their greatest hits.

The beginning of the decade was also marked by the Kosovo riots, seven years after the Serbian province gained autonomy and the status of a separate federal unit. They began as a student protest against food quality and student accommodation standards at Prishtina University, allegedly by a student of Bulgarian nationality.[71] In a series of trials, young Albanians from Kosovo were tried for belonging to 'hostile' groups such as the 'Marxist-Leninist Youth of Kosovo' which aimed to achieve republican status for Kosovo and hoped to see it eventually united with Albania.[72] From 1981 until 1984, 585 individuals (143 students) were imprisoned.[73] The students launched protest slogans such as 'Revisionists' or 'Down with the red bourgeoisie', reflecting ideological influences from Marxist-Leninist circles close to the Albanian regime of Enver Hoxha and hence raising concerns about the involvement of Albania's intelligence service.[74] Other more exclusively and nationalistically formulated demands followed, such as 'Kosova-Republic!', 'Unification with Albania!' and 'We are Albanians, not Yugoslavs!'[75] Many echoed those present on the streets of Kosovo during the protests of 1968. The crucial issue, however, seemed to have been the rapid expansion of education in Kosovo, which had created 'an academic proletariat with rising expectations'.[76] Domestic scholars also pointed to an 'autarchic economic politics and a tendency of political-cultural closure towards Serbia and Yugoslavia'.[77] The prominent Kosovan communist leader Fadil Hoxha assumed a rather ambiguous stance towards the students, echoing Tito's famous conciliatory 1968 speech following the student protests, when at the 12th provincial session of the League of Communists he stated that 'we must act and demand greater responsibility from the professors, educators and students. We must seek this from the students, since the majority of them, comrades, are with us. We must go to them, talk with them, and explain things to them. At the moment they are offended, because some of their comrades have been injured'.[78]

Despite its relative linguistic isolation and lack of visibility with regard to the rest of the Yugoslav political, media and cultural space, this generation of young Yugoslav Albanians was by no means cut off from the Yugoslav youth realm. On the contrary, the period after the establishment of the University of Prishtina in 1970 saw the emergence of many young actors, musicians, artists and youth functionaries. In the political youth realm, the SSOJ was presided over by a Kosovan twice in the period 1974–90: Azem Vllasi was its president for two mandates and Hashim Rexhepi for one. Because of the 'ethnic key' and the strict rules on proportional representation, young Albanians were present at all levels in the SSOJ in the federal units where they lived in significant numbers. Although the cultural and the media realm were indeed part of a separate 'Albanophone' sphere, writing about the Albanian rock scene in Yugoslavia in the 1970s and the 1980s, Gëzim Krasniqi observed that quite a few rock musicians of Albanian origin were part of some of the most popular Yugoslav bands (Nexhat Macula from YU grupa, Shefqet Hoxha from Vatreni poljubac [Fiery kiss], Seat Jakupi from Konkord, etc.), many Kosovan bands had Serb, Bosniak or Turkish instrumentalists and they regularly played in front of mixed audiences.[79] Furthermore, he argues, 'by being integrated into the (sub) cultural scene of Yugoslavia, this generation of artists from Kosovo reaffirmed both their Yugoslavness and Albanianness, as Yugoslavism in Tito's Yugoslavia meant above all Yugoslav citizenship, something which was not in contradiction with the particular ethnonational identities'.[80]

Yet, the decade of the 1980s was arguably also one marked by a 'politically and culturally permissive climate'[81] and it was certainly a time when already established codes of public debate and political communication began to change. The 1980s saw shifts in already established patterns of political socialisation, echoing similar trends that caused concern in the 1960s. In 1984, from the total of 2,041,270 members of the League of Communists of Yugoslavia (SKJ) 649,428 (32 per cent) were younger than twenty-eight.[82] However, in the second half of the 1980s there was a growing realisation that reforms need to be undertaken that would address the problem that the membership of the SKJ was rapidly ageing and that the participation of young people below the age of twenty-seven was steadily decreasing.

The discourse of crisis came to permeate every aspect of the social and the political life. It took two years – from 1979 until 1981 – for the political elite to 'finally acknowledge the state of crisis and to form a federal commission of around 300 politicians and scholars (the so-called Krajger commission, according to the name of the then President of the collective federal Presidency) which worked on the lenghty *Long-term Program for Economic Stabilisation*.[83] Nevertheless, Yugoslav society displayed a rather surprisingly large dose of self-criticism, genuine interest in the different manifestations and potential solutions for the all-encompassing crisis, allowing for the appearance of many open platforms for debate and exchange. As has been noted in a 1980 Radio Free Europe report: 'First, the country's economic difficulties have been piling up on a daily basis; secondly, unlike other communist countries – with the exception of Poland – the Yugoslav information media in general, and Tito's successors in particular are openly discussing the existing problems with almost no attempt made to embellish or hide anything.'[84] This preparedness to openly engage with the pending questions of reforming the system was essentially the final attempt to make Yugoslav self-managing socialism viable and functional, all the while 'genuinely aspiring to create political democracy within communism'.[85]

The main structural and symbolic pillars of Yugoslav society – non-alignment, self-management, the revolutionary legacy and brotherhood and unity, began to show the first signs of erosion and public questioning immediately after Tito's death and although the public political and media discourse continued to be marked by political phraseologies, it was also open to debate and reflection upon the envisaged paths to 'reform' and 'economic stabilisation'. Evidently, the simultaneity of all of these processes, coupled with Tito's death, 'has resulted in an accumulating systemic crisis, affecting a variety of areas at a variety of levels made worse by the way in which they interlocked causally, so that a remedy for one problem immediately raised the solution of others'.[86] Other authors have similarly observed that 'multiple crises which faced Yugoslavia in the 1980s took their toll on public confidence in the system and led to an erosion of belief in the founding myths of the state and the inherent superiority of self-management socialism'.[87] In the Yugoslav context, self-management was not limited to the notion of workers' control over the means of production. It was a principle around which all political and social life was structured. The 1974 federal Constitution was an attempt to extend self-management even in the realm of high politics: the federal assembly was referred to as 'a body of social self-management' and the federal chamber consisted of 220 delegates of self-managing organisations/communities and socio-political organisations. However, the sheer complexity of the system, in particular in the sphere of elections and delegations, made it dysfunctional and prone to abuse.[88]

The decade was marked by a deep sense of uncertainty and instability, as everything could be, and oftentimes was, publicly questioned – from the constitutional order to the official history of the Second World War. From the beginning of the 1980s, the omnipresent discourse of a multi-level (political, economic, social) crisis coincided with the emergence of a scholarly discourse within the social sciences revolving around the 'crisis generation'. This rise in youth studies/sociology of the youth could be interpreted as an evidence of a general concern for the lack of integration and political alienation of the youth. The notion of the 'crisis generation' persisted throughout the 1980s in scholarly and media discourse.

Stating that there was awareness among the young that the current crisis was part of a 'crisis of global character',[89] towards the end of the 1980s the notion of a crisis generation was supplemented by a new derivative: 'crisis of a generation'. Not abandoning Mannheim's terminology, at a conference entitled 'The Yugoslav youth of the 1980s between political apathy and autonomous political subjectivity' it was inferred that one can observe a process of '(de)homogenisation of the generation units'.[90] Srđan Vrcan, one of the most prominent Croatian and Yugoslav sociologists, similarly observed that the contemporary youth was 'a generation which lives and acts in a society caught in serious difficulties, permanent stagnant state of affairs and crisis-related processes ... It is aware that it lives in a society that belongs to a world that is in a deep and long-lasting crisis, the end of which is not visible'.[91]

Strikingly, the *JUPIO* report noted that the personal predictions about one's individual future or the future of the society were 'preponderantly optimistic',[92] as 82.9 per cent of the respondents stated that they believed their personal future would be much better or somewhat better than the present, while 62.8 per cent stated that they believed this was true for the future of the society/state.[93] Only 5.8 per cent said that they expected their personal future to be much or somewhat worse. The pessimistic view on the future of the society was clearly dependent on the federal unit in a way that the youth from the most developed Yugoslav republics, such as Slovenia, was the most pessimistic and the youth from the least developed region of Kosovo expressed the highest level of optimism: 43.5 per cent of the Slovenian respondents and 11 per cent of the Kosovan youth thought the future of the society would be worse. This led sociologists to term this particular phenomenon 'the optimism paradox'. However, as far as the view on the personal future was concerned, the figures were strikingly lower: only 6.4 per cent of Kosovans and 11.3 per cent of Slovenes thought their personal future would be worse than it was. The ability to clearly dissociate one's personal experiences from the perception of the political and the social condition of the state implies that the majority of the respondents possessed the ability to critically reflect on the sociopolitical reality, without perceiving things through their own subjective experience.

This sense of optimism that permeated the report led the author to conclude that 'the contemporary youth – socialised in a way suited to idealise certain values through the schooling process and protected within family life – had radicalised its personal expectations from society to such an extent that it is neither prepared for the time and situations of social trouble, nor able to accept the "psychology of renouncement" '.[94] This expansion of the horizon of expectations was visible, for instance, in the debates on the distribution of socially owned housing to young people/young families, as the state authorities were repeatedly reproached in the youth media and in various debates within the youth organisation for the lack of housing for the young and for the long waiting lists. As Patrick H. Patterson observed, 'in Yugoslavia, the "inflation of desire" came not from unending frustration and scarcity but instead from the *fulfillment*

Table 2 Level of interest regarding different phenomena in personal and societal realm

	'Big'	'No interest'
Friendship	69.4%	2.8%
Leisure and pastime	56.6%	3.6%
Work	54.4%	5.5%
Sex and love	48.7%	6.4%
School and education	44.6%	7.3%
Sport	41.5%	9.1%
Science/technology	36.3%	10.3%
Art and culture	31.6%	13.8%
Politics	27.3%	20.0%
Army and military affairs	28.7%	26.2%
National past	25.1%	24.2%
Religion	14.1%	52.7%

Source: Vlasta Ilišin, 'Interesiranja i slobodno vreme mladih', in Srđan Vrcan *et al.*, *Položaj, svest i ponašanje mlade generacije Jugoslavije* (Beograd: Centar za istraživačku, dokumentacionu i izdavačku delatnost Konferencije SSOJ/Zagreb: Institut za društvena istraživanja Sveučilišta, 1986), p. 115.

of desire – from the lived experience of abundance'.[95] The detected 'conformist optimism'[96] was without doubt closely related to a sense of geopolitical stability in the context of the Cold War and a perception that Yugoslavia and its institutions were relatively strong, likely to last for another hundred years, as Gregor Tomc (born 1952), member of the punk band Pankrti and sociologist, put it. Indeed, there was a shared perception similar to the one in the Soviet context that 'everything was forever'.[97] The fact that this type of question was asked in the survey may be indicative of a fear that the young were becoming depoliticised and more culture-oriented. Indeed, other sections of the survey found that 'the number of the youth interested in politics and political events has been gradually decreasing over the past two decades'.[98] A separate part of the research dedicated to religion demonstrated a high level of secularisation among Yugoslav youth – 64.2 per cent said that they never visit a place of worship. There were, however, big differences among the separate national groups: while 86.9 per cent of the Montenegrin youth, 84.5 per cent of Yugoslav youth, 77.7 per cent of the Serbian youth and 66.8 per cent of the Albanian youth said that they never went to a church/mosque, only 34.7 per cent of the Croat youth, 44.3 per cent of the Macedonian youth and 47.8 per cent of the Slovenian youth claimed the same. This partially explains why in 1986 politics, national history/relations and religion were ranked quite low on the list of interests and topics of conversation (see Table 2).

Consumer socialism in this context is an equally important piece in the mosaic of the period and of late socialist youth cultures, most notably through popular culture and travel/mobility, as it will be discussed in subsequent chapters. Namely, in the period between 1987 and 1991, the number of trips abroad by Yugoslav citizens increased from 20,013,000 in 1987 to 36,290,000 in 1990.[99] A large number of these trips were made by young people who travelled to Western Europe and perceived their own identity through the prism of an incipient Europeanism.

Finally, a prominent marker of youth culture and identity was the perception of urbanity or rurality. The rural–urban divide[100] among the young was a well-established fact which surfaced in the comprehensive surveys conducted in the 1980s. The sense of urbanity was a prominent component of the overall feeling of proximity to Europe and the modern world. What is particularly striking is the internalisation of the urban/rural dichotomy in a large part of the personal testimonies I collected. This does not come as a surprise when taking into consideration the fact that the cultural institutions within the youth infrastructure were gradually taken over by a young, educated and ambitious urban strata which embraced the novel trends in journalism, music and arts. As the rock/new wave scene was indeed based in the major Yugoslav cities, it often provides the framework for a retrospective generational framing. Musician Zoran Predin's (born 1958) reflection on the rural–urban divide conveys a shared sense of loss of urbanity which might come across as a subjective sense of elitism:

The basic division was rural–urban, that's all. We had soul-mates in Rijeka, Belgrade, Novi Sad, we felt closer to them than to someone from a nearby village. Today we can see to which extent the rural penetrated the urban … The turbo-capitalism introduced populist marketing principles which use the cheapest slogans. We were some sort of 'academia' of common sense and good taste, scattered around the republican capitals.

Moreover, the principal youth magazines were indeed at the helm of promoting what was considered to be 'urban' culture, mostly accessible to the educated, more privileged youth. As it has been argued: 'This continuous commitment of the editors to "urban" model of newspapers was instigating cultural production that used referent frames of city scenes, which did not take into account the national context of culture and its ethnic definitions, which will become so important not even a decade later.'[101] Moreover, throughout the decade, official youth bodies and forums complained and expressed concerns that the youth press was not representative of the rural and the working-class youth. Even the federal youth magazine *Mladost*, at a meeting of its publishing council, was advised to 'deal more with the problems of the rural and the working class youth'.[102]

The reality of the economic crisis which hit Yugoslavia from the early 1980s, the appropriation of a crisis discourse by the media and the political elites and, finally, a sympathetic scholarly discourse within Yugoslav youth studies/sociology of youth in the 1980s, all contributed to the proliferation of a generation defined through the all-pervasive Yugoslav late socialist crisis. This was a process of external labelling, which took place primarily within sociological research dealing with the youth, and especially due to the fact that the two big all-Yugoslav research projects on youth were conducted in 1985 and in 1989. The somewhat hyper-production in literature dealing with the youth reflects a classical Yugoslav (or for that matter, socialist) preoccupation with the young, which in times of crisis should stand at the helm of (progressive) change. Hence, it is not surprising that often politicians and authors recalled the fact that the absolute majority of those who carried out the anti-fascist liberation struggle were those under the age of thirty. This trope persisted well into the 1980s. For instance, in his speech at the 1986 congress of the League of Socialist Youth of Macedonia, Vasil Tupurkovski, former president of the federal youth organisation and member of the presidency of the Central Committee of the League of Communists of Macedonia underlined that:

> Throughout history generations of young people forcefully affirmed the continuity of the progressive and revolutionary aspirations. The most convincing and most glorious example of that is the people's liberation struggle and the socialist revolution … The revolutionary and progressive spirit of the young generations is intertwined with the historical progress and the interests of the working class in the forging of a new and humane consciousness.[103]

Similarly, a 1982 publication of the SSOJ entitled *The Young of Yugoslavia* reiterated the fact that the youth comprised three-quarters of the Yugoslav People's Liberation Army during the Second World War and that 100,000 young people and members of the Communist Youth fell as victims.[104] Indeed, due to the fact that the young had played an essential role in carrying out the revolution and in rebuilding the country in the post-war period, the older generation stuck to an unwavering conviction that the youth was crucial for the development and survival of the Yugoslav socialist project and that, under the right circumstances and guidance, the seeds of progressiveness and revolutionary potential it carried would grow as desired.

The first chapter maps the wide, decentralised youth infrastructure of the SSOJ as a form of public space which accommodated both mainstream and 'alternative' politics and cultures, outlining some of the major debates which occurred within its strictly speaking political/institutional core, as well as in its peripheral sites, i.e. its media and cultural realms. It also offers an overview of the history of the institutional youth sphere, focussing on certain crucial events, such as the events of 1968 and the 1974 reorganisation of the youth organisation which resulted in the disappearance of the Student Union(s) as a separate body. It shows how a process of negotiating new forms of youth activism (in the youth press), of questioning of inherited traditions and creating venues for democratisation of the youth organisation were made possible by the advancement of a new young political, media and cultural elite which generally sought to target the malfunctions of the system and undermine dogmatic socialism. The first half of the decade, i.e. the period immediately after Tito's death, saw different oppositional ideas and new youth cultural streams and styles were progressively invading the youth realm. Expressed reluctantly in official contexts, novel ideas and contestations were being voiced – still within the institutionalised vocabulary of Yugoslav self-managing socialism.

The second chapter focuses on the way in which parts of the youth articulated a specifically anti-regime critique and through it questioned some of the values embodied in contemporary politics and culture. In particular, it examines how older forms of political discourse and ritual – embodied by Tito's personality cult and the Youth relay race [*Štafeta mladosti*] – were critiqued in both political and new cultural forms. For the most part, this critique was not reduced to a demand for outright abolishment of Yugoslav socialism, but it was rather about challenging the norms of an older generation and reinventing socialism through the state's youth institutions.

The third chapter reflects on new youth activism within the wider context of what has been termed 'the new social movements' [*nova družbena gibanja/novi društveni pokreti*]. It addresses the broader transnational influence of movements abroad, and shows how new areas for political expression opened up around peace, anti-militarism, environmentalism/nuclear disarmament and sexuality. Late socialist Yugoslav society witnessed the proliferation of a youth arena of civil initiatives and activist citizenship, albeit fragmented and often discordant, which found shelter and support within parts of the existing youth institutional framework. Although the federal youth organisation did not explicitly endorse all of the initiatives stemming from the new social movements, it did provide spaces for some of them and increased the visibility of their demands in the public space.

The last chapter looks at the ways the youth organisation initially sought to reform and reinvent its role and mission and was later subsumed in and divided by the wider Yugoslav political debates and developments in the country. The proposed statute changes which came out of the public debate organised by the SSOJ in 1989 reflected both the gap between the Slovenian, on the one hand, and the Serbian, the Montenegrin and the Army Youth Leagues, on the other, but also shed light on a spectrum of shared visions and values which existed among the other branches. The chapter reflects upon the (lack of) consensus about the dilemma of how to modernise Yugoslav society and the sphere of institutional youth politics and culture and shows how by the end of the decade the consensus on change and reform and the discourse of 'pluralism of self-managing interests' was almost entirely replaced by a new discourse of human rights and liberal values which foreshadowed the 'exit from socialism'.

Notes

1 Documentary films such as *Srijetno dijete* [Happy child] (Igor Mirković, 2003), *Orkestar* [Orchestra] (Pjer Žalica, 2011), *The Last Yugoslavian Football Team* (Vuk Janic, 2000), *Once Brothers* (Michael Tolajian, 2010), *Dugo putovanje kroz istoriju, historiju i povijest* (Željko Mirković, 2010), *Once Upon a Time in Sarajevo* (Jacky Rowland, 2014); series dedicated to various aspects of post-Second World War Yugoslav popular culture and everyday life, such as *SFRJ za početnike* [SFRY for beginners] (Radovan Kupres, 2012) or *Robna kuća* [Department store] (Igor Stoimenov, 2009); the 'NEXT YU' season at Belgrade theatre Atelje 212 and plays such as *Rodjeni u YU* [Born in YU] (Dino Mustafić, 2010) and *Zbogom SFRJ* [Goodbye SFRY] (Kokan Mladenović, 2011); the exhibition *Poslednja mladost u Jugoslaviji 1977–1984* [The last youth in Yugoslavia] at the Museum of the History of Yugoslavia, Belgrade, 17 December 2011–15 January 2012; and scholarly and non-scholarly books which have dealt with particular cultural phenomena of the 1980s, such as Pavle Levi's *Disintegration in Frames: Aesthetics and Ideology in the Yugoslav and Post-Yugoslav Cinema* (Stanford: Stanford University Press, 2007); Dalibor Mišina's *Shake, Rattle and Roll: Yugoslav Rock Music and the Poetics of Social Critique* (Farnham: Ashgate, 2013); Ante Perković's *Sedma republika: pop kultura u YU raspadu* [The Seventh Republic: Pop Culture in the Yugoslav Dissolution] (Beograd: Službeni glasnik, 2011); Mitja Velikonja's and Vjekoslav Perica's *Nebeska Jugoslavija: interakcije politickih mitologija i pop-kulture* [Heavenly Yugoslavia: The Interaction of Political Mythologies and Pop-Culture] (Beograd: XX vek, 2012), or Željko Krušelj, *Polet – igraonica za odrasle 1976–1990* [Polet: a Playground for Adults] (Zagreb: Adamić, 2015).
All translations hereafter from Bosnian-Croatian-Serbian, Slovene or Macedonian are mine, unless stated otherwise.

2 Alexei Yurchak in his seminal study on the 'last Soviet generation' identifies one crucial 'inaugural event' around which the identity of this generation was formed – the collapse of the Soviet Union. Alan Spitzer similarly underlines this point of disjuncture, which determines a generation by referring to it as a 'social trauma', 'historical trauma' or a 'Great Divide' (a World War or a Depression generation). See: Alan B. Spitzer, 'The historical problem of generations', *The American Historical Review* 78:5 (1973), 1353–85.

3 Susan Woodward, *Balkan Tragedy: Chaos and Dissolution after the Cold War* (Washington, DC: The Brookings Institution, 1995); Sabrina Ramet, *Nationalism and Federalism in Yugoslavia 1962–1991* (Bloomington: Indiana University Press, 1992); Andrew Wachtel, *Making a Nation, Breaking a Nation: Literature and Cultural Politics in Yugoslavia* (Stanford: Stanford University Press, 1998); Dejan Jovic, *Yugoslavia: A State That Withered Away* (West Lafayette: Purdue University Press, 2009); Paul B. Allcock, *Explaining Yugoslavia* (London: C. Hurst, 2000); Valerie Bunce, *Subversive Institutions: The*

Design and the Destruction of Socialism and the State (Cambridge: Cambridge University Press, 1999); Lenard J. Cohen, *Broken Bonds: The Disintegration of Yugoslavia* (Boulder: Westview Press, 1993); V. P. Gagnon, *The Myth of Ethnic War: Serbia and Croatia in the 1990s* (Ithaca: Cornell University Press, 2004).

4 For one of the rare analyses that focuses on the intellectual realm in the 1980s, see: Jasna Dragović-Soso, *'Saviours of the Nation': Serbia's Intellectual Opposition and the Revival of Nationalism* (London: Hurst & Company, 2002). On grassroots mobilisation in the late 1980s, see: Nebojša Vladisavljević, *Serbia's Antibureaucratic Revolution: Milošević, the Fall of Communism and Nationalist Mobilization* (Basingstoke and New York: Palgrave Macmillan, 2008). Where scholars have dealt with alternatives, they have mostly focused on the 1990s. See, for example: Eric Gordy, *The Culture of Power in Serbia: Nationalism and the Destruction of Alternatives* (University Park: Pennsylvania State University Press, 1999) or Bojan Bilić, *We Were Gasping for Air: [Post] Yugoslav Anti-War Activism and Its Legacy* (Baden-Baden: Nomos, 2012).

5 See: Bojan Bilić and Vesna Janković (eds), *Resisting the Evil: [Post] Yugoslav Anti-War Contention* (Baden Baden: NOMOS, 2012); Jelena Obradović Wochnik, *Ethnic Conflict and War Crimes in the Balkans: The Narratives of Denial in Post-Conflict Serbia* (London: I. B. Tauris, 2013); Igor Duda, *Pronađeno blagostanje. Svakodnevni život i potrošačka kultura u Hrvatskoj 1970-ih i 1980-ih* (Zagreb: Srednja Evropa, 2010); Rory Archer, Igor Duds and Paul Stubbs (eds), *Social Inequalities and Discontent in Yugoslav Socialism* (London and New York: Routledge, 2016).
Studies of everyday life and social and cultural history have become more prominent in recent years: Patrick Hyder Patterson, *Bought and Sold: Living and Losing the Good Life in Socialist Yugoslavia* (Ithaca: Cornell University Press, 2011); Hannes Grandits and Karin Taylor (eds), *Yugoslavia's Sunny Side: A History of Tourism in Socialism (1950s–1980s)* (Budapest and New York: Central European University Press, 2010); Breda Luthar and Maruša Pušnik (eds), *Remembering Utopia: The Culture of Everyday Life in Socialist Yugoslavia* (Washington, DC: New Academia, 2010).

6 Andreas Wimmer and Nina Glick Schiller, 'Methodological nationalism and beyond: Nation-state building, migration and the social sciences', *Global Networks* 2:4 (2002), 301–34.

7 See: Blaž Vurnik, *Med Marxom in Punkom: Vloga Zveze socialistične mladine Slovenije pri demokratizaciji Slovenije (1980–1990)* (Ljubljana: Modrijan, 2005); Milan Balažic, *Slovenska demokratična revolucija 1986–1988* (Ljubljana: Liberalna akademija, 2004); Patrick Hyder Patterson, 'The east is red: The end of communism, Slovenian exceptionalism, and the independent journalism of Mladina', *East European Politics and Societies* 14 (2000), 411–59.

8 Aleš Erjavec, 'Neue Slowenische Kunst – new Slovenian art: Slovenia, Yugoslavia, self-management, and the 1980s', in Aleš Erjavec (ed.), *Postmodernism and the Postsocialist Condition: Politicized Art under Late Socialism* (Berkeley, Los Angeles and London: University of California Press, 2003), p. 154.

9 Anna von der Goltz, 'Introduction: Generational belonging and the "68ers" in Europe', in Anna von der Goltz (ed.), *'Talkin' 'bout My Generation': Conflicts of Generation Building and Europe's "1968"* (Göttingen: Wallstein Verlag, 2011), p. 12.

10 Donald J. Raleigh, *Soviet Baby Boomers: An Oral History of Russia's Cold War Generation* (Oxford and New York: Oxford University Press, 2013); Anna Saunders, *Honecker's*

Children: Youth and Patriotism in East Germany, 1979–2002 (Manchester: Manchester University Press, 2011); Juliane Fürst, *Stalin's Last Generation: Soviet Post-War Youth and the Emergence of Mature Socialism* (Oxford and New York: Oxford University Press, 2010); Alexei Yurchak, *Everything Was Forever, Until It Was No More: The Last Soviet Generation* (Princeton: Princeton University Press, 2005).

11 Christian Joppke, 'Transformation of citizenship: Status, rights, identity', *Citizenship Studies* 11:1 (2007), 37–48.

12 Jordan Aleksić, 'Mlada generacija i Savez Komunista Jugoslavije', in Srđan Vrcan *et al.* (eds), *Položaj, svest i ponašanje mlade generacije Jugoslavije* (Beograd: Centar za istraživačku dokumentacionu i izdavačku delatnost Konferencije SSOJ/Zagreb: Institut za društvena istraživanja Sveučilišta, 1986), p. 190.

13 Jordan Aleksić *et al.*, *Omladina i politika: jugoslavenska omladina između političke apatije i autonomnog političkog subjektiviteta* (Split: Marksistički centar Međuopćinske konferencije SKH za Dalmaciju, 1988), p. 28.

14 Pamela J. Conover makes a distinction between the affective (identity and meaning one gives to their membership in a particular political community) and the cognitive pole (the understanding and framework of beliefs one develops about their relationship to the state and to other citizens). See: Pamela J. Conover, 'Citizen identities and conceptions of the self', *Journal of Political Philosophy* 3 (1995), 133–65.

15 *Youth Prospects in the 1980s: Synthesis Report Presented to the General Conference of UNESCO at its Twenty-First Session* (Paris: UNESCO, 1980), p. 29.

16 Karl Mannheim, 'The problem of generations', in Paul Kecskemeti (ed.), *Essays on the Sociology of Knowledge* (London: Routledge, 1964), p. 292. The concept of 'youth culture' first appears in a 1942 essay by American sociologist Talcott Parsons ('Age and sex in the social structure of the United States', *American Sociological Review* 7:5 (1942), 604–16). He approaches youth culture from a functionalist perspective, emphasising youth culture's 'important positive functions in easing the transition from the security of childhood in the family of orientation to that of full adult in marriage and occupational status', in contrast with the later British cultural studies approach (the Birmingham Centre for Contemporary Cultural Studies) with a greater focus on class, as established in the seminal 1975 study edited by Stuart Hall and Tony Jefferson, *Resistance through Rituals: Youth Subcultures in Post-War Britain.*

17 Philip Abrams, 'The conflict of generations in industrial society', *Journal of Contemporary History* 5:1 (1970), 175–90.

18 Age cohort, like age group, can denote 'a grouping of individuals who share the same significant event, especially their birth, at or within a given period of time'. Jane Filcher, *Age & Generation in Modern Britain* (London: Oxford University Press, 1995), p. 134.

19 Hilde Katrine Haug, *Creating a Socialist Yugoslavia: Tito, Communist Leadership and the National Question* (London: I. B. Tauris, 2012), p. 318.

20 Lenard Cohen, *The Socialist Pyramid: Elites and Power in Yugoslavia* (Oakville, New York and London: Mosaic Press, 1989), p. 423.

21 *Ibid.*

22 Vladisavljević, *Serbia's Antibureaucratic Revolution*, pp. 45–6.

23 Mannheim, 'The problem of generations', p. 304. For the use of 'generation' and 'youth rebellion' as explanatory frames, see: Detlef Siegfried, 'Understanding

1968: Youth rebellion, generational change and postindustrial society', in Axel Schildt *et al.* (eds), *Between Marx and Coca-Cola: Youth Cultures in Changing European Societies* (New York: Berghahn, 2006), pp. 74–6.

24 On combining these approaches, see: June Edmunds and Bryan S. Turner, *Generations, Culture and Society* (Milton Keynes and Philadelphia: Open University Press, 2002). On the construction of generation, see: Mark Roseman, 'Introduction: Generation conflict and German history, 1770–1968', in Mark Roseman (ed.), *Generations in Conflict: Youth Revolt and Generation Formation in Germany, 1770–1968* (Cambridge: Cambridge University Press, 1995), pp. 4–5; Thomas Burgess, 'Imagined generations: Constructing youth in revolutionary Zanzibar', in Jon Abbink and Ineke van Kessel (eds), *Vanguard or Vandals: Youth Politics and Conflict in Africa* (Leiden: Brill, 2005); Stephen Lovell, 'Introduction', in Stephen Lovell (ed.), *Generations in Twentieth-Century Europe* (Basingstoke: Palgrave Macmillan, 2007), p. 13.

25 Srećko Mihailović *et al.*, *Deca krize: Omladina Jugoslavije krajem osamdesetih* (Beograd: Institut društvenih nauka/Centar za politikološka istraživanja i javno mnenje, 1990), p. 320.

26 Smiljka Tomanović *et al.*, *Mladi – naša sadašnjost. Istraživanje socijalnih biografija mladih u Srbiji* (Beograd: Čigoja/ Institut za sociološka istraživanja Filozofskog fakulteta, 2012), p. 30.

27 Srđan Vrcan *et al.*, *Položaj, svest i ponašanje mlade generacije Jugoslavije* (Beograd: Centar za istraživačku, dokumentacionu i izdavačku delatnost Konferencije SSOJ/ Zagreb: Institut za društvena istraživanja Sveučilišta, 1986), p. 14.

28 Djordjije Uskoković, 'Neke najčešće teorijsko-metodološke teškoće i jednostranosti empirijskih istraživanja društvenog položaja i svesti mladih u Jugoslaviji', in *Mlada generacija, danas: društveni položaj, uloga i perspektive mlade generacije Jugoslavije* (Beograd: NIRO Mladost/Predsedništvo konferencije SSOJ, 1982).

29 On tracing the construction of generation in 'memory', see: von der Goltz, 'Introduction', pp. 9–32.

30 See: Aleš Debeljak, *Twilight of the Idols: Recollections of a Lost Yugoslavia* (Buffalo: White Pine Press, 1994).

31 Tomaž Mastnak, 'From social movements to national sovereignty', in Jill Benderly and Evan Kraft (eds), *Independent Slovenia: Origins, Movements, Prospects* (London: Macmillan, 1994), pp. 94–5.

32 Open Society Archive, digital archive (hereafter OSA), Slobodan Stankovic, 'Intellectual ferment in Yugoslavia', *Radio Free Europe* Background Report, 11 November 1980.

33 Saunders, *Honecker's Children*, p. 226.

34 Tomaž Mastnak (ed.), *Zbornik Socilistična civilna družba* (Ljubljana: RK ZSMS/UK ZSMS, 1986), p. 25; Danica Fink Hafner, *Nova družbena gibanja: subjekti politične inovacije* (Ljubljana: FDV, 1992), p. 19.

35 Mirjana Ule, 'Stoletje mladine', in John R. Gillis, *Mladina in zgodovina* (Ljubljana: Aristej, 1999), p. 279.

36 Obrad Savic, 'Concepts of civil society in former Yugoslavia', in Dane R. Gordon and David C. Durst (eds), *Civil Society in Southeast Europe* (Amsterdam and New York: Rodopi, 2004), p. 78.

37 Gregor Tomc, 'Civilna družba pod slovenskim socializmom', *Nova revija* 57 (1987), 144–50.

38 Rupnik (1979) in Krishan Kumar, 'Civil society: An inquiry into the usefulness of an historical term', *The British Journal of Sociology* 44:3 (1993), 375–95, p. 386.

39 Kumar, 'Civil society'.

40 Chris Hann, Caroline Humphrey and Katherine Verdery, 'Introduction: Postsocialism as a topic of anthropological investigation', in Chris Hann (ed.), *Postsocialism: Ideals, Ideologies and Practices in Eurasia* (London and New York: Routledge, 2001), p. 9.

41 Engin Isin and Greg Nielsen (eds), *Acts of Citizenship* (London: Palgrave Macmillan, 2008); Engin Isin, 'Citizenship in flux: The figure of the activist citizen', *Subjectivity* 29 (2009), 367–88.

42 Engin F. Isin, 'Theorizing acts of citizenship', in Isin and Nielsen, *Acts of Citizenship*, p. 36.

43 *Ibid.*, p. 39.

44 Yurchak proposes this notion in order to deconstruct the often taken for granted assumptions that socialism was 'bad' or 'immoral', i.e. 'the use of binary categories to describe Soviet reality such as oppression and resistance, repression and freedom, the state and the people, official economy and second economy, official culture and counterculture, totalitarian language and counterlanguage, public self and private self, truth and lie, reality and dissimulation, morality and corruption, and so on'. See: Yurchak, *Everything Was Forever*, pp. 4–5.

45 Francesca Polletta, '"Free spaces" in collective action', *Theory and Society* 28 (1999), 1–38.

46 While the 'liminal' is strictly speaking related to more primitive societies, to rites of passage and is about obligation, the 'liminoid' is about play and choice. Liminoid phenomena are individual, though with collective or mass effects; they are part of social critiques, exposing injustices or inefficiencies of mainstream economic, political and social structures. Spaces such as bars, pubs, cafes, social clubs, etc. are considered to be permanent 'liminoid' settings. See: Victor Turner, *From Ritual to Theatre: The Human Seriousness of Play* (New York: PAJ Publications, 1982).

47 Mirjana Ule, 'Odnos omladine prema mladosti, odraslosti i budućnosti', in Vrcan *et al.*, *Položaj, svest i ponašanje*, pp. 101–13. Similarly, Dave Laing in *One Chord Wonders: Power and Meaning in Punk Rock* (Milton Keynes and Philadelphia: Open University Press, 1985) showed that many punk musicians (43 per cent) actually came from middle-class families.

48 Ljubica Spaskovska, 'The Yugoslav chronotope: Histories, memories and the future of Yugoslav studies', in Rory Archer, Armina Galijas and Florian Bieber (eds), *Debating the Dissolution of Yugoslavia* (London: Ashgate, 2014).

49 Mikhail Bakhtin, 'Forms of time and of the chronotope in the novel', in Michael Holquist (ed.), *The Dialogic Imagination: Four Essays* (Austin: University of Texas Press, 1981), p. 84.

50 Paul Thomson, 'The voice of the past: Oral history', in Robert Perks and Alistair Thomson (eds), *The Oral History Reader* (London and New York: Routledge, 1998), p. 22.

51 Alessandro Portelli, *The Death of Luigi Trastulli, and Other Stories: Form and Meaning in Oral History* (Albany: SUNY Press, 1990), pp. viii–ix.

52 Kathryn Anderson and Dana C. Jack, 'Learning to listen: Interview techniques and analyses', in Robert Perks and Alistair Thomson (eds), *The Oral History Reader* (London and New York: Routledge, 1998), p. 166.

53 Alistair Thomson, 'Unreliable memories: The use and abuse of oral history', in William Lamont (ed.), *Historical Controversies and Historians* (London and New York: Routledge, 1998), p. 27.

54 Lynn Abrams, *Oral History Theory* (London: Routledge, 2010), p. 19.

55 *Omladina Beograda: statistika i istraživanja* (Beograd: Marksistički centar organizacije SK u Beogradu, 1983); *Omladina SR Srbije u brojkama* (Beograd: Istraživačko-izdavački centar SSO Srbije, 1986); Dragomir Pantić, *Vrednosne orijentacije mladih u Srbiji* (Beograd: Istraživačko-izdavački centar SSO Srbije, 1981); Dragomir Pantić *et al.*, *Interesovanja mladih* (Beograd: Istraživačko-izdavački centar SSO Srbije, 1981); Snežana Joksimović *et al.*, *Sadržaj i oblici neformalnog okuljanja mladih u Beogradu* (Beograd: Centar za idejni rad SSO GK Beograd, 1986); Mirjana Ule, *Mladina '85* (Ljubljana: Institut za kriminologijo pri pravni fakulteti, 1985); *Mladina Slovenije '82* (Ljubljana: Republiška konferenca ZSMS, 1982); Mirjana Ule, *Mladina in ideologija* (Ljubljana: Delavska enotnost, 1988).

56 Benjamin Perasović, 'Razgovor: Nebojša Popov, predsjednik Jugoslavenskog udruženja za sociologiju. Sloboda je nedjeljiva', *Studentski list* 2:966 (27 January 1988), 5.

57 Vrcan *et al.*, *Položaj, svest i ponašanje*, p. 7.

58 Aleksić, 'Mlada generacija', p. 188.
The analysis was done on a sample of 6,215 respondents between the ages of fourteen and twenty-seven (twenty-nine for the young farmers), consisting of five principal contingencies: secondary school youth, university students, unemployed youth, employed youth and young farmers. The summary report published in the form of an edited volume consists of separate chapters with elaborate data on different themes ranging from the 'values of the young generation' to the 'attitudes of the young towards nation and religion' and generally reflects the major themes and preoccupations of the time (proliferation of the religion in public, decline in youth membership in the League of Communists, decline in support for self-management, proliferation of the North–South divide, etc.), as well as some 'frozen narratives' tending to represent the youth as a victim of a system which did not allow enough space for the realisation of its potentials.

59 Mihailović *et al.*, *Deca krize*.

60 *Youth Prospects in the 1980s*, p. 7.

61 *Ibid.*, p. 9.

62 *Ibid.*, p. 10.

63 Johanna Wyn and Dan Woodman, 'Generation, youth and social change in Australia', *Journal of Youth Studies* 9:5 (2006), p. 499.

64 *Youth prospects in the 1980s*, p. 17.

65 'Delegati u radničkim savetima organizacija udruženog rada', *Statistički godišnjak Jugoslavije 1985* (Beograd: Savezni Zavod za statistiku, 1985), p. 79.

66 'Delegati u skupštinama društveno-političkih zajednica prema zastupljenosti žena i omladine i stručnom obrazovanju u 1982', *Statistički godišnjak Jugoslavije 1985*, p. 106.

67 'Diplomirani studenti 1981', in Dušan Davidović (ed.), *Mladi Jugoslavije: opšti pregled* (Beograd: Centar za istraživačku i dokumentaciono-izdavačku delatnost Predsedništva Konferencije SSOJ, 1982), p. 35.

68 Slobodan Stanković, *The End of the Tito Era: Yugoslavia's Dilemmas* (Stanford: Hoover Institution Press, 1981), p. 121.

69 Bogdan Denitch, *Limits and Possibilities: The Crisis of Yugoslav Socialism and State Socialist Systems* (Minneapolis: University of Minnesota Press, 1990), p. 109.

70 Šta bi vam Tito danas rekao?', *Stav* 21 (23 September 1988), 22–3.

71 See: Ramadan Marmullaku, 'Albanians in Yugoslavia: A personal essay', in Dejan Djokic (ed.), *Yugoslavism: Histories of a Failed Idea, 1918–1992* (Madison: University of Wisconsin Press, 2003); Aleksandar Petrović and Đorđe Stefanović, 'Kosovo, 1944–1981: The rise and fall of a communist "nested homeland"', *Europe-Asia Studies* 6:7 (2010), 1073–106.

72 *Yugoslavia: Prisoners of Conscience* (London: Amnesty International Publications, 1985).

73 Dušan Bilandžić, *Historija Socijalističke Federativne Republike Jugoslavije: glavni procesi 1918–1985* (Zagreb: Školska knjiga, 1985), p. 495.

74 Momčilo Petrović, *Pitao sam Albance šta žele, a oni su rekli: republiku … ako može* (Belgrade: Radio B92, 1996).

75 Marmullaku, 'Albanians in Yugoslavia', p. 305.

76 OSA, Patrick Moore, 'The Kosovo events in perspective', *Radio Free Europe* Background Report, 28 April 1981.

77 Bilandžić, *Historija Socijalističke Federativne Republike Jugoslavije*, p. 497.

78 OSA, Louis Zanga, 'The Kosovar dilemma', *Radio Free Europe* Background Report, 20 May 1981.

79 Gëzim Krasniqi, 'Socialism, national utopia, and rock music: Inside the Albanian rock scene of Yugoslavia, 1970–1989', *East Central Europe* 38 (2011), 336–54.

80 *Ibid.*, p. 340.

81 Ana Dević, 'Anti-war initiative and the un-making of civic identities in the former Yugoslav republics', *Journal of Historical Sociology* 10:2 (1997), 150.

82 Slobodan Bjelajac and Stojan Obradović, 'Omladina u Savezu komunista', in *Klasno-Socijalna Struktura Saveza Komunista Jugoslavije* (Beograd: Izdavački centar Komunist, 1984).

83 Bilandžić, *Historija Socijalističke Federativne Republike Jugoslavije*, p. 474.

84 OSA, Slobodan Stanković, 'The Yugoslavs openly discuss the country's problems', *Radio Free Europe* Background Report, 20 November 1980.

85 Pedro Ramet, 'Contradiction and reform in Yugoslav communism: A conclusion', in Pedro Ramet (ed.), *Yugoslavia in the 1980s* (Boulder: Westview Press, 1985), p. 326.

86 George Schopflin, 'Political decay in one-party systems in Eastern Europe: Yugoslav patterns', in Ramet, *Yugoslavia in the 1980s*, p. 314.

87 Daniel J. Goulding, *Liberated Cinema: The Yugoslav Experience 1945–2001* (Bloomington: Indiana University Press, 2003), p. 145.

88 See: Adam Roberts, 'Yugoslavia: The constitution and the succession', *The World Today* 34:4 (1978), 136–46, p. 139. On the practical malfunctions of socialist self-management in the 1980s, see: Harold Lydall, *Yugoslavia in Crisis* (Oxford: Clarendon Press, 1989).

89 Aleksić *et al.*, *Omladina i politika: jugoslavenska omladina između političke apatije i autonomnog političkog subjektiviteta*, p. 13.

90 *Ibid.*, p. 21.
91 Srđan Vrcan, 'Suvremeno pokoljenje mladih – novo i osobito pokoljenje', in *Mlada generacija, danas*, p. 137.
92 Vladimir Obradović, 'Društveni položaj omladine u Jugoslaviji', in Vrcan *et al.*, *Položaj, svest i ponašanje*, p. 49.
93 Ule, 'Odnos omladine prema mladosti', p. 111.
94 Obradović, 'Društveni položaj omladine', p. 49.
95 Patrick Hyder Patterson, *Bought and Sold: Living and Losing the Good Life in Socialist Yugoslavia* (Ithaca: Cornell University Press, 2011), pp. 314–17.
96 Aleksić *et al.*, *Omladina i politika*, p. 22.
97 Yurchak, *Everything Was Forever.*
98 Srećko Mihailović, 'Odnos omladine prema politici', in Vrcan *et al.*, *Položaj, svest i ponašanje*, p. 175.
99 Derek R. Hall, 'Tourism change in Central and Eastern Europe', in Armando Montanari and Allan M. Williams (eds), *European Tourism: Regions, Spaces and Restructuring* (Chichester: John Wiley & Sons, 1995), p. 229.
100 For analyses of the rural–urban dichotomy in the Yugoslav context, see: Xavier Bougarel, 'Yugoslav wars: The "revenge of the countryside" between sociological reality and nationalist myth', *East European Quaterly* 32:2 (June 1999), 157–75; John B. Allcock, 'Rural–urban differences and the break-up of Yugoslavia', *Balkanologie* 6:1/2 (2002), 101–25. On perceptions of urbanity and antinationalism in the post-Yugoslav context, see: Stef Jansen, *Antinacionalizam: etnografija otpora u Zagrebu i Beogradu* (Belgrade: Biblioteka XX vek, 2005); Stef Jansen, 'Cosmopolitan openings and closures in post-Yugoslav antinationalism', in Magdalena Nowicka and Maria Rovisco (eds), *Cosmopolitanism in Practice* (Aldershot: Ashgate, 2008), pp. 75–92.
101 Dejan Kršić, *Mirko Ilić: Fist to Face* (New York: F+V Media, 2012), p. 52.
102 Boško Grbić, 'Omladinska štampa: položaj, delovanje, tretman', *Mladost* 1277 (22 March 1982), 3.
103 *XII конгрес на Сојузот на социјалистичка младина на Македонија* (Скопје/Кочани: Републичка конференција на ССММ: Младост, 1986), p. 32.
104 Davidović, *Mladi Jugoslavije*, p. 53.

'Pockets of freedom': the youth sphere and its spaces of negotiation and dissent

Moje su nebo vezali žicom
Po mome mozgu crtaju šeme
Žele još jednu kopiju svoju
Da njome vrate nestalo vreme.
Al' ne dam svoje ja ideale
I ješću snove umesto hleba
Ja svoju sreću nosim sa sobom
Ona je parče slobodnog neba.[1]

'Nebo', Električni orgazam (1981)

In the 1980s, the voices of dissent coming from the young Yugoslav generation were not, for the most part, expressed within a clearly delineated alternative sphere, but rather within the wide framework of the SSOJ. Whilst most work on political alternatives in late socialism has focused on the rise of alternative spheres or parallel societies, contention and negotiation from within official institutions has seldom been studied in detail.[2] Addressing the last Yugoslav generation through the ways it articulated its generational specificities and preoccupations in the institutional youth sphere – more specifically in media and culture – this chapter maps the wide, decentralised youth infrastructure of the SSOJ as a form of public space. It outlines the processes of change in the late socialist youth institutional realm and reflects specifically on the ways contestations nested, became voiced or accommodated within the existing framework of the SSOJ. Arguably, the very existence of its decentralised network allowed for novel youth cultures and politics to emerge and develop – through the venues, events and in particular through the youth media/press network. In addition, the chapter reflects on the limits of toleration, the appropriate forms of expression, and the acceptable boundaries of freedom and criticism.

As was the case with other socialist states, the youth was considered one of the most important pillars of Yugoslav society. The widely popular slogan *Tito–Partija–Omladina–Armija* [Tito–the Party–the Youth–the Army] points to the importance given to the youth, as a separate pillar in the socialist order. Hence the SSOJ was established as one of the five 'socio-political organisations' in socialist Yugoslavia, alongside the Socialist Alliance of Working People (SSRNJ), the Union of Fighters of the National-Liberation Struggle, the Alliance of Trade Unions and the SKJ. As such, it was formally part of the political system, in particular through its delegates to the SSRNJ and to the various chambers of the municipal, republican and federal assemblies.[3] However, not all members of the SSOJ were members of the Party. Membership in the SKJ was voluntary, albeit desirable; from the 1960s onwards, and in particular during the 1980s, the number of SKJ members below the age of twenty-eight began to decrease. Seen as a critical pillar of the Yugoslav socialist project, the state invested in the youth both symbolic and economic capital with the hope that the sense of 'Yugoslav socialist patriotism' would supersede and replace narrower circles of belonging or ethnic and class divisions.

The sense of a multi-level crisis and the decline of trust in the Party and in the SSOJ in the first half of the 1980s led many young activists to argue that the institutional youth sphere had to be reformed. In the early 1980s, youngsters who wished to express alternatives found possibilities in the 'peripheral' parts of the SSOJ, i.e. in the cultural realm and the youth media. It was in particular the decentralised nature of the SSOJ which allowed 'pockets of freedom' to be created or (re)claimed by a new generation of political activists, journalists, musicians and artists, within its very institutional infrastructure – consequently producing cross-fertilisations of ideas and initiatives that did much to promote a burgeoning music/media scene. By the late 1980s, most of the major youth magazines contained hardly any trace of what was their originally conceived role of acting as official organs of the branches of the SSOJ. While differences between federal units and regional variation have to be acknowledged, a new pan-Yugoslav network of alternative voices was created though the SSOJ's cultural and media infrastructure. Yet, in the first half of the 1980s, these challenges remained on the periphery: it was not until the second half of the decade that the SSOJ began to reinvent itself as a space where *political* alternatives could be articulated and where a more pronounced challenge towards the institutional set-up as a whole emerged.

The processes of contention, negotiation and change unfolding within the youth sphere were certainly embedded within the larger societal and political developments and the all-pervading discourse and sense of crisis. A history of a relatively liberal youth culture and a semi-free press coupled with ongoing processes of freer public debate and a consensus on political reform contributed to the creation of the youth media as an arena for various articulations of demands for freedom of speech and critical reflection on the contemporary socio-political reality. Essentially, the last Yugoslav generation chose not to withdraw or completely opt out of the institutional framework, but met the state in its own 'official' territory and challenged it there.

Evidently, the debates and changes which ensued in the institutional youth sphere were a consequence of the crisis and set the organisation on a path to reinvent itself, deal with withdrawal in active membership and participation and respond to increased criticism both from without and from within. The principal question this chapter engages with is how the transformation of the official rhetoric, politics and practices within the institutional youth sphere unfolded. How did the youth organisation engage with and respond to the wider socio-political crisis and its own internal crisis in terms of cadres, democratisation and reform? It was the 'peripheral' parts of the youth infrastructure (the youth cultural venues) which were the most porous and open to alternative culture and new forms of expression, with the youth press as the most vocal, popular and visible part of the youth institutional framework. It progressively carved out new spaces for debate and rethinking of the socio-political reality and articulated demands for freedom of speech, all the while navigating a series of bans, court cases, pressures and public stigmatisation.

Children of socialism: Yugoslav 'socialist democracy' and its (dis)contents

Stemming from the interwar youth revolutionary wing of the Yugoslav Communist Party founded in 1919, the youth organisation went through several organisational reforms.[4] In the immediate post-war period it was led by and composed of youngsters who had some experience or memory of the Second World War. Although by the mid-1950s the Yugoslav elite had relinquished socialist realism for high modernism, and Western cultural influences including rock and jazz were making inroads into youth culture, it was not until the late 1960s that a whole new generation born in the 1940s had come of age and marked a radical, enduring shift in Yugoslav youth politics and culture. Their coming of age coincided with the significant reform wave in politics and economics after 1965 – most notably the sacking of the secret police chief Aleksandar Ranković in 1966 and the launch of the first foreign capital investments in 1968. The 'sixty-eighters' were indeed the first children of Yugoslav self-managing socialism, but they were also well versed in European and global contemporary philosophical, cultural and political theories, events and debates. This knowledge and Yugoslavia's openness significantly informed their critique targeting the 'old', revolutuionary partisan generation as well as their subversive

cultural activism which nevertheless nested within the existing youth infrastructure. From the perspective of official youth politics, 'internationalism' was seen
as 'an integral part of the socialist upbringing of young people'.[5] The desired
level of familiarity with contemporary international relations, the social and
political movements around the world, the international labour movement, and
the politics of peaceful coexistence was to be achieved through programmes of
youth exchange and mobility. Hence, anti-imperialism and solidarity with the
liberation movements formed only one part of what 'internationalism' stood
for in the Yugoslav context: support for anti-colonial movements, safeguarding
peace, a global struggle for socialism and progress underpinned by the ideas of
(national) freedom and (socialist) democracy. A spontaneous anti-imperialist fer-
vour marked the protests following the execution of Patrice Lumumba in 1961
and the mass anti-war Vietnam demonstrations in 1965.[6] The intellectual, political or artistic outlook and activism of the post-war generation and in particular
of a significant part of the sixty-eighters was informed by contemporary developments and debates globally, and in particular by those launched by the 1968
student protets in Western Europe. In the words of Borka Pavićević (born 1947),
a playwright and cultural activist who took part in the 1968 student protest, 'I
think for my generation internationalism was something completely natural. It
need not be labelled as such, but it was that ideational, public and literary convergence – Marx, Mao, Marcuse, the Frankfurt School. All of that existed as one
spiritual milieu'.[7] Velimir Ćurgus Kazimir (born 1948) was also part of the 1968
student movement. His testimony echoes that sense of a European progressive
left consciousness and pinpoints a crucial issue that would be taken up by the
1980s generation – freedom of speech:

> Most of us were leftist, but we were not communist. That's the big difference,
> in particular [relevant] today, when one speaks from an anti-communist posi-
> tion which assumes that everyone who belongs to the Left deep inside is a
> Stalinist. And here we come to this paradox, when talking about 1968, and
> I belong to that generation, that we were the critics of what we were calling the
> 'red bourgeoisie', the undemocratic nature of the system, the manipulation of
> the press. One of our primary demands was freedom of speech and freedom
> of the media. ... We never perceived the Soviet Union as a place where we
> would like to live, that was rather the West, Scandinavia, even the USA.

It was in particular after the 1968 student riots that there was an increase
in the number of scholarly studies of the youth. Perceived both as a potential
problem and as a resource, the youth was put under scholarly scrutiny throughout the 1970s and the 1980s with the aim of 'establishing the reasons for its
discontent, but also of proving its attachment to socialism'.[8] A 1971 study on
Yugoslav youth pointed to its 'litmus-paper-like nature', i.e. its ability to act as a

'sensible indicator' for various societal phenomena or anomalies, assuming 'an a priori criticism towards the ruling structures'.[9] Sociologists preserved this lens of observing the youth as potentially rebellious. By the second half of the 1980s it was openly admitted that the critique of the new generation had shifted from the 'ruling structures' to the very 'ideological labels':

> In the eyes of the ideologues and the institutions, the young individual acts as a subject whose 'desires' are already known to society and which the society tries to satisfy, while in his/her own eyes s/he acts as subject which often 'doesn't know what it wants', which is in search of him/herself, entangles him/herself in conflicts with the representatives of 'society', which less and less identifies him/herself and the rest of the youth with the ideological labels of our society.[10]

In the second half of the 1980s, a process of moving away from the institutionally-coded socialist youth movement signalled an attempt for the creation of a new form of politics/culture, one that did not necessarily reject Yugoslavia or progressive (liberal or centre-left) politics, but searched for a new version of it. The way in which the young generation in the 1980s was, for the most part, positively rethinking Yugoslav socialism was a question which had its roots in the late 1960s and early 1970s. The student movement in this period essentially targeted the ruling elite 'for inefficiency in carrying out the socialist revolution – that there was not enough egalitarianism, self-management, or solidarity with other revolutionary movements'.[11]

Mainly directed against the independence of the Student Union(s) and the events of 1968, the decision to reform the youth organisation in 1974 reflected a growing concern with the role of the major Yugoslav universities as relatively autonomous breeding grounds for oppositional ideas and critical thought – in particular within the fields of philosophy and sociology. Consequently, in the period from the student protests in 1968 until 1974 '[Belgrade] University became the focus of cultural and political events. A dialogue developed on the ideas of counter-culture and the "new left" in frequent public discussions, magazines and periodicals, far more so than in the regular classroom sessions'.[12] While the youth organisation was generally criticised 'for its lack of purpose and inactivity' even by Party officials, the Student Union 'moved into a position of more open conflict with the League of Communists than any other political organisation during the period 1966–71'.[13] Indeed, one of the most often repeated arguments was that the Student Union must not act as a transmission belt of the Party.[14] However, the 1968 protests were not without a precedent. As early as 1959, soon after the opening of the 'Student Centre' in Zagreb, which was hailed as the most modern student complex in the country (consisting of dormitories, restaurants, cinema, etc.), the students organised a protest against food quality which later moved to the streets, sported some anti-regime slogans and was stopped by an intervention from the police. The protests in Zagreb sparked similar demonstrations in Skopje and Rijeka[15] and overcrowded universities and graduate unemployment would remain high on the agenda until the very end.

President Tito's conciliatory speech in June 1968, which effectively put an end to the student protest, did not manage to appease all of its protagonists, however. In October 1970, 6,000 students at Belgrade University staged another strike in protest of the sentencing of Vladimir Mijanović – one of the leaders of the 1968 Belgrade protest – to a twenty-month prison sentence for 'hostile anti-state propaganda'.[16] Mijanović was the chairman of the Student Union's committee at the Faculty of Philosophy and was accused, among other things, of publicly opposing the electoral lists proposed by the Socialist Alliance in 1969, for distributing leaflets calling for Yugoslavia to stop exporting its workers to West European capitalist states and urging the Bosnian miners from Kakanj to continue their strike. In January 1971, Noam Chomsky wrote a letter to the editors of *The New York Review of Books* entitled 'The Conscience of Yugoslavia' in protest to Mijanović's sentencing where, among other things, he stated that 'Mr. Mijanović and those associated with him are the hope and the conscience of the Yugoslav revolution'.[17]

What the political elite identified as 'new left' ideas or 'ultra-left radicalism' mainly penetrated the youth through contacts with progressive/anti-imperialist student groups in the West and through intellectual circles and university professors associated with the Praxis group and its journal which was banned in 1975. The 'unreserved support'[18] the students got from some of their professors features in many individual testimonies. Talking about the 1968 Belgrade student protest, Borka Pavićević recalled that sense of solidarity: 'There was a fundamental debate about the values between us … The professors were our teammates, our co-disputants. A good product of that was that our exams were not examinations, but dialogues … What is important about sixty-eight, is that one learned how not to fear anyone – neither the police, nor the professors, the [Party] city committee, God, anyone.'[19] Indeed, as Rusinow observed, 'at least the student elite among the children of the Yugoslav revolution had apparently absorbed some of its ideals and taken them seriously'.[20] However, many professors, as well political officials (most notably Second World War veteran and future federal foreign secretary Miloš Minić, who suffered physical injuries during the confrontation with the riot police) who were themselves student activists in the interwar period as part of the underground progressive communist movement, openly or tacitly aided the student protestors because they could identify with aspects of their struggle. Ljubiša Ristić (born 1947), a well-known theatre director who was a drama student in 1968, recalled how the dean of the Belgrade Academy for theatre, film, radio and television, Radoš Novaković, an established film director, a Second World War veteran and a Party activist, handed him the keys of the building and allowed the student 'action committee' to use the 'Gestetner' duplicating machine for their leaflets and other material during the June protests.[21]

However, radical left tendencies were only one aspect of what were identified as manifestations of an anti-socialist consciousness among the young: bureaucratism, technocratism, nationalism, different bourgeois orientations, dogmatic neo-Stalinism.[22] The protagonists of the 1968 events are unanimous that although the student discontent and demands boiled down to a critique from the left targeting the rise of a 'red bourgeoisie', increasing social inequality and an abandonment of the original revolutionary socialist principles, the calls for freedom of expression and demands for resignations of the federal, republican and city secretaries for interior affairs due to the excessive use of force by the riot police against the student protestors, testified to the presence of a broader ideological spectrum, 'from those who adhered to the idea of a socialism with a human face to those who were anti-socialist', according to Kemal Kurspahić (born 1946), editor at the student magazine *Student* at the time of the protests.[23] For different reasons, he claims, royalists, anarchists, anti-communists and Stalinists all supported the students in 1968.

Indeed, the second half of the 1960s could be pinpointed as a critical period for the diversification of the Yugoslav youth sphere, something that would have a lasting legacy up until the break-up of Yugoslavia. The critique that stemmed from the 1968 student protests was resignified by the generation of the 'eighty-eighters'. The first Yugoslav post-war generation – the 'sixty-eighters' – was the one that pioneered novel, subversive political and artistic tendencies. Hence, it is possible to identify several features that defined this generation and the ways in which it articulated its critique through various cultural acts, which constitute a set of continuities and models found twenty years later in the political and cultural struggles of the 1980s generation:

- increased mobility/travel outside of Yugoslavia that contributed to a sense of internationalism;
- open and more covert struggles for freedom of expression;
- a sense of elitism, considering the absolute majority of activists were educated, urban youth rather than young (industrial) workers or farmers;
- fragmentation of and tension/conflict within the institutional youth sphere;
- targeting of the authoritarian traits of socialism though comparing/equalising Nazism and Stalinism/communism;
- insistence on a generation gap, i.e. a self-fashioned generational identity in contrast to an older – in this case the Second World War revolutionary – generation.

By 1968 it was also becoming clear that the Yugoslav Party was growing old and that this in turn revealed a growing sense of disillusionment with the state

Figure 2 Caricature from Macedonian youth magazine *Fokus*, 1971

of Yugoslav socialism and the prescribed boundaries of institutional political activism (see Table 3).

As a consequence of all of this, the Third Conference of the SKJ in December 1972 was partially dedicated to the youth. A long resolution entitled 'The struggle of the SKJ for a socialist orientation and active participation of the young generation in the development of the socialist self-managing society' was adopted.[24] The adjective 'socialist' was added to the official name of the youth organisation at its ninth congress in 1974: from the 'Yugoslav Youth League' [*Savez omladine Jugoslavije*] it became the 'League of Socialist Youth of Yugoslavia' [*Savez socijalističke omladine Jugoslavije*]. That was also the moment when the Yugoslav Student League [*Savez studenata Jugoslavije*] ceased to exist as a separate youth organisation, as it was merged with the Yugoslav Youth League to form the new 'League of Socialist Youth of Yugoslavia'.[25] This attempt at political and organisational homogenisation of the youth could be interpreted, first, as an effort to tighten the control over the relatively independent university-based student organisations, and, second, as an attempt

Table 3 Youth Party membership relative to total Party membership 1958–66

Year	Total Party membership	Up to the age of 25	% of total Party membership
1958	829,953	196,019	23.6
1961	1,035,000	224,077	21.6
1962	1,018,331	184,186	18.1
1963	1,919,013	156,367	15.3
1964	1,031,634	140,052	13.6
1965	1,046,202	131,749	12.6
1966	1,046,018	120,234	11.5

Source: According to data from 1967 cited in Slobodan Stankovic, 'On the Eve of the Yugoslav Youth Party Congress', Radio Free Europe (Research), 7 February 1968, *Open Society Archive* (digital archive).

to bridge the increasing gap between the urban, intellectual, university-based student youth, on the one hand, and the working class/rural youth, on the other. Azem Vllasi, representing the autonomous province of Kosovo, was elected president of the newly consolidated SSOJ in 1974 and remained at the post for two mandates until 1978. According to him, prior to 1974, there were *de facto* two separate youth organisations and the decision to merge them was an attempt to reinforce the coherence of the institutional youth sphere. Indeed, the 'passivity' and the 'insufficient inclusion' in all aspects of the social and economic life of working class and rural youth were often juxtaposed in official discourse with the 'increasing visibility/exposure of the student youth'.[26] Evidently, two major events on the Yugoslav political scene at the beginning of the 1970s – the 1971 Croatian 'mass movement' (MASPOK), the purge of its 'nationalist' leaders and the 1972 removal of Serbian 'liberals' played an equally important role in the decision of the Party to curb the autonomy of the student unions. The Croatian case exposed the porousness of the borders between the political and the youth/student realms, as the propagated ideas resonated with a significant number of students at Zagreb University who took part in the demonstrations.[27]

The attempted unification of the youth organisation under the banner of 'socialism' appeared effective, at least until the first years after President Tito's death. The 1972 Party resolution had urged the young to embrace 'socialist patriotism', actively partake in the strenghtening of global socialism, intensify relations with revolutionary and liberation movements and become good 'internationalists'.[28] At the very beginning of the new decade, the political wing of the youth organisation still unanimously followed the main political line in celebrating the Yugoslav revolutionary heritage, socialist self-management, non-alignment and co-operation with Third World countries. Hence, in a bold display of commitment to Yugoslav non-alignment and in response to the Soviet invasion of Afghanistan, between the two international youth seminars in Kumrovec in 1980 and 1981 the SSOJ left the Prague-based and Moscow-sponsored International Union of Students (IUS). Although local problems concerning student standards and employment were always on its agenda, the SSOJ chose to finance the participation of fifty delegations (out of ninety-nine in total) at the 1981 Kumrovec youth seminar, including different socialist or leftist youth unions from Australia, Brazil, Ghana, Honduras, Congo, Madagascar, Malta, Seychelles, Sierra Leon, Uganda, Palestine and South Africa, in what could be interpreted as an intent to mirror the official state politics of commitment to non-aligned internationalism.[29]

The youth organisation in the 1980s

The 1980 UNESCO report on youth noted that 'Schools, political parties, trade-unions and governments enter the 1980s under the threat of massive withdrawal of confidence by the younger generation'.[30] Furthermore, youngsters 'seem to find little reflection of those goals of social progress and justice in day-to-day workings of governments and political parties'.[31] In a similar vein, the 1986 *JUPIO* report underlined in its introductory notes the fact that

> the contemporary youth is living in conditions of relatively wide-spread democ-ratisation of social life ... Hence, the youth lives in a context where it is no longer possible to implement some earlier mechanisms of prohibition of certain aspects of the socio-political reality, through systematic institutional closures or limitations of people's existential and spiritual horizons ... Ultimately, the youth lives in a general context where it is absolutely no longer possible to achieve the desired socio-political goals through a comprehensive, consistent and limited political indoctrination, as well as through occasional virulent ide-ological campaigns.[32]

Writing about the Yugoslav political realm of the early 1980s, Haug notes that 'The seeming inability of the SKJ leaders to deal with the crisis seriously shook public confidence in the Party. This led the SKJ to immerse itself in a large-scale self-criticism exercise'.[33] Archival material from the League of Socialist Youth, as well as official reports from the League's congresses, demonstrate a replication of the extensive 'self-criticism exercise' within the multi-level structure of the Yugoslav youth organisation. Internal documents emphasised that 'the SSO lacks a long-term and well-planned activity for [its] engagement in the Socialist Alliance [of Working People]'.[34] Indeed, the SSOJ was reproached at different levels and resorted to self-critique concerning the low numbers of youth delegates to the SSRNJ and the other organs of the political system. In 1982, for instance, of the 1,431 delegates to the republican assemblies and the 308 to

the federal assembly, only 121 and 6 respectively belonged to the young generation.[35] Studies on the institutional youth structures in other socialist states have
pointed to similar, yet context-specific, phenomena. Writing about the Hungar-
ian youth organisation, Laszlo Kürti noted that 'the most serious wound to the
youth organisation was self-inflicted by its self-preoccupation and political pressure to maintain a hegemonic status quo over its youth through participation in
its activities'.[36] Indeed, the detected sense of 'self-preoccupation' resonates with
the above-mentioned observation by Haug and is visible in debates within the
SSOJ from that time.

It was at approximately the same time that a more vibrant discourse on the
necessity for 'democratisation' emerged. In April 1983, the presidency of the
Conference of the SSOJ at its eighth session decided to initiate a country-wide
discussion on 'Some questions on the democratisation of relationships within the
League of Socialist Youth of Yugoslavia'.[37] Among other things, the existence of
widerspread discontent was acknowledged and it was concluded that the youth
organisation cannot become a genuine social actor as long as there were different
types of ' "benevolent mentors", tutors, techno-bureaucratic structures [which]
would be able to impose work content, to create politics and even impose leaderships'.[38] In compliance with the guidelines, the SSO of Bosnia-Herzegovina
launched a programme of 'broad discussion' round-tables and public debates in
May 1983 within all of its associated branches and youth bodies, with the aim of
'assessing the basic causes which lead to the slowing down and weakening of the
development of democratic relations in a number of organs and organisations
of the League of Socialist Youth'. However, four months later, once the deadline
for the organisation of public discussions passed, the presidency of the Bosnian
SSO concluded that the discussion 'was not implemented well, nor it had the
breadth and the mobilising component, as it had been outlined'.[39]

As it has been noted above, the Yugoslav youth sphere in the 1980s was permeated by such ongoing debates taking place at the official political level, by
various youth-related phenomena coming from below, as well as by issues central to the maintenance of the SSOJ as a mass youth organisation.[40] During
the first half of the 1980s, criticisms were voiced and debates were articulated
with certain reluctance and in a manner that was still tailored to fit the socialist
self-management discourse. Although there was public acknowledgement that
the number of young people in the different self-managing organs and decision-
making bodies was decreasing and that the youth organisation had not managed to engage and mobilise enough young people, publicly the focus was the
economic decline and the possible ways of improving the existing political and
socio-economic framework. Domestic debates revolved exclusively around the
Yugoslav crisis and the malfunctions of self-management. Nevertheless, youth
unemployment and deprivation was a global problem, as demonstrated by the

1980 UNESCO report which underlined that 'What is scarce, therefore, and will become scarcer, is not only energy, investment capital, and domestic and international credit, but the jobs that carry with them the adult rights and responsibilities that the young expect'.[41]

The opening speech of the 11th congress of the SSOJ in December 1982 by its President Bogić Bogićević was in line with the inherited political rhetoric and conveyed the sense of determination to pursue self-management and preserve the legacy of President Tito: 'At this occasion too, we clearly underline that we are resolutely against anything that is anti-self-management and anti-socialist, that is contrary to the ideology and the politics of the SKJ.'[42] He reminded the audience that it was the first youth congress 'without Josip Broz Tito, the most cherished friend and teacher'. The question of the extent to which this already presented only a formalised discourse versus a genuine articulation of political values remains open. While lauding the role and legacy of Marshal Tito, the official stance of the federal youth organisation critically targeted and denounced the various flaws and abuses of self-management (corruption, lack of discipline at the workplace, failure to attend meetings and effectively participate in self-managing organs, social inequality). In the years immediately following Tito's death, there was a tacit consensus among the political elites for pursuing a discourse of unity and perseverance on the road paved by the old revolutionary generation. However, the socialist parlance in its specific Yugoslav variant, which had functioned as a sort of a frozen narrative or a form of political correctness, began to fade away progressively – especially in the second half of the decade.

The first signs that the SSOJ could become a site for voicing critique targeting the system came from a critique denouncing entrenched party interests, abuses and corruption. For most of the first half of the decade, the official youth milieus at federal level engaged in a debate that revolved around the discourse of the economic crisis, unemployment and the malfunctioning of self-management. The SSOJ appears to have demanded more socialism, i.e. strengthening of the self-management system in all of its complexity and more discipline in all social spheres through a status quo with regard to the existing political framework and the established social values. Denouncing the reality of a 'red bourgeoisie' through a radical leftist critique, the president of the youth organisation targeted 'the fraudulent behaviour or privatisation of socially owned property, bribe and corruption. The SSOJ is going to uproot those and similar phenomena, exposing the hypocrisy of those who "sacrifice themselves in the struggle for socialist progress" while unjustifiably amassing and acquiring material wealth with no great effort and refusing to share the fate of the working class'.[43] Although it was not clearly stated in his speech, this critique also targeted the youth officials and high functionaries within the branches of the SSOJ, who enjoyed a number of privileges and often turned into permanent and not-so-young position holders. Even two years earlier, there was a manifest awareness within the official youth circles that the SSOJ promotes conformism, careerism and materialism through its personnel policy, rather than progressive action. At the end of his mandate as president of the SSOJ in December 1980, Vasil Tupurkovski, aged twenty-nine at the time, voiced unsparing criticism: 'Many youth functionaries believe they are irreplaceable, so we have arrived at a strange situation in which to discuss the problem of rejuvenating the youth federation's leadership.'[44] As an illustration, the average age of those employed in the municipal branches [*opštinska konferencija*] in the Bosnian Youth League was 27.4, in the city branch [*gradska konferencija*] 28.4, while at republic level [*republička konferencija*] the average age was 33.5.[45] This was an indicator that the higher levels of the youth organisation were in a way usurped by career-seeking individuals whose activism was formalised and represented a mere stepping stone on their way to political careers in other 'socio-political organisations' and bodies at republican or federal level.[46] The problem of position-seeking cadres appears to have persisted throughout the decade. Research conducted on the subject of youth functionaries in Serbia in 1984 demonstrated that the top positions in the SSO branches were held by people with questionable academic or professional skills: three-quarters had only finished secondary school and 80 per cent of those who were enrolled at universities had failed one or more years of study, their main motivation for taking up the position being the relatively high salary.[47]

Igor Vidmar's testimony (born 1950) reveals this perception that the young political elite, i.e. the youth functionaries in the SSOJ, were purely conformist, at the same time acknowledging that, after all, that was an individual, rather than a generational trait:

> They were always careerist – from the very beginning. First, they were orthodox Marxists, then, they were entrepreneurs, then they were the liberal youth organisation guys, and then they were the civic movement guys, and then [Igor Bavčar] the Minister of Interior … I mean … It's that kind of people. Very ambitious, very opportunistic … But that is a matter of individual character.

Nevertheless, after a decades-old practice of generally acting as junior branches of the Party, the youth organisation was indeed facing a decline in membership. As it was observed: 'The young more visibly manifest distrust and even *enmity* towards their own youth organisation which de facto has lost its members and artificially constructs its leadership pyramid.'[48] Indeed, there was a widespread sentiment of contempt among the youth, in particular among those from the alternative cultural circles, towards the 'little bureaucrats' in the SSOJ, as several of my interviewees had referred to them. This excerpt from the interview with

Petar Janjatović (born 1956), journalist and rock-critic, confirms this widespread perception, or a negative stereotype which existed among the urban youth:

> Firstly, it was only the least intelligent and the most appalling, slimy students which got involved in the youth organisation at school. They knew it was the way to forge a career – literally from seventh grade onwards, they were like – I'll be the president of the class, I'll join the League of Communists, me this, me that … We had an aversion towards that … But once I started moving around the editorial boards of the youth press, I saw that the people who sit on those boards were perfectly normal.

By 1985 a more elaborate discourse of the crisis penetrated the youth organisation, as it began to organise round-tables addressing its impact on the younger generation. The SSOJ was progressively opening up to critical thought and began to act as a forum for different debates. For instance, the proceedings from a public debate entitled 'Close perspective on Yugoslavia with a focus on the societal position of the youth' began with the following statement:

> Over the past few years our society has found itself in a socio-economic crisis which manifests itself in different ways: dropping rates of economic growth and stagnating production, growing unemployment, decrease in income levels, extreme debt … dying out of self-management and strengthening of polycentric etatism, disorder, idleness, lengthy meetings, erosion of the moral and the legal system, rise of nationalism, irresponsibility, corruption and increase of criminal activity … If we want to leave the crisis behind, we need to get rid of the dogmas … we must adjust the definitions of socialism and self-management to our objective circumstances and possibilities.[49]

It is worth noting that this and many other similar public discussions were not only organised by the federal youth organisation, but the publication of the proceedings in a book format (i.e. not only as a report or an addendum in a youth newspaper) was financed and undertaken by the SSOJ itself. Since debate was systematically and institutionally encouraged, the battle of opinions and visions therefore progressively intensified.

After stepping down as president, Tupurkovski also pointed to the lack of democracy in the decision-making process within the SSOJ, its inability to appeal to and mobilise the university student population, and, most intriguingly, to the existence of 'two sorts of young people: those in the forums and those outside them'.[50] This was indeed one of the most prominent division lines within the youth sphere: the youth that gravitated around the alternative cultural spheres or was associated with the vibrant youth press was generally apolitical, indifferent and/or inimical to the official youth organisation and its functionaries. As an illustration, in a survey conducted at the University in Skopje (Macedonia) in 1981 only 5.4 per cent of the students considered themselves politically 'very active': 23.2 per cent saw themselves as politically 'not active at all'; 28 per cent 'little active'; 24.4 per cent 'average'; and 16.9 per cent 'active'.[51]

By 1990, the trend of distancing and retreat from the political institutions became a well-established fact. However, the results from the 1989 all-Yugoslav survey showed a striking difference between the attitude towards the youth organisation and the Party. While only 15 per cent said they were members of the SKJ and more than half (52 per cent) were not and would not like to become members, 65 per cent said they were members of the SSOJ, 18 per cent were not, but would like to become, and only 17 per cent were not and would not like to be its members.[52] By integrating many of the alternative/new social movements and groups within its structure and by consensually abolishing the grand celebration of Tito's birthday in early 1988, as will be discussed in the following chapter, the SSOJ was reforming faster than its original senior sibling – the SKJ. This is captured by the following excerpt from the interview with Janjatović:

> When you look back now, you realise that the entire rock, punk and new wave at the time was financed by the League of Socialist Youth! [...]
>
> In the summer of 1982, we organised a two-day festival of new punk bands which was called ABRS – Alternative Belgrade Rock Scene. You know the ARA album – Artistic Work Action. So, the idea was to promote those bands. Our guest bands were Idols, Electric Orgasm and Šarlo Akrobata, along with the pile of those new bands. The organisation went smoothly, because they gave us the money for it. We commissioned the best sound engineer from Zagreb, we got Tašmajdan [hall] or we rented it, I can't remember, but nothing was complicated. You would submit a project proposal and they'd say – yes, here's the money.
>
> Today, if [a governmental body] gives you the money, you'd be forced to make a lot of compromises. At the time they didn't ask us to do anything in return, no speeches, no flags. [...]
>
> What is crucial is that absolutely no one made us get involved into any type of propaganda. That's the key story. And what's more, you didn't have anywhere a big sign or a logo saying – 'The League of Socialist Youth'. Nothing. Once or twice they asked us to organise a round-table, a public lecture along the lines of the creativity of the youth in the socialist something. But later they realised it doesn't make sense and it never happened again.[53]

Similarly, Igor Vidmar noted in an anecdotal manner that 'they' in the youth organisation eventually had to join 'us', and changed their course sometime in the middle of the 1980s, allowing the SSOJ to recover its legitimacy and support among the young:

> The Youth Socialist League sometimes helped, sometimes tried to hinder, control things, but without much success – they were hopelessly behind with their 'official' youth culture, until they joined 'us' by the mid-1980s.

So, despite a general withdrawal in trust from political institutions which could have exacerbated the decline of the SSOJ, it forced its reinvention, as a place where multiple communities and spheres could interact. Hence, scholars were right to observe that 'there is an impression that in certain parts of the country ... the interest for this [youth] organisation has been revived, alongside the confidence in it'.[54] Dejan Jović (born 1968), himself younger than Vidmar and Janjatović, witnessed the liberalisation and de-ideologisation of the youth organisation in the second half of the decade. He testified to the unravelling of the strictly socialist ideological frame of the institutional youth realm:

> Over time, the criteria for being chosen [to work] at the youth organisation stopped being of ideological nature. Only in extreme cases, for example – not allowing someone to become a president unless one was a Party member [...]
>
> I think the majority of the people [in the SSOJ] were progressively oriented and very successful at what they were doing, as was proven later ... After all, you had to win some sort of elections [in order to move up the hierarchy, starting from primary school and the elections for president of the class]. At least there was one additional candidate ... For example, I lost the election for the city [youth] organisation, but it was a fair battle ... You had to have the ability of persuasion and lobbying and that is the thing I personally think I learned in that organisation. You see politics from the inside. I found it immensely boring to sit at those meetings ... However, you saw it was real politics. You couldn't impose anything.

Although the progressive transformation of the official youth rhetoric, politics and practices reflected wider societal debates and calls for reform, it was essentially a product of internally generated debates and concerns, some of which were penetrating the higher political levels of the SSOJ from the League's 'peripheral' domains, such as the youth media and the new music cultures. Questioning of the inherited traditions and reflecting upon venues for democratisation and reinvention of the youth realm were made possible by the advancement of a young political elite which internalised the critique of the youth organisation and the youth cadres.

Mapping the youth infrastructure

Due to its highly decentralised set-up, the youth organisation was ideally positioned and equipped to channel creativity, alternative and novel approaches to art and journalism, *post festum* facing bans of whole magazine issues or public criticism for certain events or opinions. The complex youth infrastructure which stretched beyond the strictly political core of the SSOJ (see Figure 1) consisted of event venues, publishing houses, weekly and scholarly magazines, student centres and radio stations and it was further expanded and diversified after the

Table 4 Youth media outlets by federal unit

Federal unit	Magazine of the League of Socialist Youth (SSO)	Magazine of the University branch of the SSO in the capital
SR Slovenia	*Mladina*	*Tribuna*
SR Croatia	*Polet*	*Studentski list*
SR Bosnia-Herzegovina	*Naši dani*	*Valter*
SR Serbia (proper)	*Omladinske novine/Nove omladinske novine* (NON)	*Student*
SR Montenegro	*Omladinski pokret*	*Univerzitetska riječ*
SR Macedonia	*Млад борец*	*Студентски збор*
SAP Vojvodina	*Glas omladine* (*Stav* – from 1987)	*Index*
SAP Kosovo	*Zani i rinisë/ Zëri i rinisë* (1968–86)/ *Zëri*	*Novi svet /Bota e re*
SFR Yugoslavia	*Mladost*	*Ideje* – jugoslovenski studentski časopis

1968 events. Each one of the eight federal units had a principal youth venue,[55] weekly or bi-weekly magazines of the republican branch of the SSO, of the university branch(es) of the SSO (see Table 4) and most had dedicated radio programmes or channels.[56]

An observation from the 1980 UNESCO report that 'In the more desperate structural crisis of the coming years, the young may turn to the camera and microphone in order to protest against the economic and social limitations impinging on their lives'[57] proved true in the Yugoslav context. Because of its complex structure which also included 'collective members' such as the organisations of the Red Cross, the Scout Union, the Music Youth, the Literary Youth, etc., as well as a network of youth newspapers, magazines and scientific/research and publishing centres, the SSOJ directly or indirectly involved hundreds of well-educated, creative young people who did not even distantly fit the stereotypical profile of the conformist, careerist young functionary. Hence, the youth organisation was far from a monolithic structure; on the contrary, it provided platforms for critical rethinking of political dogmatism and exposure to counter-cultural styles and alternative standpoints. In the early 1980s, political change in the SSOJ's elite echelons was still blocked; however, within culture, and at the youth sphere's peripheral locations, the SSOJ's infrastructure encouraged the emergence of new political and cultural alternatives. Although there were apparent manifestations and consequences of regional variation and of what has been termed 'republicanization of sovereignty'[58] – since the youth infrastructure did function along the lines of the federal units – nevertheless, a pan-Yugoslav cultural sphere and a media space gained strength, linking progressive groups in different cities. Senad Pećanin (born 1965), former editor-in-chief of the Bosnian daily *Dani*, was part of the team which worked in the Youth Program [*Omladinski program*] at Radio Sarajevo and was actively involved as a young journalist in the Bosnian youth magazines *Naši dani* and *Valter*. As he recalled:

> We had an excellent cooperation with Radio Index [from Belgrade] ... For example, every Wednesday I had a program called 'Youth YU media', which used to give an overview of the youth press – from Novi Sad's *Stav*, to Belgrade's *NON*, Yugoslav *Mladost*, *Mladina*, Maribor's *Katedra*, *Polet*, the radio stations like Index, B92, Radio 101, Radio Študent. That program ran from 1988 until 1990. Definitely there was a supranational sphere, we had great cooperation.

Petar Janjatović similarly recalled this arena of young journalism and youth media co-operation:

> At the moment when rock n' roll became very intriguing, and through writing about music I realised that one can write about everything – politics, literature ... and then we began to sneak around the different music festivals and to meet people who did the same in other cities. I started writing for [Slovenian] *Mladina*, for *Naši dani* in Sarajevo. Between *Jukebox* and [Croatian] *Polet* there was a natural co-operation. The youth press gave an additional layer of freedom, one was totally ... disburdened. ... As if the network of the youth press was composed of very like-minded people. At one point when *Polet* was very famous, almost the entire editorial board was bought out and moved to [Croatian weekly] *Start*. Even today those people are the media elite of Croatia.

An urge for greater freedom in cultural expression which had been growing within the youth realm since the mid-1960s was to play an important role in creating the possibilities for alternative expression in the 1980s. The youth realm provided many venues which were meant to cater for the various cultural/artisitic and media interests of the young. In addition, the network also consisted of publishing houses related to the SSO branches, such as the Centre for Research, Documentation and Publishing Activity of the Presidency of the Conference of the SSOJ [*Centar za istraživačku, dokumentacionu i izdavačku delatnost predsedništva Konferencije SSOJ*], the Research and Publishing Centre of the Serbian SSO [*Istraživačko-izdavački centar SSO Srbije*], or the Centre for Social Activity of the Croatian SSO [*Centar društvenih djelatnosti SSOH*]. Beside the weekly magazines, most of the republics' youth organisations and their associated publishing centres also published journals. These often featured academic articles and more in-depth analyses of different social phenomena,[59] among which the journal of the federal youth organisation 'Ideas – journal for the theory of contemporary society' [*Ideje – časopis za teoriju suvremenog društva*], the journal of the Croatian Youth League 'Questions – journal for theoretical and social questions' [*Pitanja – časopis za teorijska i društvena pitanja*], or Bosnian 'Faces – youth review for social questions, culture and art' [*Lica – revija mladih za društvena pitanja, kulturu i umjetnost*].

The Student Cultural Centre in Belgrade [Studentski kulturni centar- SKC] is certainly one of the most iconic student venues. The officers' cultural venue of the pre-Second World War Yugoslav monarchy and a building used by the Yugoslav secret police from 1945 until 1968, it was handed over to the students of Belgrade University after the 1968 student riots. After an extensive renovation, it opened its doors in 1971. According to Dunja Blažević, who was the director of the Belgrade Student Cultural Centre Art Gallery from 1971 to 1980, the way SKC's structure was conceptualised was inspired by the London Institute of Contemporary Arts, i.e. the prospect of hosting different programmes under the same roof.[60] The Student Cultural Centre in Belgrade came to be perceived not only as a cradle and safe haven for alternative and progressive youth culture – from art, to debating, publishing and music – but also as a space which embodied a spirit of internationalism and provided a platform for all that was new, progressive, transnational:

> SKC from the very beginning was an important and cult place, and remained one until today. It was completely normal to encounter there Bob Wilson, to have a drink in the late hours with Sam Peckinpah, to have a chat about modern art with Joseph Beuys, with Luigi Ontani and Sandro Pertini about the Italian situation, with Oriana Fallaci about politics, or with Petra Kelly about ecology and the Green Party.[61]

Blažević was also editor-in-chief of the visual arts programme at TV Belgrade from 1981 to 1990, where she presented a famous programme – 'Fridays at 10pm' [*Petkom u 22*]. This excerpt from a published interview is illustrative of a trans-generational obsession with freedom and the occupation of the major cells of the youth infrastructure by people who perceived themselves as non-conformist and willing to stretch the boundaries of permitted critique:

> SKC of that time was truly a micro-territory of freedom. It offered programmes that were pushing the borders of the perception of art as well as the borders of social thought. Our projects and events had that innovative component and, in parallel, they were in line with what was called for in those days in contemporary arts and culture worldwide.
>
> … and [it was the time when I had] also complete freedom! I was given carte blanche to create this programme [Fridays at 10 pm] according to my poetics and beliefs. Thus I had the opportunity to explore continuously that which was my primary and lasting interest: the historical avant-garde and

neo-avant-garde. It was precious for me to be able to create a certain climate and provide substantial information on the tendencies in world contemporary art for such a wide audience.[62]

SKC's counterpart in Yugoslavia's second biggest city Zagreb was the Student Centre and in particular its gallery – Galerija SC. Its director in the period 1966–80 was Želimir Koščević, former curator at the Zagreb Museum for arts and crafts, who got a scholarship in 1969 for further training at the Stockholm Modern Museum. It was during this fellowship that he acquired a range of professional contacts that he later built upon and used for organising exhibitions and events at the Student Centre Gallery.[63] Throughout the 1970s these venues incited and supported new artistic practices and acted as alternative cultural spaces for an entire generation of young Yugoslav artists who were keen to experiment with multimedia and conceptual art and did not have access to the mainstream cultural institutions, museums and galleries.[64]

The lead singer of Belgrade band Električni orgazam [Electric orgasm] Srđan Gojković (Gile) (born 1961) talked at length about the importance of the Belgrade Student Cultural Centre, referring to it as 'a big factory' with regard to its wide scope of activity, but also as 'a vent pipe' which was one of the 'gains' from what initially seemed to be a successful 1968:

> I think SKC was a compromise dating back to the student revolt in 1968, when the students got some concessions from Tito and one of those concessions was SKC. It was allowed to be some sort of a vent pipe for some silly young people – they could entertain themselves in there so that they don't protest on the streets … SKC in a way was simultaneously an educational institution for us and also for the new generation which was educated through our work. This is the place where we first watched the French new wave, many Yugoslav censored films … some exhibitions by avant-garde artists, different performances – there were all sorts of things in SKC … It was like a big factory. We used to practise in the basement and we would then just climb upstairs and play a gig. It was the only place and the main one for the first two to three years, for the Belgrade alternative scene.

The Ljubljana Student Cultural Centre was also one of the most prominent places on the map of youth venues. As Barbara Borčić (born 1954), artistic director of the Ljubljana Student Cultural Centre (ŠKUC) from 1982 to 1985 recalled:

> Backed by an abundance of new theory we entered into opposition to institutional culture; we were to radicalise the relation, and the gallery took up a progressive stance. We began systematically to present alternative art production from the (former) Yugoslavia. Surprisingly, the Škuc Gallery was the first to present the most important (conceptualist) artists (for example, R. Todosijević,

G. Đorđević, M. Stilinović, T. Gotovac, V. Delimar, and others) and their radical views to the Slovene public.

ŠKUC became a meeting point of youth, and in addition it was opened for exhibitions of works by young authors not attending art academies. Its audience was specific – very critical and without any prejudices. ŠKUC became a focal point of ideas and inspirations; people gathered to plan joint projects … A whole new generation of photographers was formed … The border between art and life, between public and authors, faded – they were all included in the process, one way or another. The gallery began to publish cassettes, fanzines …

The programme in that period – in contrast to the programme before and after that – was devised according to exclusion: the Škuc Gallery organised the projects which were not admitted to other galleries, but at best to some club (FV 112/15[65], for instance). This stimulated atypical, unconventional exhibitions, special installations, multimedia projects, art performances – events that in other galleries were not possible.[66]

The 'unusually decentralised' nature of the socio-political system was replicated on the level of the institutional youth arena. This, of course, was closely related to the practical implications of the system of socialist self-management and in particular the 1976 Law on Associated Labour.[67] The 1974 federal constitution reaffirmed the doctrine of self-management which was an all-pervasive principle of social and political organisation, 'a means of restricting the accumulation of political power at the center, a guarantee against the abuse of power, and a device for making compatible the seemingly incompatible demands for a stable one-party state on the one hand, and for genuine democracy on the other'.[68] For instance, in 1989 the Student Centre [*Radna organizacija Studentski centar*] in Zagreb was composed of five 'Basic organisations of associated labour' [*Osnovna organizacija udruženog rada – OOUR*]: Student dormitories [*Studom*], Social student alimentation [*Društvena prehrana studenata*], Culture [*Kultura*], Student service [*Student servis*], Graphic service [*Grafički servis*] and Working association of common services [*Radna zajednica zajedničkih službi*].[69] The Student Cultural Centre in Zagreb was located at the 'social pavilion' [*društveni paviljon*] which opened in 1979 in the student settlement 'Stjepan Radić' and it was under the larger institutional umbrella of the Student Centre. As each working unit [*radna jedinica*] or basic organisation was free to expand its network of activities, or, according to the provisions of the Law on Associated Labour it could leave the larger working organisation which it was part of, the youth infrastructure was indeed prone to expansion and diversification.[70] Thus, it was the Student service which was financing the Zagreb Youth Radio [*Omladinski radio*] founded in 1982 at the initiative of the Zagreb city branch of the League of Socialist Youth. In 1989 the Student service also initiated a school for foreign languages, a computing workshop and facilitated student job placements abroad. OOUR

Culture, on the other hand, was the initiator of the student television STV [*studentska televizija*] in 1987–88, first as an internal media outlet and later as part of the Croatian state television.[71]

In the Macedonian capital, despite the lack of an official 'student cultural centre', it was the Youth Centre '25 May' [*Дом на млади '25 Мај'*] which acted as the principal venue for youth cultural activity. It consisted of concert halls, cinemas, exhibition spaces and performance halls. Personal testimonies confirm that like the other youth venues across Yugoslavia, it featured as an epicentre of alternative culture which was nested within and hence promoted by the institutional youth infrastructure. Toše Filipovski (born 1969) was actively involved in the post-punk and hard-core scene in the 1980s. He recalled a concert by Slovene punk band Pankrti at the Youth cultural centre and an atmosphere which in his view resembled more the streets of London than what was considered to be a socialist youth event:

> Everything was happening at MKC … One of the things that got me infected was the last concert of Pankrti in Skopje, the promotion of their Red Album – *Rdeči album* in 1984. As a fifteen-year-old kid I happened to be visiting relatives in Skopje and my older cousins took me to this concert. What I saw left a lasting imprint on my memory. That was the first time I saw so many punks in one place – a classical scene from King's Road in London – punks with Mohawk hair, chains, all that punk iconography in one place. That was the last time I saw that in Skopje … The hall was packed and I have never again seen such a packed punk concert.

Apart from the main youth cultural centres which were widely known and frequently used for concerts, debates or exhibitions, the youth infrastructure network had many other subsidiary venues, both in the capital cities and in smaller provincial towns, some of which were equally important in providing platforms for the proliferation of alternative culture. The sheer number of those made it almost impossible for the mainstream media or the Party branches to follow every event or censor every transgressive initiative. One of those smaller venues was recalled by Petar Janjatović:

> *Dadov*, the youth amateur theatre, was also very important. They had a small, phenomenal venue which could take around 200 people. Someone had an idea, probably the director of the theatre, who was also related to the Youth League, to organise gigs of unknown bands every Monday. Dragan Kremer was in charge for a while, through *Jukebox* [magazine]. So, every Monday night one could drop by, knowing that there would be at least ten people you knew. There were three bands playing and by definition at least one of them was great. That was the ideal place for us – you go out, have a beer, hang out, and you hear what's new. It was there that I saw for the first time the unknown

band Partibrejkers, for example … That was also all within their budget, you know, the equipment, the person who took care of it, none of that was cheap. Kremer was also paid for his job. There were tickets which cost the price of a beer, 100 dinars, symbolic price. That lasted for a couple of seasons, it was really important.

Certainly, it was the availability of funds for the vast youth infrastructure which was one of the main factors for the phenomenal output and cultural and media production. A former editor of the Croatian weekly *Polet* recalled:

> What is so different today from that time is the amazing amount of money that used to be invested in students and youth culture. Every youth organisation in Zagreb had its own newspaper, magazine, or theater; some even started radio stations or sponsored rock festivals. *Polet* created the punk scene and helped invent those bands. It was not private money, all of it was pumped in by the state into that scene. Youth activities, then, were sponsored at the highest level. In fact, the amount of money invested at the time was probably equal to the entire amount allocated to arts and culture by the government today.[72]

The pluralisation and fragmentation of the youth sphere was surely not a phenomenon typical of the late socialist era. With the emergence of jazz and rock 'n' roll in the late 1950s and in the 1960s, the public outlook of Yugoslav youth culture was profoundly transformed.[73] Although Yugoslavia shared many socio-political traits with other European socialist countries, from consumer socialism to censorship and one-party politics, by virtue of being open to Western culture and co-operation with both sides in the Cold War, it was clearly a very different place for a young person in the 1970s and the 1980s compared to the rest of the socialist world. In Czechoslovakia, for instance, aspiring rock musicians were required to take qualifying exams in 'Marxism-Leninism' up until the late 1980s.[74] However, at the heart of this lay the fact that Yugoslavia was a highly decentralised, *de facto* confederal state where levels of control and censorship varied among the federal units and by virtue of the fragmented nature of federal institutions (including the Party) and the doctrine of self-management, the exercise of coercion and power was diluted. Often, what was unacceptable for publication in one federal unit could pass in another. Srđan Gojković (Gile) reflected on this:

> L.S.: *Did you experience censorship?*
> No, we never had that problem … Actually, [Belgrade-based record label] PGP did not allow us to record the album with the songs 'Crocodiles are coming', 'Sky' and 'You', whose lyrics were considered problematic, but we could do it in Zagreb … I think by the mid-1980s it [censorship] was all gone. There were a couple of affairs, like 'Marshall's dead' with [Sarajevo band] *Zabranjeno pušenje*.

However, as control and acts of banning were still a reality in the first half of the 1980s, adjusting to the confines of tolerated freedom was also present, along with a practice of self-censorship and pragmatism. Gregor Tomc's testimony illustrates the willingness to compromise and an awareness that if one wanted to pursue one's artistic/musical activity, one had to step inside what was considered to be the institutional space:

> We made fun of them [the Youth League] publicly, we would always speak of them as 'official youths' – they were the official youth, we were 'unofficial'. We would always call them 'uradna mladina' – people who are youth by profession, for making money. But, in actual life, we needed them. I mean, if you wanted to organise a concert, you had to do it through the youth organisation. Although we were pretending to be in a separate world, in a communist country it was impossible to be in a separate world. You always needed the state, for anything – organising a concert, publishing a record. We didn't really care about the verses, they could change the verses. Because this was not what punk was all about. It was about the community. So, if they would say – change the words 'throwing bombs', we would change them and we would be throwing cakes, it was not a big deal. But it was a big deal for the communists because they believed in the power of the word. Their whole concept of rule was that whoever controls the word is in control of authority. So, if somebody speaks out of line, that's very dangerous. So, when punks were speaking out of line, you had to censor that. We had no project, we didn't believe in the magic power of the word, so we changed words without any problem. And people later would say – that was a compromise. Of course it was, I mean ... That was the only way you could function. If you were a completely principled person you would never have a concert.

Indeed, the punk, rock and new wave bands more often than not had the youth organisation as their patron, and were invited and paid to play concerts during youth congresses, the Youth relay[75] celebrations or at the youth voluntary work camps. One could argue that there was a two-way process of co-optation, since both sides were exposed to the influence or the interest of the other. The youth organisation pragmatically tried to appeal to its membership and appear in harmony with the contemporary trends in music and culture, while the young musicians, many of them openly apolitical or indifferent to the espoused ideology, were happy to profit from the infrastructure and the funds of the youth organisation. Vlatko Stefanovski's band *Leb i sol* [Bread and Salt], Zoran Predin's *Lačni Franz* [Hungry Franz] and Gregor Tomc's *Pankrti* [Bastards] were all awarded the prize 'Seven Secretaries of the SKOJ'[76] by the Croatian Youth League. The prize was introduced in 1964 and was awarded by the 'city conference' [*gradska konferencija*] of the League of Socialist Youth from Zagreb to young artists, writers, musicians, journalists, scientists and sportsmen below the age of thirty. Senad Avdić (born 1960) was editor-in-chief of the federal youth magazine *Mladost* in 1987–88 and was also active in the SSO in Bosnia-Herzegovina. Like other interviewees, he referred to the professional youth functionaries in a sarcastic, if not derogatory manner, underlining that 'even' they had realised that the old concepts and ways have lost their appeal:

> It was a pretty confusing time … The [new] times had already prevailed over the old matrix … Even the 'small youth communists' had understood that those times are gone. At that time Pankrti got the 'Seven Secretaries of SKOJ' award, which was shocking! So, a thaw was commencing … though it took them some time [to realise change was needed].

Vlatko Stefanovski (born 1957) similarly reflected on what he perceived to be a pragmatic attitude by the youth political elites within the SSOJ:

> That mainstream youth-functionary scene, the young little bureaucrats, they understood that things were turning sour, that there was no joking any more, and they were trying to fuse the Youth relay with rock 'n' roll. And they were successful in it … We were playing concerts which reconciled those two principles – young socialists and young rockers. The authorities realised that you can't leave rock 'n' roll on the margins. … I know that those youth organisations were trying to reconcile the rock musicians with the rest of the youth.

Zoran Predin was leader of the Slovenian band Lačni Franz [Hungry Franz]. He was blunt about his band's own pragmatic relationship with the youth organisation:

> So, we charged a fee every time we performed at youth congresses. When they would ask us why we perform for a specific congress, we would say – no, we perform for money. That's why we weren't so popular [with the regime], there were those other so-called regime bands, such as *Plavi orkestar*, or *Bijelo dugme*.

Young journalists and researchers were similarly paid by the same organisation which they openly targeted for its malfunctioning and were employed by the functionaries whose competence they publicly questioned. This could be interpreted as an indicator of the latent and gradual democratisation of Yugoslav society in the 1980s. Described as 'schizophrenic' by some of my informants, the outlook and content of the official youth print media in the 1970s and in particular in the 1980s was eclectic to the extent that on one page it would feature a report from a session of the Party, an interview with a legal theorist on the contested 'verbal crime' article, and on the next a critical review of the new album by David Bowie, or an article on female orgasm and the G-spot![77] Although by the late 1980s it was taken for granted that the majority of the main youth magazines hosted polemical views, debates, open critique and did not reflect the official policies and politics of the youth organisations which financed them and figured as their founders, as early as the beginning of the decade the official bodies and institutions publicly acknowledged the fact that 'in some cases [there is] even complete alienation of the magazine from the organisation it belongs to'.[78] This and similar observations were expressed at a one-day round-table dedicated to the youth press by the Commission for Information of the SSOJ and the Section for Information and Public Opinion of the SSRNJ.[79] Petar Janjatović emphasised this aspect and the phenomenon of a bi-polar youth media space:

> When the youth press begins to open up towards non-conventional topics, which you have probably noticed, they begin to appear totally schizophrenic. On the first ten pages – workers, miners … after that come the music and pop culture pages and there you have f*** sakes and going to hell, boobs and bums, funny comics, totally Frankenstein-like! We can only guess what happened there. My take on it is that at some point, within those structures, there began to appear people who were not only careerist, but were talented and figured out that the structure of the League of Socialist Youth should be used for doing something original, individual. Vlada Bajac, a well-known writer and the owner of the publishing house *Geo-poetika*, at the time was an editor of the weekly program 'Young, crazy world' [Mladi, ludi svet] at Studio B, a program which was financed by the Belgrade League of Socialist Youth. Then someone decided that the program should be aired five times per week and Vlada Bajac asked me to be the music editor. The program changed its name into 'Ritam srca' [Rhythm of the heart] and that was the first time I began to encounter the presidents of the youth organisation, the president of this or that commission and I realised that half of those people are actually okay. The other half was real imbeciles, but, all of a sudden, you see people who really know what they are doing.

Similarly, the Research and Publishing Centre of the Serbian Youth League (*Istraživačko-izdavački centar SSO Srbije*) among its mainstream publications featuring sociological analyses of the youth or documents and reports from the youth congresses, also financed high quality journals and edited volumes dealing with the new (sub-)cultural phenomena. Most prominently these included the remarkable 1983 edited volume entitled *Drugom stranom – Almanah novog talasa u SFRJ* [The other side – almanac of the new wave in SFRY], featuring essays on graffiti, fanzines, photography and lyrics from the acclaimed Yugoslav new wave bands; as well as the extraordinary journal *Potkulture* [Subcultures] published from 1985 until 1989, approaching the phenomenon in a broader and more scholarly manner. The journal featured translated articles by British scholars and experts on youth sub-cultures such as John Clarke and Tony Jefferson, texts by Polish and Russian authors on sub-cultures in

Eastern Europe, or by Yugoslav theoreticians and young intellectuals on gay counter-culture, lesbian literature and the Yugoslav artistic alternative scene, for instance.[80] Trans-national cultural flows, gazes directed at both East and West and appropriation of the youth venues as 'spaces of freedom' were not phenomena that were unique to the decade of the 1980s. However, while one of the main novelties in youth culture in the late 1960s and the 1970s was conceptual art, the scope of the notion of sub-cultures in the 1980s was so wide that it could include anything from new music trends such as punk, new art forms, video art, photography, or new literary trends. Velimir Ćurgus Kazimir was the editor of the Research and Publishing Centre of SSO Serbia from 1979 until 1988. His testimony reveals trans-generational patterns of identification and commonalities:

> It was an institution which had a political roof, but inside people worked on many serious and interesting things which had little to do with the official establishment. One stream was the research on the value orientations of the youth, and the second was the publishing stream. I think we published around 150 titles … After all, it was us who published the first book by Zoran Đinđić *Subjectivity and violence*, along with other titles which dealt with Trotskyism, democratic pluralism … And, of course, there was our pioneering attempt to deal with subcultures. *Potkulture* was the first journal to deal with subcultures from various aspects … Those were texts by our young sociologists who were at the beginning of their careers. There was no other space where they could publish such texts. We also made the *Almanac*, the story about the new wave and its impact, which at that time was not recognised as being political. One of the main criticisms, also coming from our circles, was that the music is totally apolitical, not engaged. Later it became apparent that that music was a very direct, political answer to the situation of the 1980s. That represents an interregnum which marked a certain kind of a liberalisation of the state which primarily did not unfold in a political, but in a cultural way … It was extremely exciting … That was a time when we shed light on something which existed, but was concealed and we said – we have to deal with this in a serious way, it's here, we can't pretend that it doesn't exist.

Petar Janjatović also recalled the initiative for the publishing of the *Almanac*:

> He [Velimir Ćurgus Kazimir] proposed that we compile an encyclopedia of Yugoslav rock 'n' roll, provided it was ready in five months' time. I told him that was impossible. Not only it was impossible, it was also stupid, because there was so much going on, almost every week a new album was released. We suggested that we do something dealing with punk and new wave and we got a complete support from the publishing house! You saw it, it's huge and it materialised thanks to Kazimir. Kazimir also had to answer in front of someone, he had to convince someone to assign a budget for that, but it seems all of those structures realised that something significant was going on.

Apparently, more senior figures in the management of the youth publishing houses and media outlets took a decision to promote, support and protect these and many other similar initiatives. As Senad Pećanin noted:

> In essence, there were no real consequences, I can't say there were. At work we didn't suffer any serious consequences because we had Boro [Kontić], he protected us, he took upon him everything, we didn't feel anything.

Boro Kontić (born 1955), although not significantly older, was higher on the institutional ladder in terms of professional seniority and as an editor of the youth program at Radio Sarajevo, he acted as the main mediator between the governing organs who had to make sure programmes do not stray away from the Party line and the young journalists and comedians at the radio:

> I was fined several times because of TLN [*Top Lista Nadrealista*][81] or PRIMUS and those fines were usually in the amount of 10 per cent of the [monthly] salary. It was awful ... Once they removed the entire show [TLN] without my knowledge.

He was also fined several times 'because of the Slovenes' in 1987: 'I say – by virtue of playing Laibach music I certainly deserved to have a Slovenian passport.'

In the 1980s, the peripheral parts of the youth sphere – the numerous youth and student cultural venues and media outlets – hosted and promoted novel forms of youth culture which progressively worked to pluralise and modernise

Figure 3 'Surrealists' Top Chart', Radio Sarajevo, 1983

the organisation. As has been observed, 'Under socialism you could (mis)use the socialist infrastructure and framework in order to establish your own "free territories"'.[82] The political core of the SSOJ and the professional youth cadres were initially perceived as out of step with the popular trends in youth culture and journalism. A process of negotiation, compromise and reform from within gradually replaced an initial sense of mutual distrust and hostility between the youth functionaries and the young journalists, musicians and artists. Through what could be identified as a reluctant, pragmatic, if not populist move to neutralise growing criticism from within and from without the youth organisation and appeal to its 'base', the peripheral parts of the youth infrastructure opened up the SSOJ to new trends in culture, journalism and publication.

The youth press and freedom of expression

In November 1980, the editor-in-chief of *Polet* Zoran Franičević (1957–2008) wrote:

> It is apparent that in the context of the crisis of the youth organisation, the state of the economy and the socio-political relations, as they are, the youth press has an opportunity and space for a more decisive and more concrete action … We know the enemy, as well as their means … It seems that our (youth) press is preparing to become more open, more engaged and more protruding than the organisation which is paying us. For that battle of ours we should not, of course, expect to have our housing question solved, [to receive a] better pay and nice office space, but some possible bruises – yes![83]

Indeed, throughout the 1980s the youth press sought to expose the contradictions within the Yugoslav legal framework with regard to freedom of speech and freedom of expression. This led foreign scholars to observe that 'Of all the periodical publications appearing in Yugoslavia, it is the youth press which has proven the most consistently nettling to the authorities. Outspoken to the point of rebelliousness, the young editors … have repeatedly ignored even the most fundamental taboos'.[84] Yet, this was not without a precedent. In the late 1960s the youth and student press displayed a similar level of outspokenness and were therefore subject to political pressure, public critique and bans – in particular during and after the 1968 student protests.[85] Writing about the (lack of) freedom of the press in the 1960s and the 1970s, April Carter argued that 'journalists and writers often did show considerable independence of mind and party leaders were far from united in the desire to impose timid conformity'.[86] Similarly, a 1970 Radio Free Europe report dedicated to the youth press observed that 'Criticism is usually merciless. The youth press shows no respect for any social or political elements in the country'.[87] The subsequent federal Constitution nominally guaranteed freedom of thought and freedom of expression in the public and the media space, as Article 166 of the 1974 Constitution stipulated that 'Freedom of thought and deciding shall be guaranteed' and Article 169 guaranteed that 'Scientific and artistic creation shall be free'.[88] On the other hand, however, Article 133 of the Penal Code proscribed any type of 'hostile propaganda':

> Whoever in an article, leaflet, drawing, speech or in some other way calls on or incites the overthrow of the government of the working class and working people, the unconstitutional change of the socialist self-management social system, breaking-up of the brotherhood and unity and equality of nations and nationalities, overthrow of the organs of social self-management and authorities and their executive organs, resistance to decisions of competent organs of authorities and of self-management which are significant for the protection and development of socialist self-management relations, the security or defense of the country; or whoever maliciously and untruthfully represents the social and political situation in the country, shall be punished by imprisonment for a term exceeding one year but not exceeding 10 years.[89]

Article 133, along with Article 157 which related to 'Damaging the reputation of the Socialist Federal Republic of Yugoslavia'[90] and Article 134 which prohibited 'Inciting national, racial or religious hatred, discord or hostility',[91] represented the core of what was considered non-negotiable and hence inviolable in political/constitutional terms. In the wider public sphere the struggle for change and greater freedom of expression had begun earlier in the decade with several petitions which targeted this part of the legislation. Serbian lawyer Srđa Popović, who was engaged in many court proceedings defending individuals accused of 'verbal crimes' and 'hostile propaganda', submitted a formal request with the federal presidency in 1980 demanding amendment of Article 133 – a petition which bore the signatures of 103 intellectuals and public figures predominantly from Zagreb, Belgrade and Ljubljana.[92] That same year in Zagreb 43 public figures (including former rector of Zagreb University Ivan Supek, the future Croatian nationalist President Franjo Tuđman, the personal physician of Croatia's Party leader Vladimir Bakarić and representatives of the Catholic Church) also petitioned the Yugoslav presidency asking for a new amnesty law that would free all political prisoners.[93] In 1981 the President of the Federal Court in an article in the law journal *Naša zakonitost* acknowledged that the formulation of Article 133 was not precise, while at the 1983 conference of Yugoslav criminologists several professors of law called for the repeal of the article.[94]

When in 1984 the Croatian youth magazine *Polet* commissioned film, conceptual and performance artist Tomislav Gotovac (1937–2010) to take part in a marketing project on the streets of Zagreb, acting as a 'colporteur' and dressed up as anything from a mummy, Superman, a worker with a hammer and a sickle, or Santa Claus, it was not the first time that non-conformist art, performance and photography was being transplanted from print media and the conventional confines of the gallery space onto the public cityscape. Yet, it was without a precedent that an official youth magazine stepped into a provocative event intelligently fusing marketing and art – Gotovac was detained by the police almost on every occasion, while the City Secretariat for Internal Affairs received more than 200 complaints from disturbed citizens.[95] The awareness that there was a space which allowed for the claiming of freedom of expression in the youth media, albeit with certain risks, was present in the absolute majority of the testimonies I collected. They were all aware that there were ways to navigate a spectrum of restrictions and were not reluctant to take up certain risks. Oral history gives us important evidence from below concerning the changing rules over public expression and the new spaces available within the youth press for discussion of public issues.

Dragan Kremer (born 1960) was a music critic and journalist in several youth media in the 1980s. He recalled that sense of limited freedom:

> It was indeed possible to push certain attitudes through those media which were indeed alternative in outlook. The media themselves were not alternative per se, however. There was that level of tolerated freedom – there was a line which could not be crossed, but also a space beyond that line where one could do whatever one wanted.

Sašo Ordanoski (born 1965) was a young journalist in Macedonia. He similarly recalled:

> Yugoslavia was not a dictatorship, but it was a communist state and the public debate on certain issues had a significant effect. At the same time, the youth press in Macedonia and in Yugoslavia was living its renaissance. I was a correspondent for Belgrade's *NON*, I was also writing for [youth federal magazine] *Mladost* and I was employed for several years in [Macedonian] *Mlad borec*. All of these magazines were at the forefront of promoting those novel ideas which would later in a way produce the cadres and the platforms of the nineties … I was twenty-something, with no other obligations, no family, well-paid … We used to read a lot – it was still the time of books … we travelled a lot, we were very mobile, especially within Yugoslavia, which was one boiling scene.

Senad Pećanin related the loosening of 'the communist bondage' with the rise of a generation of young journalists who dared 'shift the boundaries of freedom':

> Working for the [Sarajevo] Youth Program was a brilliant experience, it was the last time there was such a generation, an entire generation of exceptional journalists … My generation and I were lucky to make a start in the period when the communist bondage began to loosen and not to feel a real pressure of censorship. There were certain problems here and there, but Boro [Kontić]

was managing it brilliantly and reduced the damage. He took upon himself all those pressure, fines, salary cuts, while protecting us. We thought that was a normal way of communicating – talking freely. We were really shifting the boundaries of freedom.

As the decade wore on, the overall public debate on freedom of the media was intensifying. A book by Professor Mihajlo Bjelica published in 1985 entitled *Велике битке за слободу штампе* [Great battles for the freedom of the press] raised questions about auto-censorship, the prospect of establishing private newspapers in Yugoslavia and the ways to fight for freedom of the press in the context of a societal and economic crisis. However, the Yugoslav reality of a semi-free media space and a relatively permissive post-1968 youth sphere did not necessarily imply an absence of arbitrary clamp-downs or strictly enforced boundaries of expression. Pećanin also recounted at length a close encounter with 'the regime' on the occasion of the withdrawal of the candidature for a member of the federal presidency by politician Nenad Kecmanović after he was told that Kecmanović might have co-operated with the British intelligence service:

> No one knew why he did it, he didn't say anything, while everyone was speculating that it was under pressure, it was a Yugoslav topic … In the media we were all trying to find out the reasons, since we knew he didn't do it willingly … The programme was on at 2 p.m., we announced that at 2:15, I read it, of course we didn't reveal the source … That was a blast. At 2:17 the director of the Radio called Boro to stop the program, because we used to have live phone calls in the programme without censorship, which was revolutionary for the time. We had to stop the programme and the next morning at 5 a.m. there was a knock at the door – I used to live in the student dormitory with my girlfriend … The guy showed his ID from the state security agency and said I had to go with him. I told my girlfriend to call Boro if I don't come back. And then there were 5–6 hours of questioning, threats, yelling – I endangered I-don't-know-what, I put into question the relations between Yugoslavia and Great Britain.

Negotiating the boundaries of freedom was thus a prevalent practice in a context where public debate on certain issues was limited and where there were acknowledged, yet navigable, restrictions in the public space. Hence, in order to embed one's non-conventional artistic or media practice within the existing infrastructure, one had to work with the conventions and find a way through the institutional set-up to carve out 'spaces of freedom'. Individuals used different strategies in what sometimes resembled a process of delicate bargaining, a complex web of practices, or simply 'a game' of testing the boundaries. Miha Kovač (born 1960) was editor-in-chief at Ljubljana's Radio Student and later at the Slovenian youth magazine *Mladina*. He was also member of the Association for Yugoslav Democratic Initiative (UJDI) formed in 1989. He stressed his one-month work experience in London in 1988 – at Simon & Schuster where he was 'learning book publishing'. He underlined the art of negotiating one's way within the formally proscribed boundaries of youth journalism, as well as the fact that conflicts with the authorities for the most part did not materialise into legal prosecution or imprisonment:

> All the time we were playing a game with the authorities ... After being banned, I sometimes took a problematic text to the print shop three days in advance and if I got a call – 'You will be banned!', I would remove it and I would publish it two weeks later [...]
>
> I mean, we never took the system seriously. So, the bottom line is that in those days in Slovenia the communist system was already somehow disintegrating. Although there were conflicts all the time, they never took us to prison, or whatever. They were yelling at us, pressuring us, but we were, you know, negotiating, making two steps back and one step forward, as Lenin would say.
>
> L.S.: *What kind of pressure was that? They would summon you to the Party?*
>
> Yes ... They would call us ... There were some funny things. For example, May the 13th was the official day of the Yugoslav police. And on that day we played the Lili Marlene tune and we said we are testing how long the police needs to come and arrest us. They needed about half an hour [laughs]. We were released very quickly, in a few hours. There were some hard-liners in the Party who were trying to close down the radio station, but the soft line in the Communist Party defended the radio station. We always somehow survived. The bottom-line is that the situation was not black and white, in the sense that on one side there was an opposition and on the other side there was the Communist Party. There was very ... how to say ... It was a kind of web of very strange relations and everybody was playing his or her own game. I would say that for most of us who were involved in this movement, we were to a certain extent very, very pragmatic, willing to make compromises, but pushing the limits of the possible further on all the time.

This excerpt reaffirms the fine line which existed between transgression/contention and calculated negotiation within the existing political and institutional boundaries. The navigation of the institutional and political boundaries oftentimes required intelligent manipulation and improvisation, as Boro Kontić recalled:

> After we had done the montage, I knew exactly which parts could be problematic – the fifth, the eighth minute, after this and that line ... Now it might seem ridiculous, but that was the way it was. I play the tape, we sit down with him [the editor], we keep silent and listen to the programme. Precisely when that part approaches ... I mean, I swear, I didn't do it because someone had told me [to do it], it was pure instinct ... During that sequence I ask him if he

wants a cigarette and he replies yes or no. The sequence is over and later I start coughing and ask him to open the window ... And so on, the programme ends, he tells me – 'Well you've got one boring programme there', I reply – 'The next one will be better', and so on. I mean, hilarious stuff, but that was the only way.

Cross-republican influences were also crucial in shaping attitudes and media activism. Kovač emphasised the importance of the trial of the six Belgrade intellectuals arrested in 1984 and charged with counter-revolutionary activity:[96]

Actually, many things in Slovenia started to happen because of the 'Belgrade Six' ... Radio Student and *Mladina* were writing a lot about this trial ... We were claiming that we will not solve the Yugoslav economic crisis by arresting people who think and discuss about what's going on. This trial helped form quite strong links between Ljubljana and Belgrade ... So, for a while, we were quite close. But those disintegrative pressures finally destroyed UJDI too.

Robert Botteri (born 1963) was appointed editor-in-chief of Slovenian *Mladina* in 1987 after having worked as an editor in the student magazine *Tribuna*. He recalled that he began working for *Tribuna* at the time of the 'Free University' affair in Belgrade in 1984, i.e. the above-mentioned 'trial of the Belgrade six' and, like Kovač, he emphasised its importance in enhancing the debate on Article 133 and freedom of speech:

Mladina and *Tribuna* were the only media in Yugoslavia which dared report about that trial in a non-conformist way. They labeled us counter-revolutionaries, to which we replied that we are professionals and we only report about the court case and [we asked] whether that was a 'crime'. It turned out that they are tried for 'verbal crime' and that goes against freedom of speech. So, we immediately initiated a campaign in the student press ... We made badges with the number 133 crossed out. That was one way how the idea of freedom of speech was being spread around. Things then came one after the other. First it was freedom of speech, then the petition against the death penalty, a petition for the liberation of all political prisoners, for civil military service, for the rights of homosexuals, and at the end came the Youth Baton. We said that seven years after the death of the Marshal it is ... idolatry, carrying the Baton and bowing to a dead man was anachronistic. All our actions were condemned, while the real confrontation happened around the Baton and the army, it was where it climaxed.

Indeed, over time the struggle for greater freedom of expression worked to expand the scope of the debate and the range of demands. The Slovenian youth press was at the forefront of these debates and acted as a model for young journalists in the other republics. Eventually, the spectrum of demands and debates which were voiced in the youth press, boiled down to the questions of democratisation/pluralisation in general and freedom of expression, in particular. There is a consensus among the interviewees who were active in the youth media that

Figure 4 *Mladina* front cover, 1988

an aspiration for the democratisation of Yugoslavia was what underpinned their activism. Its formulation in these precise terms could be equally interpreted as a *post-hoc* construction. Botteri summarised it thus:

> From the mid-1980s we were constantly advocating democratisation. To us, human rights were sacrosanct. That is why we were signing the petitions for the release [from prison] of Vojislav Šešelj, Vladimir Šeks and Alija Izetbegović … That is why we also published interviews with all of them. With Šešelj in particular we had many problems, the interview was banned, then we published

only the questions, and later the answers … That is where we located the only chance for that state, the chance of its democratisation … I still believe that everything could have been solved like in the Czech case. Had the ruling party accepted that model of democratisation and had it put a halt to nationalism in the beginning … If Serbia had a liberal leadership things would have turned out differently.

Because of the very nature and political organisation of socialist Yugoslavia as a highly decentralised ethno-territorial federation, comprehensive analysis of the response of the authorities is quite challenging. Dealing with the elite discourse on 'tolerated freedom' in the youth realm necessitates an analysis of the separate republics' contexts and the responses of the respective Party branches and the republics' political/legal authorities. Although Yugoslavia was arguably the 'cutting edge of East European socialist theory and practice, the most open and liberal society in the region, the socialist country with the region's highest per capita income, and deemed most likely to join the European Community',[97] until the final days of the federation the Party played the central role in almost all spheres of social and political life in what was a *de facto* 'confederal party-state'.[98] Nevertheless, by the mid-1980s the federal Party, no matter how fragmented and far from being unanimous, was arguably dominated by reformist forces.[99] Moreover, by the end of the decade there was a shared sense among federal circles that Yugoslavia's future lay with an indispensable 'europeanization', as 'there was a consensus within the federal government (including the army) in favor of westernization and liberalization'.[100]

However, factions within the republics' Party branches were a reality, and although cleavages along 'reformists v. conservatives' lines were not always easily discernible, shifts in policies towards the youth organisations, the alternative cultural practices and the youth media were largely conditioned by party factionalism and/or changes in the Party's top echelons. The responses of the republics' political authorities to the various 'affairs' in the youth domain differed from federal unit to federal unit. More often than not it was local, republican media outlets which channelled the critique and different form of public discrediting aimed at what was perceived to be subversive youth behaviour. For example, in 1984 Sarajevo-based band *Zabranjeno pušenje* was attacked in the Bosnian press in an article entitled 'The toxic fumes of "Smoking Forbidden"', which was followed by the band being temporarily banned from performing and from radio and television shows. The so-called 'Crk'o Marshall' [The Marshall's croaked] affair was taken up by the media and the local authorities after a concert in the Croatian town of Rijeka, where the band leader's comment after their Marshall amplifier had broken was interpreted as an act of ridiculing, a distasteful allusion to (Marshal) Josip Broz Tito. The journalist concluded that 'This short period of time was enough for the youth eager for fun and spectacles to be imbued with new thoughts, with continuous underestimating of everything we have achieved so far and the banal, vulgar ridiculing of the fundamental slogan from the People's Liberation Struggle "What belongs to others we don't want, what is ours we will never surrender"'.[101]

Dejan Jović was involved both in the youth press and in the Croatian SSO. He raised the issue of Party factions' impact on the youth media and the youth organisation, as he recalled the removal of the editor of Croatian youth weekly *Polet*:

> I was angry when [editor Mladen] Babun was removed, to me that seemed inappropriate … We regarded that as an intra-Party conflict which was reflected upon our editorial staff. He [Mladen Babun] was indeed close to [Stipe] Šuvar's [102] [Party] faction, as all of us were, but we didn't like the way the faction led by Mika Špiljak transferred the intra-Party conflict onto the youth organisation. And that happened quite often. Not only in *Polet*, but also in the daily press. The intra-Party conflicts were always reflected there … There were big conflicts and from that you can conclude that there was proto-pluralism, huge conflicts in the media.

In a similar vein, Botteri located a major shift in the Slovenian youth realm after the 1986 Krško congress of the ZSMS, which coincided with a change in the Party leadership and a new liberal camp. At the same time, a younger genera-tion took over the youth organisation and over *Mladina*. Outside of the official framework, he claims, they had normal, good interaction and communication even with the federal youth president Hashim Rexhepi (born 1958, originally from Kosovo):

> Even the politicians in private conversations used to tell us – 'We know that, but it is still not the right time, wait a little …' Everyone shared the opinion … It was becoming clear that some sort of democratisation is indispensable. Those waves were already underway in Eastern Europe as well.

Yet, court cases and bans on specific issues of youth magazines persisted throughout the decade. Often, the bans followed the legal framework which regulated the press and were not necessarily related to the federal Penal Code and the infamous Article 133. From 1950 practices of pre-censorship had been abolished, the 'Law on prevention of abuse of the freedom of the press and of other types of information' [*Zakon o sprečavanju zloupotrebe slobode štampe i drugih vidova informisanja*] from 1976 provided the legal framework and it was the public prosecutor who could act 'only ex-post facto, after a broadcast, publication or film presentation'.[103] It is what happened on 16 March 1988, when the public prosecutor in Ljubljana ordered the confiscation and a ban on circulation of the eleventh issue of the youth weekly *Mladina*. The article in question was the editorial signed by the 'Counter-revolutionary editorial staff' and entitled 'In the name of the people – to the defenders of the Revolution'.[104] The editorial was addressed to the Yugoslav leadership and appears to have summed up the main points of contention and debate, as it accused the elite of wasting time dealing with the youth press and suggested that it should rather focus on financial affairs and corruption; on the public debt of more than twenty billion dollars which was spent on elite villas and privileges; on a foreign policy which diminished Yugoslavia's reputation abroad; and an inhumane and greedy sale of arms. In addition, the text outlined fourteen 'counter-revolutionary demands', including the establishment of a market economy, direct elections, doing away with the monopoly of the Party and public control of the army.[105] Although many of these points overlapped with the views reflected in the other Yugoslav youth media, *Mladina*'s approach and articulation were sharper and hence more prone to criticism and controversy. Also, what set them apart in this case was the demand for a public control over the army and a halt to arms sales. The precedent to this was a highly controversial and debated article entitled 'Mamula go home' which labelled the federal defence secretary a 'merchant of death':

> the guilt of the Yugoslav commander of the armed forces is even bigger because he is selling rifles with roses of non-alignment in the barrels and with fake smiles about non-interference in interior affairs … It was damn clear to Mamula why and against whom the Yugoslav arms in Ethiopia and Uganda are going to be used: in the civil wars, i.e. against the domestic guerrilla.[106]

Although Slovenian *Mladina* was most of the time at the centre of what was seen as controversial youth journalism, the bans and court cases were in no way unique to the Slovenian youth press. The prosecutor's office on 28 January 1988 issued a temporary ban (upheld by the District Court) and on 2 February issued a permanent ban for issue number 3 of Zagreb's *Studentski List* from 27 January 1988, quoting a number of problematic articles among which 'We are condemned to a status quo', 'Oasis of fake liberty' and 'Media courtesans'.[107] The first article reported on a lecture by Dr Marijan Korošić in ŠKUC and quoted a comment and a question from the audience which implied that a coalition between Stipe Šuvar and [Serb Party leader] Slobodan Milošević was hampering the process of democratisation, calling it a 'military-police-party lobby'.[108] Another problematic argument was from an article entitled 'Oasis of fake liberty', which dealt with the attacks on the magazine of the students of Maribor University in Slovenia and similarly targeted the Party as 'a factor that progressively deepens our crisis and uses national hatred for the protection of its own interests'.[109] The editorial staff replied by publishing part of the poem

'To those who follow in our wake' by Bertold Brecht,[110] in addition to a reprint of the official decision of the public prosecutor and a reply which qualified the act of the ban as 'civilizational anachronism' and quoted a number of official figures, politicians and other statements in mainstream newspapers and magazines which raised similar issues regarding the inefficiency and disunity of the Party without being criminalised or banned.[111] Not long afterwards, the public prosecutor issued another ban for the issue number 9 for the article 'The dictator is coming' dedicated to the visit by Congolese (Zaire) president Mobutu Sese Seko. The prosecutor's decision quoted 'the offensive claims [which damage] the honour and reputation of the Republic of Zaire and its President Mobutu Sese Seko', as well as the friendly relations between the two countries.[112] After the ban, the magazine published an overview of the recent history of Congo and more strikingly, a series of quotes by President Tito dating from 1960 and 1961, where he had openly attacked the overthrow of Patrice Lumumba: 'Since all manner of expression of our own opinion about [our] friend Mobutu, [including] the quoting of foreign sources or even quoting from our own press could lead us again into a situation where SL could be banned, we decided to look into what was said about our friend Mobutu by the man whose opinion, although sharper than ours, could help us avoid a ban.'[113] The 'publishers' of the magazine – the university assembly [*skupština Sveučilišta*] and the city branch of the Croatian SSO renounced their right of appeal and the Council of the magazine (presided by a delegate from the city conference of the Croatian SSRN) called for the resignation of Ivica Buljan, the magazine's editor [*odgovorni urednik*] and attacked the magazine for not being representative of the city youth it was meant to address. On 27 April 1988, after the appointment of a new editor, the magazine published a statement by the 'former' editorial board following its collective resignation entitled 'The limit of political compromise':

> Our intention was to initiate a serious and well argumented dialogue about the most sensitive questions and problems of Yugoslav society. Our efforts, however, were declared politically illiterate and irresponsible. It was said, in one way or the other, that 'the time is not yet ripe' for whatever we were attempting [to raise] … without doubt the times that are coming are going to be even worse if we don't start discussing about it today … We wish the new editorial board both courage and knowledge, and of course, less political wisdom than the times require.[114]

This episode offers an illustration of the common, often arbitrary legal obstacles the youth press used to encounter throughout the 1980s. It also points to a specific way of 'disciplining' young journalists in a context where the mainstream media were openly discussing many of the sensitive issues which the youth press was often sanctioned for. For instance, that same year at the end of May, the Party held its first conference (a smaller forum between two congresses) where party leaders and delegates formulated an openly expressed critique addressing the very issues which were subject to criminalisation upon appearance in the youth press: 'corruption in the party, the possibility of leadership changes and the party's relinquishment of the monopoly on power, and the need for different opinions to be recognised.'[115] In essence, the youth press was attacked and subject to temporary or permanent bans because it was seen as overstepping the boundaries of its prescribed scope of topics in this sphere. Political critiques did occur publicly at different political levels, but the youth press was not considered an appropriate venue for such discussions: rather, the authorities often argued that the youth press should focus on issues of importance for the young and the student population, by which they generally meant a focus on culture and entertainment.

Indeed, political developments in the country, social and economic issues, i.e. 'high politics', did come to occupy a significant portion of all of the main youth magazines in the 1980s. Articles appeared which exposed the socio-economic structural inequalities and the many forms of corruption, especially among top Party officials, linking these phenomena as the products of the authoritarian traits of Yugoslav socialism, in particular the Party's monopoly on power. In December 1984 *Polet* published an ironic call for the 'Big, bigger, the biggest Yugoslav competition for the photograph of the most beautiful, richest, most luxurious and most unavailable house for the working class on the territory of the former Yugoslavia', printed over a black and white photo of a big mansion.[116] It also noted that 'precedence will be given to the photographs which will also supply information about the location, the size, the owners and their occupation'. As Paul Betts observed in the context of the GDR, 'nasty sarcasm was much more typical of the 1970s and 1980s … Yet the shift in tone can also be seen as a changed idea of citizenship, in that people addressed the state less as supplicants than as equal and deserving citizens. They were more demanding of their socialist rights … and often brazenly pointed out misuse of resources in the public interest'.[117]

It was the federal youth magazine *Mladost* that boldly referred to 'our socialist oligarchy' and the existence of legal, institutional channels embedded in Yugoslav self-management conducive to social/wealth inequality.[118] Similarly, an article published in the main Bosnian youth magazine *Naši dani* addressed a big public debate which exposed the practice of building summer villas by high Bosnian political officials at the seaside resort of Neum.[119] The article unreservedly attacked high ranking politicians and named them individually: 'To nationalise what had been robbed. To take away once and for all from the red bourgeoisie and give to the working class.'[120] Finally, a similar affair burst into the open when Slovenian *Mladina* accused Minister of Defence General Branko Mamula[121] of having army recruits construct a summer villa in the sea resort of Opatija.

Although reflective of the critique voiced by the 1968 generation regarding the betrayal of the revolutionary and socialist ideals, these acts by the youth press, however, need to be seen as embedded within the context of the time, i.e. within the public debates on the economic and political crisis which were already under way both in the mainstream media and in politics.[122] From a contemporary perspective, however, those acts might appear naive, as Senad Pećanin reflected on their attacks in the press targeting late socialist functionaries:

> It's ridiculous – we used to publicly destroy them for having roast lamb for lunch, for eating on invoice. Today I feel like the biggest idiot for doing that ... This post-war Bosnian elite here, and I could see some evidence – millions of marks were spent ... Raif [Dizdarević] says ... as member of the presidency he had a car and a driver, a flat for temporary use while on the post, two phone lines – the bills for one of which he had to pay himself ... at the first or second presidency meeting he proposed and the comrades agreed that the cost for the food at the restaurant at the presidency building would be deducted from their salaries at the end of the month. Oh! – I am thinking – f***, what are we talking about? These [post-socialist elites] swept away hundreds of millions ... And we brought down that elite at the time ... for a weekend house in Neum. The man worked for forty years, he was a revolutionary, held all kinds of offices – and we questioned why he owned a weekend house in Neum and a 40 square metre flat!

Although the political elite of the youth organisation was not challenged until later in the decade, its cultural and media spheres within a very decentralised structure increasingly provided prominent outlets for alternative expression. The first half of the decade, i.e. the period immediately after Tito's death, was the time when different oppositional ideas and radically new youth cultural streams and styles were progressively invading the youth realm. Expressed reluctantly at official level and still within the institutionalised vocabulary of Yugoslav self-managing socialism, novel ideas and contestations were fermenting under the shrinking layer of the politically correct discourse of socialist self-management. The internally engendered critique aimed at careerist and position-seeking cadres and at the alienation of the SSOJ was upheld by the youth press which began to drift away from its originally conceived role as a media platform of the Youth League(s). The increasing involvement of the youth media in contemporary political debates was met by a range of obstacles – from bans and dismissals, to public attacks. In the context of progressive liberalisation of an already highly decentralised federation and a youth infrastructure, young musicians', artists' and journalists' acts in the public sphere frequently cut across the fine line between negotiation and dissent. Although the 1986 *JUPIO* report underlined the limiting of the spaces for autonomy and free initiative of the young, as well as societal tendencies which aim for 'maximal politicisation and ideologisation of everything',[123] the youngsters active in the peripheral parts of the youth infrastructure – the cultural and media circles – found ways to navigate the system and carve out spaces of independent initiative and non-conformist art and media culture. As it was already mentioned, these phenomena were not particular to the decade of the 1980s. As Valerie Bunce notes, 'The result was that socialist Yugoslavia was, by regional socialist standards (especially from the late 1960s onward) unusually decentralized, unusually liberalized, and unusually situated with respect to East-West economic and political-military rivalries'.[124] This came not only as a result of the unique Yugoslav political and theoretical takes on classical Marxist theory – most notably the concept of the withering away of the state[125] – but also as a result of the existence of a critical mass of young people who took advantage of the resources and the spaces of the youth sphere.

Notes

1 'They tied my sky with wire / They are drawing schemes on my brain / They want another copy of them / To help them bring back the long gone times. / But, I am not giving up my ideals / and I will eat dreams instead of bread / I carry my fortune with me / It is a piece of the free sky' (from the song 'Sky').

2 An obsession with anti-communist resistance, separate from the values of the state, was the product of post-communist nationalist historiographies – approaches that are still dominant in the work of e.g. institutes of national memory or institutes for the investigation of communist crimes. However, challenges to this approach that stress the embeddedness of late socialist dissent within regime discourses and practices, are growing. See, e.g. Anna Saunders, *Honecker's Children Youth and Patriotism in East Germany, 1979–2002* (Manchester: Manchester University Press, 2011); Paul Betts, *Within Walls: Private Life in the German Democratic Republic* (Oxford and New York: Oxford University Press, 2010).

3 For example, the 'basic organisations' of the SSOJ in the various companies, factories and educational institutions used to delegate members to the chamber of associated labour in the municipal assembly, which then sent delegates to the same chamber in the Republic's parliament and to the federal chamber of the federal assembly. The 'municipal conference' of the SSOJ delegated members to the socio-political chamber of the municipal assembly, while the 'republican conference' of the youth organisations had its delegates in the socio-political chamber of the Republics' assemblies.

4 The League of Communist Youth of Yugoslavia (*Savez komunističke omladine Jugoslavije – SKOJ*) existed under that name from 1919 until 1948, when it changed its name into People's Youth (*Narodna omladina*) and kept it until 1963. The organisation was known as the League of Youth (*Savez omladine*) and was separate from the Student Union (*Savez studenata*) until 1974.

5 Archive of Macedonia, Skopje (hereafter AM), *Сојуз на студенти на Македонија*, box number 2 (1971–73), 'Актуелните прашања на општествената положба на младата генерација во самоуправното социјалистичко општество', November 1972, pp. 16–17.

6 See: James Mark, Peter Apor, Radina Vucetic and Piotr Oseka, '"We are with you, Vietnam": Transnational solidarities in Poland, Hungary and Yugoslavia', *Journal of Contemporary History* 50:3 (2014), 439–64.

7 Borka Pavićević, 'Nama i Merkator', in Đorđe Malavrazić (ed.), *Šezdeset osma – lične istorije: 80 svedočenja: objavljeno povodom 40 godina od velikih studentskih demonstracija u Beogradu* (Beograd: Radio Beograd 2/Službeni glasnik, 2008), p. 372.

8 Smiljka Tomanović *et al.*, *Mladi – naša sadašnjost. Istraživanje socijalnih biografija mladih u Srbiji* (Beograd: Čigoja/Institut za sociološka istraživanja Filozofskog fakulteta, 2012), p. 129.

9 Stanko Posavec, 'Politička ideologija i omladina', in Stanko Posavec *et al.*, *Omladina i socijalizam – ostvarenja i mogućnosti* (Zagreb: Centar za društvene djelatnosti omladine, 1971), pp. 27–9.

10 Mirjana Ule, 'Odnos omladine prema mladosti, odraslosti i budućnosti', in Srđan Vrcan *et al.*, *Položaj, svest i ponašanje mlade generacije Jugoslavije* (Beograd: Centar za istraživačku, dokumentacionu i izdavačku delatnost Konferencije SSOJ/Zagreb: Institut za društvena istraživanja Sveučilišta, 1986), p. 104.

11 Gregor Tomc, 'The politics of punk', in Jill Benderly (ed.), *Independent Slovenia: Origins, Movements, Prospects* (London: Macmillan, 1997), pp. 113–35. On the 1968 student protests in Yugoslavia, see: Hrvoje Klasić, *Jugoslavija i svijet 1968* (Zagreb: Ljevak, 2012).

12 Nebojša Popov, 'The university in an ideological shell', in Nebojša Popov (ed.), *The Road to War in Serbia: Trauma and Catharsis* (Budapest: Central European University Press, 2000), p. 311.

13 April Carter, *Democratic Reform in Yugoslavia: The Changing Role of the Party* (London: Frances Pinter, 1982), p. 172.

14 'Skupština Saveza studenata', *Studentski list* 9 (25 March 1969), pp. 4–5; Ilija Moljković, *'Slučaj' Student: dokumenti* (Belgrade: Službeni glasnik, 2008).

15 Tomislav Ćorić, *Pola stoljeća Studentskoga centra u Zagrebu (1957.–2007.)* (Zagreb: Sveučilište u Zagrebu/Studentski centar u Zagrebu, 2007).

16 Open Society Archive, digital archive (hereafter OSA), Slobodan Stankovic, 'Belgrade student unrest', *Radio Free Europe* Background Report, 29 October 1970.

17 Noam Chomsky, 'The conscience of Yugoslavia', *The New York Review of Books* (7 January 1971), www.nybooks.com/articles/1971/01/07/the-conscience-of-yugoslavia/ (last accessed 7 December 2015).

18 'Stvara se studentski pokret na Beogradskom univerzitetu', *Student* (vanredni broj) (4 June 1968), p. 1.

19 Borka Pavićević, 'Nama i Merkator', in Malavrazić, *Šezdeset osma – lične istorije*, pp. 374–5.

20 Dennison Rusinow, *The Yugoslav Experiment 1948–1974* (Berkeley: University of California Press, 1978), p. 234.

21 Ljubiša Ristić, 'Sunčeve pege', in Malavrazić, *Šezdeset osma – lične istorije*, p. 358.

22 AM, Сојуз на студенти на Македонија, box number 2 (1971–1973), 'Актуелните прашања на општествената положба на младата генерација'.

23 Kemal Kurpashić, 'Moja '68: poziv na ljudskiji, pravedniji, bolji svet', in Malavrazić, *Šezdeset osma – lične istorije*, p. 202.

24 Marko Lolić, *Revolucionarni omladinski pokret u Jugoslaviji (SKOJ-SSOJ, 1919–1984)* (Beograd: Radnička štampa, 1984).

25 See: *Statut SSOJ* (Belgrade: NIRO Mladost, 1986), p. 8.

26 AM, *Сојуз на студенти на Македонија*, box number 2 (1971–1973), 'Актуелните прашања на општествената положба на младата генерација во самоуправното социјалистичко општество, Скопје, ноември 1972 год.', p. 3.

27 See: Jill Irvine, 'The Croatian spring and the dissolution of Yugoslavia', in Jasna Dragović-Soso and Lenard J. Cohen (eds), *State Collapse in South-Eastern Europe: New Perspectives on Yugoslavia's Disintegration* (West Lafayette: Purdue University Press, 2007), pp. 149–78.

28 OSA, Slobodan Stankovic, 'After the third Party conference in Belgrade', Radio Free Europe (Research), 11 December 1972.

29 Archive of Yugoslavia, Belgrade (hereafter AY), *Savez socijalističke omladine Jugoslavije* SSOJ 114, folder 298, 'Pregled organizacija kojima PK SSOJ plaća putne troškove za učešće na međunarodnom seminaru omladine i studenata'.

30 *Youth Prospects in the 1980s: Synthesis Report Presented to the General Conference of UNESCO at its Twenty-First Session* (Paris: UNESCO, 1980), p. 21.

31 *Ibid.*, p. 40.

32 Vrcan *et al.*, *Položaj, svest i ponašanje mlade generacije Jugoslavije*, p. 11.

33 Hilde Katrine Haug, *Creating a Socialist Yugoslavia: Tito, Communist Leadership and the National Question* (London: I. B. Tauris, 2012), p. 309.

34 Archive of Bosnia and Herzegovina, Sarajevo (hereafter ABH), *Republička konferencija SSOBIH*, 'Komisija za društveno-politički sistem', box 108, 'Ostvarivanje ustavnih funkcija socijalističkog saveza /teze za raspravu/', Beograd', May 1983.

35 Statistical data shows that the number of youth delegates to the workers' councils rose progressively: from 9,175 in 1953, to 31,578 in 1968 and 53,566 in 1983. However, out of the total number of 484,784 delegates, only 53,566 belonged to the category of 'youth'. *Statistički godišnjak Jugoslavije 1985* (Beograd: Savezni zavod za statistiku, 1985), pp. 79/106–8.

36 Laszlo Kurti, *Youth and the State in Hungary: Capitalism, Communism and Class* (London: Pluto Press, 2002), p. 179.

37 ABH, *Republička konferencija SSOBIH*, 'Program vođenja javne rasprave o materijalu "Neka pitanja demokratizacija odnosa u Savezu socijalističke omladine Jugoslavije"', box 108, 7 May 1983.

38 Archive of Slovenia, Ljubljana (hereafter AS), *RK ZSMS 1974–1990*, AS 538, technical unit 334, 'Izveštaj o radu Konferencije SSOJ, njenih organa i tela za period decembar 1982-decembar 1984 (predlog)', November 1984.

39 ABH, *RK SSOBIH*, box 108, 'Informacija o provedenoj javnoj raspravi', 19 October 1983.

40 According to the 1981 census, 4,858,425 (21.7 per cent) belonged to the category of youth. In 1984, the SSOJ officially had 3,703,658 members. *Statistički godišnjak Jugoslavije 1985*, pp. 111–13.

41 *Youth Prospects in the 1980s*, p. 18.

42 *Jedanaesti kongres SSOJ* (Beograd: NIRO Mladost, 1983), p. 23.

43 *Ibid.*, pp. 14–15.

44 OSA, Slobodan Stanković, 'Changes in the Yugoslav Communist Youth Federation', *Radio Free Europe* Background Report, 5 January 1981.

45 ABH, *RK SSOBIH*, box 108, 'Prostorni i materijalni položaj opštinskih, gradske, medjuopštinskih i republičkih konferencija Saveza socijalističke omladine Bosne

i Hercegovine i organa društvenih organizacija koji okupljaju mlade na nivou opština, grada i republike (interno)', February 1984.

46 A more creative and cynical response to the same problem was voiced in the 1980 LP *Dolgcajt* [Boredom] by the Slovenian punk rock band Pankrti [Bastards]: 'He always knows where the wind is blowing / where it did and where it will. / He also likes to awaken memories / of the times when he was not yet alive. / Else he likes to argue about things / about which he has no clue / and because these are very common / at least that he does well / 17, 17, young perspective cadre / 17, 17, instead of a head a radar'. See: Oskar Mulej, ' "We are drowning in red beet, patching up the holes in the Iron Curtain": The punk subculture in Ljubljana in the late 1970s and early 1980s', *East Central Europe* 38 (2011), 373–89.

47 Milan Bečejić, 'Krvna slika predsednika – omladinski kadrovi: kontinuitet prosečnih?', *NON – List mladih Srbije* 497 (4 November 1984).

48 Jordan Aleksić, 'Zagonetka društveno-političkog aktivizma mlade generacije', in *Mlada generacija, danas: društveni položaj, uloga i perspektive mlade generacije Jugoslavije* (Beograd: NIRO Mladost/Predsedništvo konferencije SSOJ, 1982), p. 79.

49 Dragoje Žarković, 'Aktuelni problem našeg društva (posebno omladine) i putevi njihovog rešavanja', in *Bliska perspektiva Jugoslavije s posebnim osvrtom na društveni položaj omladine* (Beograd: Predsedništvo konferencije SSOJ, 1985), pp. 5–6.

50 OSA, Slobodan Stanković, 'Changes in the Yugoslav Communist Youth Federation', *Radio Free Europe* Background Report, 5 January 1981.

51 Vladimir Goati and Dimitar Mirčev, 'Društveno-političko i samoupravno delovanje omladine', in *Mlada generacija, danas*.

52 Bora Kuzmanović, 'Socijalni i politički aktivizam omladine', in *Deca krize: Omladina Jugoslavije krajem osamdesetih* (Beograd: Institut društvenih nauka/Centar za politikološka istraživanja i javno mnenje, 1990), p. 81.

53 Rock music became progressively embraced by the youth organisation mainly as a response to wider societal developments within culture and the domestic music industry. Namely, 70 per cent of the authors in the area of pop and rock music at one of the largest music production companies in Yugoslavia, *Jugoton*, were younger than thirty. Only in 1983, *Jugoton* received 300 rock demo recordings. The youth organisation followed suit and different branches found different ways of accommodating the new music cultures. For instance, the SSO branch in the Croatian town of Rijeka had a sub-commission for rock music within its commission for culture. Borislav Knežević, 'Crnci u produkciji', *Polet* 273/274 (3 August 1984), p. 28.

54 Bora Kuzmanović, 'Socijalni i politički aktivizam omladine', in *Deca krize*, p. 81.

55 ŠKUC – Ljubljana; Studentski centar (SC) – Zagreb; Dom mladih (Skenderija) – Sarajevo; Studentski kulturni centar (SKC) and Dom omladine – Belgrade; Dom omladine 'Budo Tomović' – Podgorica; Дом на млади „25 Мај,, – Skopje; Kulturni centar mladih 'Sonja Marinković' – Novi Sad (from 1984: Kulturni centar Novog Sada); Pallati i rinisë, kulturës dhe sporteve 'Boro dhe Ramizi' – Prishtina.

56 Radio Študent in Ljubljana; Omladinski radio/Radio 101 in Zagreb; Omladinski program/Omladinski radio in Sarajevo; Radio Index in Belgrade; Клуб 100 in Skopje.

57 *Youth Prospects in the 1980s*, p. 38.

58 Valerie Bunce, *Subversive Institutions: The Design and the Destruction of Socialism and the State* (Cambridge: Cambridge University Press, 1999), p. 51.

59 For example, one 1987 issue of *Ideje* featured articles on the 'European stag-flation', on the history of socialism, the relationship between socialism and democracy and the Serbian youth movement in the nineteenth century. Another 1987 issue was dedicated to 'Contemporary Albania and Yugoslav-Albanian relations'.

60 Dunja Blažević, 'Before and after: 2 examples', personal communication.

61 Slavko Timotijević *et al.*, *Ovo je Studentski kulturni centar / This is the Students Cultural Center: prvih 25 godina: 1971–1996* (Beograd: BMG, 1996).

62 Katarina Pejović, 'Pioneering as a lifestyle: A conversation with Dunja Blažević', www.bifc-hub.eu/interview/pioneering-as-a-life-style-a-conversation-with-dunja-blazevic (last accessed 9 December 2015).

63 Darko Glavan, 'Experiment and initiative', in *Students' Centre Gallery: 40 Years* (Zagreb: Studentski centar, 2005), p. 12.

64 See also: Ana Janevski, *As Soon As I Open My Eyes I See a Film: Experiments in Yugoslav Art in the '60s and '70s* (Warsaw: Museum of Modern Art in Poland, 2011); *The Misfits: Conceptualist Strategies in Croatian Contemporary Art* (Zagreb: Muzej suvremene umjetnosti, 2002); Laura J. Hoptman and Tomáš Pospiszyl, *Primary Documents: A Sourcebook for Eastern and Central European Art since the 1950s* (New York: Museum of Modern Art, 2002).

65 The 'FV 112/15' theatre took its name from France Verbinc's *Dictionary of Foreign Terms*, page 112, heading 15, which read: *C'est la guerre*. They drew inspiration from the historical avant-garde and the American beatniks. In 1981 the group took over the organisation of the Tuesday disco nights at the student dormitory and through 'Disco FV' the FV brand was established. See: Nikolai Jeffs, 'FV and the "Third Scene"', 1980–1990', in *FV – Alternative Scene of the Eighties* (Ljubljana: International Center for Graphic Arts, 2008).

66 'Barbara Borčić 1982–1985', www.galerija.skuc-drustvo.si/textborcic2.html (last accessed 27 February 2014). See also: Barbara Borčić, 'The ŠKUC gallery, alternative culture, and Neue Slowenische Kunst in the 1980s', in Zdenka Badovinac, Eda Čufer and Anthony Gardner (eds), *NSK from Kapital to Capital: An Event of the Final Decade of Yugoslavia* (Cambridge, MA: MIT Press, 2015), pp. 299–318.

67 See: *Zakon o udruženom radu* (Zagreb: Vjesnik, 1976).

68 Adam Roberts, 'Yugoslavia: The constitution and the succession', *The World Today* 34:4 (1978), 136–146, p. 139.

69 Ćorić, *Pola stoljeća Studentskoga centra u Zagrebu*.

70 For example, following a referendum in 1987 the working unit 'Cinema and bookshop' decided to leave the OOUR 'Kultura' and form a separate OOUR 'Cinema Student Centre', but the decision was annulled by the District Court in Zagreb. In 1990 the Student Radio left the institutional framework of the Student Centre and formed a separate joint-stock company 'Radio 101'.

71 Ćorić, *Pola stoljeća Studentskoga centra u Zagrebu*.

72 Kršić, *Mirko Ilić*, p. 49.

73 See, for example: Radina Vučetić, *Coca Cola Socialism: The Americanization of Yugoslav Popular Culture in the 1960s* (Belgrade: Službeni glasnik, 2012).

74 Sabrina Petra Ramet, 'Rock music in Czechoslovakia', in Sabrina Petra Ramet (ed.), *Rocking the State: Rock Music and Politics in Eastern Europe and Russia* (Boulder: Westview Press, 1994), pp. 55–72. See also: William Jay Risch (ed.), *Youth and Rock in the Soviet*

Bloc: Youth Cultures, Music and the State in Russia and Eastern Europe (Lanham: Lexington Books, 2015).

75 Officially known as *Štafeta mladosti*, the main event was held every year on 25 May at the stadium of the JNA in Belgrade – officially celebrated as the Day of Youth [*Dan mladosti*] and Tito's birthday. It was preceded by a Yugoslav-wide relay race held every year from 1945 until 1987.

76 The 'seven secretaries' refer to the seven youngsters who held this position within the underground communist youth organisation in the interwar period in the Kingdom of the Serbs, Croats and Slovenes – later renamed the Kingdom of Yugoslavia. They were all brutally killed at the end of the 1920s and the beginning of the 1930s.

77 Dragan Todorović, 'Ženski orgazam G-tačka', *NON – List mladih Srbije* 497 (4 November 1984), p. 37.

78 Boško Grbić, 'Omladinska štampa: položaj, delovanje, tretman', *Mladost* 1277 (22 March 1982), p. 3.

79 *Ibid.*

80 Dick Hebidge's *Subculture: The Meaning of Style* was translated and published in Yugoslavia in 1980, only one year after its appearance in Great Britain.

81 *Top Lista Nadrealista* [The Surrealists' Top Chart] was a widely popular comedy show which aired on TV Sarajevo from 1984 until 1991. It was originally part of the youth radio programme. At the end of the 1980s it ridiculed the absurdity of the rising conflicts in Yugoslav politics. It is mostly remembered for its political satire and some of its sketches which dwelled on the prospect of war and the ensuing divisions have been seen as 'prophetic'. One of its leading characters – Nenad Janković (Nele Karajlić) fronted the band *Zabranjeno pušenje* [Smoking forbidden]. Their first album *Das ist Walter* was released in 1984 in 3,000 copies by Zagreb's record label *Jugoton* (after being refused by Belgrade's PGP-RTB) and eventually sold around 100,000 copies. The show and the band form the core of the *Novi primitivizam* [New primitivism] movement which based its aesthetics on local Bosnian humour and urban/youth Sarajevo sub-culture. On New Primitivism and The Surrealists' Top Chart, see: Pavle Levi, 'Yugoslavism without limits', *Disintegration in Frames: Aesthetics and Ideology in the Yugoslav and Post-Yugoslav Cinema* (Stanford: Stanford University Press, 2007), pp. 57–85; Dalibor Mišina's, *Shake, Rattle and Roll: Yugoslav Rock Music and the Poetics of Social Critique* (Farnham: Ashgate, 2013).

82 Rajko Muršič, 'Punk anthropology: From a study of a local Slovene alternative rock scene towards partisan scholarship', in Laszlo Kűrti and Peter Skalnik (eds), *Postsocialist Europe: Anthropological Perspectives from Home* (New York and Oxford: Berghahn Books, 2009), p. 199.

83 Zoran Franičević, 'Uvodnik', *Polet* 141 (12 November 1980), p. 4.

84 Pedro Ramet, 'The Yugoslav press in flux', in Pedro Ramet (ed.), *Yugoslavia in the 1980s* (Boulder: Westview Press, 1985), p. 111.

85 'Privremena zabrana rasturanja lista Student, po drugi put', *Student* (vanredni broj 3), 11 June 1968, p. 4; Ilija Moljković, *'Slučaj' Student: dokumenti* (Belgrade: Službeni glasnik, 2008). See also: Marko Zubak, 'Omladinski tisak i kulturna strana studentskoga pokreta u Socijalističkoj Federativnoj Republici Jugoslaviji (1968.–1972.)', *Časopis za suvremenu povijest* 1 (2014), 37–53.

86 April Carter, *Democratic Reform in Yugoslavia: The Changing Role of the Party* (London: Frances Pinter, 1982), p. 200.

87 OSA, Zdenko Antic, 'Yugoslav youths' rebellious press', *Radio Free Europe* Background
    Report, 29 May 1970.
88 Article 167 related to the freedom of the press: 'Freedom of press and other
    forms of informing and public expressing, freedom of associating, freedom of
    speech and public coming out, freedom of gathering and other public gath-
    ering shall be guaranteed. Citizens shall have the right to express and publish
    their opinions through the means of informing', as well as Article 168: 'Press,
    radio and television and other means of public informing and communicating
    shall be obliged to inform public truthfully and objectively, and also to pub-
    lish opinions and information of bodies, organisations and citizens which are
    of interest for public'. In November 1990 the federal government led by Ante
    Marković permitted private ownership of the press (including foreign participa-
    tion) and practically did away with all existing limitations concerning freedom
    of expression.
89 In June 1984 the Federal Public Prosecutor reported that of the 545 individuals
    charged with political crimes in 1983, 76 per cent were charged with 'verbal crime'
    [*verbalni delikt*]. See: *Yugoslavia: Prisoners of Conscience* (London: Amnesty International
    Publications, 1985).
90 'Whoever brings into derision the Socialist Federal Republic of Yugoslavia, its
    flag, coat of arms or national anthem, its highest authorities or representa-
    tives thereof, its armed forces or the supreme commander, shall be punished
    by imprisonment for a term exceeding three months but not exceeding three
    years.'
91
    (1) Whoever by means of propaganda or in some other way incites or fans
         national, racial or religious hatred or discord between peoples and nationali-
         ties living in the SFRY, shall be punished by imprisonment for a term exceed-
         ing one year but not exceeding 10 years.
    (2) Whoever, by insulting citizens or in some other way, incites national, racial
         or religious hostility, shall be punished by imprisonment for a term exceeding
         three months but not exceeding three years.
    (3) If an act referred to in paragraphs 1 and 2 of this article has been committed
         systematically or by taking advantage of one's position or office, as part of a
         group, or if disorder, violence or other grave consequences resulted from these
         acts, the offender shall for an act referred to in paragraph 1 be punished by
         imprisonment for not less than one year and for an act referred to in para-
         graph 2 by imprisonment for a term exceeding six months but not exceeding
         five years.
         The complete text of the Penal Code is available at: www.refworld.org/docid/
         3ae6b5fe0.html (last accessed 23 September 2016).

92 'Član 133', *Studentski list* 7:970 (24 February 1988), pp. 14–15.
93 OSA, Slobodan Stankovic, 'No permission for Yugoslavia's first "free and demo-
    cratic magazine"', *Radio Free Europe* Background Report, 2 December 1980.
94 *Yugoslavia: Prisoners of Conscience*, p. 29.
95 Milena Dragićević-Šešić, *Umetnost i alternativa* (Beograd: Fakultet dramskih umet-
    nosti, 1992), p. 166.

96 For the links between Serbian and Slovenian intellectuals in the 1980s, see: Jasna Dragović-Soso, *'Saviours of the Nation' – Serbia's Intellectual Opposition and the Revival of Nationalism* (London: Hurst & Company, 2002).

97 V. P. Gagnon, 'Yugoslavia in 1989 and after', *Nationalities Papers* 38:1 (2010), 23–39, p. 23.

98 *Ibid.*, p. 26.

99 *Ibid.*

100 Susan L. Woodward, *Socialist Unemployment: The Political Economy of Yugoslavia 1945–1990* (Princeton: Princeton University Press, 1995), p. 350.

101 Pavle Pavlović, 'Otrovni dim Zabranjenog pušenja', www.media.ba/mcsonline/files/shared/Pavle_P.pdf (last accessed 27 February 2014). The famous slogan was often purposefully and sarcastically (mis)quoted as 'What belongs to others we (don't) want, ours – we don't have'.

102 Stipe Šuvar (1936–2004), one of the leading Croatian and Yugoslav politicians in the 1980s, who was also a university professor of sociology. Openly critical of the rise of nationalism in Yugoslavia, targeted by nationalist forces and Party factions in Serbia and Croatia after he came into conflict with Slobodan Milošević, 'he was perhaps the last outstanding non-Serbian politician who seriously tried to create a common Yugoslav political and cultural space'. Andrew Wachtel and Predrag J. Marković, 'A last attempt at educational integration: The failure of common educational cores in Yugoslavia in the early 1980s', in Jasna Dragović-Soso and Lenard J. Cohen (eds), *State Collapse in South-Eastern Europe: New Perspectives on Yugoslavia's Disintegration* (West Lafayette: Purdue University Press, 2008), p. 215.

103 Gertrude J. Robinson, *Tito's Maverick Media: Politics of Mass Communication in Yugoslavia* (Urbana, Chicago and London: University of Illinois Press, 1977), p. 62. By the mid-1980s, the Yugoslav media network was significantly fragmented, decentralised, yet numerically impressive. In 1987 Yugoslavia had 2,825 newspapers and 202 radio and TV stations. The 1985 press law did not effectively neutralise the decentralising tendencies. See: John B. Allcock, *Explaining Yugoslavia* (London: C. Hurst, 2000), p. 292.

104 'Mladinu su (opet) zaplijenili', *Studentski list* 10:973 (1988), pp. 4–5.

105 OSA, Milan Andrejevich, 'A challenge from Slovenian journalists', *Radio Free Europe* Situation Report, 2 May 1988.

106 The following year *Mladina* again raised the same issue in its editorial – this time related to a visit of a Yugoslav delegation to Chile: 'Of course, we can only rhetorically wonder which weapons Yugoslavia sold to the Chilean dictatorship.' Botteri and Suhadolnik, 'Eskadroni smrti, go to hell', *Mladina* 14 (14 April 1989), p. 1.

107 'Odgovor SL-a na prijedlog javnog tužioca o privremenoj zabrani lista: Mirno more, dobro zdravlje', *Studentski list* 4:967 (3 January 1988), p. 5.

108 Zoran Oštrić, 'Osuđeni smo na status quo', *Studentski list* 2:966 (27 January 1988), p. 7.

109 Igor Mekina, 'Oaza lažne slobode', *Studentski list* 2:966 (27 January 1988), p. 18.

110 'Truly, I live in dark times! / An artless word is foolish. A smooth forehead / Points to insensitivity. He who laughs / Has not yet received / The terrible news. / What times are these, in which / A conversation about trees is almost a crime / For in doing so we maintain our silence about so much wrongdoing! / And he

who walks quietly across the street, / Passes out of the reach of his friends /
Who are in danger? / It is true: I work for a living / But, believe me, that is a
coincidence. Nothing / That I do gives me the right to eat my fill. / By chance
I have been spared. (If my luck does not hold, I am lost.) / They tell me: eat
and drink. Be glad to be among the haves! / But how can I eat and drink /
When I take what I eat from the starving / And those who thirst do not have
my glass of water? / And yet I eat and drink. / I would happily be wise. / The
old books teach us what wisdom is: / To retreat from the strife of the world /
To live out the brief time that is your lot / Without fear / To make your way
without violence / To repay evil with good – / The wise do not seek to satisfy
their desires, / But to forget them. / But I cannot heed this: / Truly I live in
dark times!'

111 'Odgovor SL-a na prijedlog javnog tužioca o privremenoj zabrani lista: Mirno
     more, dobro zdravlje', *Studentski list* 4:967 (3 January 1988), p. 5.

112 'Zašto je zabranjen SL? Kako smo zaboravili Lumumbu', *Studentski list* 12:975 (6
     April 1988), p. 6.

113 'Tito o Mobutuu: eksponent, agent, zločinac …', *Studentski list* 12:975 (6 April
     1988), p. 7.

114 'Saopćenje bivše redakcije "SL-a": Granica političkog kompromisa', *Studentski list*
     14:977 (27 April 1988), p. 4.

115 OSA, Milan Andrejevich, 'An assessment of the party conference', *Radio Free
     Europe* Yugoslavia Situation Report, 7 June 1988.

116 'Veliki, veći, najveći', *Polet* 292 (21 December 1984), p. 10.

117 Paul Betts, *Within Walls: Private Life in the German Democratic Republic* (Oxford and
     New York: Oxford University Press, 2010), p. 189.

118 Duška Maksimović and Raško Kovačević, 'Dali smo opljačkali državu?', *Mladost*
     13 (10–23 March 1986), pp. 8–11.

119 A 1969 issue of *Naši dani* which raised a similar issue was banned by the public
     prosecutor after it published an article entitled 'Comrade Boss' which claimed
     that the working class is being exploited. For this and other bans in the youth and
     student press in the late 1960s, see: April Carter, *Democratic Reform in Yugoslavia: The
     Changing Role of the Party* (London: Frances Pinter, 1982).

120 Radmilo Milovanović, 'Neum ili dolje crvena buržoazija', *Naši dani* 949 (2
     September 1988), p. 7.

121 Born in 1921, Admiral Mamula was one of those on the late Yugoslav political
     scene who belonged to the 'partisan generation'. He joined the partisan units
     under Tito's command in 1941 and by the end of the war acted as the political
     commissar of the Naval Headquarters for the Northern Adriatic.

122 A wave of workers' strikes swept the country throughout the decade. In 1986
     alone there were 851 registered strikes and in 1987 that number increased to
     1685! The strikes were a display of inter-ethnic solidarity and the protest slogans
     used by the workers reflected the same anti-regime sentiment which prevailed
     in the youth press: 'Down with the red bourgeoisie!', 'You betrayed Tito', 'We
     want change'. See: Goran Musić, 'Jugoslovenski radnički pokret 1981–1991', in

Đorđe Tomić and Petar Atanacković (eds), *Društvo u pokretu: novi društveni pokreti u Jugoslaviji od 1968 do danas* (Novi Sad: Cenzura, 2009), pp. 160–8.

123 Vrcan *et al.*, *Položaj, svest i ponašanje*, p. 13.

124 Bunce, *Subversive Institutions*, p. 53.

125 See: Dejan Jović, *Yugoslavia: A State That Withered Away* (West Lafayette: Purdue University Press, 2009).

2

'Comrades, I don't believe you!': youth culture and the rethinking of historical legacies

The image of freedom changes over time;
The freedom that is possible in a period of plenitude
is no longer viable when want reigns.
Our freedom is the freedom of those who think alike.[1]

Laibach (1982)

In January 1980, the jury of the federal board for the celebration of 25 May – 'Youth Day' and president Tito's birthday – concluded that they had only received five scenario proposals for the final stadium event [*slet*], none of which satisfied the criteria: 'The response to the call for proposals was very small, while the quality of the received works was such that none qualifies for the award. The Jury suggests that the Presidency of the SSOJ establishes a working group for the drafting of a scenario for the final Day of Youth event.'[2] The single most important youth event began to appear anachronistic and incapable of inspiring youth from below, even before Tito passed away. However, understandably, in an atmosphere of a somewhat Soviet-inspired paranoia after the invasion of Afghanistan and Tito's illness and subsequent death, there was reluctance in the very early 1980s to openly pose these questions at an official level. Not only did this commemorative and festive occasion fail to spark genuine interest or to mobilise the youth as it had done twenty years before, it also consumed a significant part of the SSOJ's budget. Millions of dinars were spent not only on the organisation of the final event on 25 May at the Belgrade Yugoslav People's Army (JNA) stadium, but throughout the year in related events all over the country.

Challenges to earlier conceptions of the Youth Day, however, need to be put in the context of changing debates over Tito's role. The unraveling of Tito's mythical aura began not long after his funeral on 8 May 1980 in Belgrade. Vladimir Dedijer's *Novi prilozi za biografiju Josipa Broza Tita* [New contributions for the biography of Josip Broz Tito] was published in 1981 and Dedijer, Tito's

official biographer, was hailed as someone 'who began reducing Tito's personality cult to human proportions'.[3] Although the text did not radically challenge
Tito's stature, its publication sparked controversy since it was seen as 'eroding
many of the myths officially fostered in Yugoslavia during the last three and a
half decades'.[4] Dedijer was quoted saying that 'one does a disservice to such
a great personality by writing of him according to protocol, like a Pharaoh,
extolling him to the sky and hiding his faults'.[5]

Two years later, in 1983, after the main event commemorating 25 May at the
Belgrade stadium, a wave of reactions from senior officials and political bodies
swept the media space. Stana Tomašević-Arnesen, a Second World War veteran
and at the time president of the SSRNJ Committee for commemorating Tito's
legacy, insisted that 'It is intolerable that, under the pretext of praising Tito, a
personality cult, religion, and mysticism have been allowed to develop … At
the central celebration Tito descended on clouds that stayed in place like the
"throne of the Almighty," while bluish light filtered through the backdrop'.[6] It
is thus important to note that among both the most senior political officials and
youth circles there was a shared sense of disapproval regarding the nine-metre
figure of Tito which rose among clouds of smoke at one end of the stadium.
This ushered in a new, 'modernised' form of celebrating the Youth Day the
following year, where in addition to the revolutionary and socialist slogans, rock
'n' roll was prominent as a music background both at the final celebration at
the JNA stadium and on the streets of Belgrade, which in 1984 also hosted the
'Yugoslav meetings of the youth' [*Jugoslovenski susreti mladih*].[7]

It was representatives of this new generation who articulated an unprecedented critique in the realms of culture and youth commemorations. Indeed,
they conceived of their challenge in explicitly generational terms, questioning
some of the values embodied in contemporary politics and culture, but above all
in an older generation which was seen to perpetuate inherited rituals and rhetoric without being able to respond to the contemporary challenges and crises.
Without doubt there was a parallel process of 'cautious political liberalisation'[8]
unfolding at the institutional/political level and the atmosphere of open public
debate and acceptance of the reality of the crisis fed into the debates within
the youth realm. However, for the most part, this critique was not reduced to a
demand for outright abolishment of Yugoslav socialism, but it was rather about
challenging the norms of an older generation and reinventing socialism through
the state's youth institutions. This critique often manifested itself in cultural
forms. Hence, this chapter addresses some of those cultural responses as sites
for generational contestation. In particular, it reflects on how mainstream political discourse and inherited youth rituals were questioned in debates over the
personality cult and the Youth relay race, and explores how mainstream socialist
youth culture was critiqued through new music trends.

What was defined in the Introduction as the second generational marker – a new 'sense of citizenship' – manifested itself through a new way of articulating conceptualisations of 'rights' and 'identity'. Despite a sense of crisis, fundamental aspects of Yugoslav identity and belonging survived. Indeed, surveys confirmed that most still belived that change could be engineered through institutional forms. Nevertheless, the role of the inherited youth rituals such as the voluntary work actions and the celebration of 25 May changed irrevocably. Finally, a series of debates provoked by the rise of new youth music scenes, some of which were seen as contesting Yugoslavia's anti-fascist legacy, provided the countours for an anti-regime critique which sought to expose the authoritarian traits of the Yugoslav socio-political system and to stretch the discursive boundaries of rights and freedom(s).

A new sense of citizenship

Surveys and interviews from the 1980s demonstrate different degrees of crisis of faith in the status quo. However, they also demonstrate, especially amongst the younger generation, a fundamental faith in the Yugoslav project, both in terms of national/ethnic identifications, and with regard to the future of a form of socialism. Indeed, even some of the most critical voices believed that change could be engineered through institutional forms. Although the rights and identities that constituted citizenship were being rethought, this was nearly always done within a Yugoslav framework.

Respondents in the 1986 *JUPIO* study expressed a high dose of pessimism concerning the future of Yugoslav society. Nevertheless, few could envision a radical transformation or a disappearance of the Yugoslav framework: rather, 'the main concern of the vast majority of the population was their economic well-being in the face of the economic crisis'.[9] When asked what were the most important problems the society was facing, the majority of respondents in the *JUPIO* survey located the core problems with the economic sphere – most prominently youth unemployment and the representatives of the state bureaucracy who in the eyes of the young generation failed to live up to their roles and could not be held accountable for political or economic decisions. The *JUPIO* research also demonstrated a relatively high degree of identification with Yugoslavia. The part dedicated to the 'national attachment' (see Table 5) revealed a rather low interest in and identification with ethno-national or religious terms.

By summarising the results according to the federal units and taking into account the last three degrees (medium, strong and extreme), the research revealed that the highest degree of national attachment was among the youth in Kosovo (72.5 per cent + 5.7 per cent + 0.4 per cent = 78.6 per cent) and in Macedonia (60.2 per cent + 3.7 per cent + 0 per cent = 63.9 per cent), while the lowest was found among the young of Bosnia-Herzegovina (30.3 per cent +

Table 5 National attachment

Degree of national attachment	% of respondents
Absence of national attachment	11.9
Weak national attachment	43.8
Medium national attachment	41.9
Strong national attachment	2.3
Extreme national attachment	0.1

Table 6 Nationally mixed marriages are doomed to fail (percentage of those who agree)

Nationality	% who agree	Political membership status	% who agree	Employment status	% who agree
Yugoslavs	10	Members of the SSO	15	University students	11
Croats	12	Non-members of the SSO	43	Employed	15
Slovenes	14	Not sure of their SSO membership status	23	Students (high school)	19
Montenegrins	15	Members of the SKJ	14	Unemployed	20
(Bosnian) Muslims	15	Non-members of the SKJ	19	Farmers	27
Serbs	17				
Macedonians	29				
Albanians	45				
Average agreement: 18%					

Source: Sergej Flere, 'Odnos mladih prema etnosu', in Vrcan *et al., Položaj, svest i ponašanje mlade generacije Jugoslavije*, pp. 136– 7.

1.5 per cent + 0 = 31.8 per cent).[10] The results according to 'contingency strata' showed that the level of national attachment was lowest among students (30.4 per cent) and highest among farmers and 'rural youth' – 57.5 per cent. The survey also showed a high percentage of acceptance of nationally mixed marriages (see Table 6), which echoes the tendency of valuing individual (as opposed to cultural/ethno-religious) traits when choosing a marriage partner or a friend.[11]

As the majority of the 5.4 per cent of the Yugoslav population who declared 'Yugoslav' in the 1981 federal census were young people, scholars among other things sought to measure the levels of national and Yugoslav attachment. In order to map certain conclusions on the sentiment of Yugoslav belonging as supranational or national, the *JUPIO* research posed several different questions. The percentage of those who agreed with the statement 'The feelings of Yugoslav belonging and my national belonging are not the same, but I care about both of them' was 61 per cent. The highest percentage was among the Macedonians (69 per cent) and the lowest among the Albanians (56 per cent) – although in all of the cases that meant that the majority espoused a Yugoslav identification as a supplementary, supranational sentiment, where the ethno-national and the Yugoslav were not mutually exclusive. On the contrary, this points to the fact that this generation embodied what I call 'layered Yugoslavism', i.e. it had internalised the basic postulates of the Yugoslav polity – its parallel ethno-territorial and its supranational character. Having been born and socialised within the quasi-confederal political framework of Yugoslavia, where the separate national/federal units and identities publicly and institutionally coexisted with the Yugoslav level/sense of identity and citizenship, this generation had internalised a two-tier sense of belonging and self-perception, where the national/republican, on one hand, and the Yugoslav dimension, on the other, were perceived and appropriated as complementary. Second, coming of age and being active in the 1970s and 1980s, this generation was particularly exposed to the tension between the strong centrifugal and weakening centripetal forces and tendencies at institutional and everyday level. In addition, the research quoted the 'surprising finding' of 72 per cent of young people across the entire survey who declared that they agreed with the statement: 'I am a Yugoslav and I can't give priority to any other affiliation/belonging.' The highest percentage was among the Bosnian Muslim youth (80 per cent), the Macedonians (78 per cent) and the Serbs and Montenegrins (76 per cent), while the lowest was among the Slovenes (49 per cent). The fact that even the lowest percentage implies that half of the respondents demonstrated a surprisingly high level of 'Yugoslav orientation' is very telling of the way this generation perceived Yugoslavism and self-identified in broader terms, beyond the traditional ethno-national framework. Although it was predominantly among the Bosnian youth that the Yugoslav was adopted as a 'primary identification', even the youth belonging to the other national groups which demonstrated a relatively high level of national attachment/ethnocentrism (such as the Albanians, Macedonians and Slovenes), accepted the Yugoslav as an additional (civic, political, cultural) layer of identification or sense of belonging. The research concluded that 'there is a very high potential for Yugoslav identification [*opredeljivanje*] among the young ... which is not a matter of fashion and transience, but of more profound integrative processes'.[12]

The testimony of Sašo Ordanoski offers a synthesis of all of these points by reflecting on what Yugoslavism represented and meant at individual level:

> First of all, there was a sentimental dimension to the Yugoslav identification. A sentiment related to the fine, decent life which certain social strata nowadays

can only long for. There was also a political platform within it – no matter how caricature-like it sounds today, the idea of brotherhood and unity did not sound like a pamphlet … Ultimately it appealed to a core human emotion and that is the fundamental need for security. That idea allowed people to feel safer and engendered a need to preserve that union, which consequently resulted in the large number of people who declared Yugoslav [in the census]. In any case, the feeling of being Macedonian, Serb, etc. came a little later, when the conflict intensified and when eventually the people were pushed into their national corrals and forced to identify according to their primary ethnic belonging. The Yugoslav idea was a synthetic idea, a more cosmopolitan idea, hence it could not be negative in itself. It didn't however imply an erasure of the consciousness of ethnic belonging, but a desire to pluralise that ethnic belonging and to integrate it with other ethnic belongings into a new quality – more powerful, bigger, more comfortable … The instigators of the events which destroyed this proved to be more powerful than the instigators of the integrative idea – 'and the rest is history'.

The idea that Yugoslavism was not understood as an attempted 'erasure of the consciousness of ethnic belonging', but it was rather a 'cosmopolitan idea' which essentially helped to 'pluralise' and raise the ethnic onto a higher level, echoes the finding of the *JUPIO* study. The majority of my interviewees spoke of 'togetherness' as a way to avoid using the notion of 'brotherhood and unity' which might appear 'caricature-like' nowadays. It is also important to note the capacious quality in both spatial and abstract terms, raised in many testimonies, implying that Yugoslavism allowed plurality and was able to accommodate difference. Yugoslavia, in this sense, was understood both as a spatial framework which was bigger and hence more commodious than the narrower national/federal unit, and as a wider identity framework which offered more freedom and an extended scope for self-identification.

In an atmosphere where scholars were observing a trend of a progressive increase in the ethnic distance from the 1960s onwards, the last all-Yugoslav research on youth published in 1990 revealed some astounding results which echoed those from 1986. When asked to declare whether and to what extent (medium, high or very high) they are prepared to personally engage in the preservation and realisation of certain group interests and tendencies ('my generation', 'my nation', 'my religion', 'Yugoslavia as a whole'), the majority (54 per cent/'very high') chose 'SFR Yugoslavia as a whole'.[13] Although the authors noted that there were differences along national/regional lines, the research found that the preparedness for engagement for the interests of one's nation and the interests of Yugoslavia as a whole are actually connected as 'for the majority of the young these two attitudes *do not appear as incompatible*'[14] (emphasis mine). Indeed, an ethno-national and a Yugoslav sense of belonging seen as complementary rather than mutually exclusive persisted until very late into the decade. Although ethnic distance had increased between 1985 and 1989, in 1989, the majority of the respondents understood Yugoslavism as a 'sense of togetherness' [*osećanje zajedništva*]. The Slovenian youth was the only exception – for 43 per cent of them Yugoslavism represented 'citizenship', while for 14 per cent – an expression of unitarism and centralism.[15] Although the survey revealed that 86 per cent of the respondents declared general preparedness for engagement for the interests of Yugoslavia, with generational interests (82 per cent) and national interests (74 per cent) ranked just below that, it concluded that the youth mostly identified with the social/class group it belonged to.[16] The sense of belonging to a socially, culturally or generationally defined group with a relative disregard for the ethno-national aspect indeed surfaced in many of the interviews I conducted. Robert Botteri's testimony is particularly illustrative:

> I have to say I never identified as Yugoslav. I was at the age when I would rather identify as a punk than a Yugoslav. I used to claim that I have more in common with a punk from Belgrade, than with someone who is into folk music from Ljubljana [laughs]. So, we had a rather internationalist understanding/outlook. We felt closer to the punks in England. So, we never perceived it in a nationalist way. Moreover, being a Yugoslav at that time was also some kind of nationalism. It was an antipode. We saw nineteenth-century remnants in all of the nationalists. We thought they wouldn't be able to re-surface, we thought the world was becoming global and it didn't matter what you were. We probably underestimated the power of nationalism. Especially with those who were not supposed to be nationalist ... Because the top echelons of the communist parties were always describing themselves as internationalist. If there was anything valuable in [the Yugoslav interpretation of] Marxism, it was internationalism.

The sense of multiple layers in one's identification with Yugoslavia is evident in the majority of the testimonies I collected. The awareness of one's ethno-national belonging is clearly present and discernible, whereas the Yugoslav identification is present, but stripped of national content. Dejan Jović's testimony provides an illustration of this:

> Formally I never declared Yugoslav ... In the student index there was a box for 'nationality', which I left blank. I enrolled at university in 1986. And that was how I felt. The student index is the evidence. First of all, I considered that question inappropriate, intrusive. It was completely incomprehensible for me why one was asked to declare their nationality. It made you wonder – what is the purpose of that question? On the other hand, as I have dual national belonging, Croatian and Serbian, I found it difficult to decide and I simply never wanted to decide. If I had to, I used to say I have dual belonging, Serb and Croat, to be fair to both. Formally, in the censuses I was 'undeclared', but not 'Yugoslav'. Why? Because I think I bought in, I followed the dominant politically correct logic, which was that Yugoslavs in the ethnic sense do not exist. That was what we were taught in school, that 'Yugoslav' is not an ethnic category. Yes, all of us are Yugoslav, that's how we feel, but in the ethnic sense we are Serbs, Croats ... So,

I was not that big of a rebel in that sense to dare say – 'I am an ethnic Yugoslav, precisely because everyone says they don't exist', as many people actually did.

Culture played an important role for this generation in the 1980s in how they made sense of Yugoslavism. The majority of my interviewees identified Yugoslavism in broad cultural terms. Gregor Tomc drew a line between the political and the cultural poles of the Yugoslav project, pinpointing, as did the majority of the interviewees, 1987–88 and the rise of Milošević as the turning point:

> For me it was a cultural concept. ... I wrote a text in *Nova revija 57* where I said that I don't feel as Slovenian, but I feel much more as a citizen of Ljubljana and a fan of my football team, and I like Yugoslavia as a multicultural event, but I really hate the political system. So, I always hated Yugoslav politics, but I had no problem with Yugoslav culture. But, unfortunately, we had such incapable politicians that messed up the whole project and it can never be revived.
> But this was never translated into secessionism until Milošević. Milošević had to come up with this very aggressive nationalism for people to start thinking – look, maybe we should redefine this cultural idea into a political concept. ... Later everybody became anti-Yugoslav because we simply ... when you watched those generals threatening you on TV ... these were not the kind of people I wanted to be in the same country with.

This was also a generation that was defined in terms of a crisis in political socialisation by contemporaries. The beginning of the 1980s saw an emergence of debates about the ideological fragmentation of the youth and its disillusionment or lack of support for socialist self-management. Moreover, throughout the decade scholars and politicians sought explanation for the rapidly declining number of young members of the SKJ. The number of the youth in the SKJ, like the total number of party members, was steadily increasing from 1969 until 1980: from 295,115 (23.3 per cent) to 614,106 (32.6 per cent) in 1979. In 1980, 32 per cent (649,428) of the 2,041,270 members of the SKJ were young people below the age of 28. However, in 1985, the number was already down to 504,368 (23 per cent).[17] By 1989, 43 per cent of the respondents in the last youth survey thought that the work of the SKJ (referred to as a 'senior organisation' [*seniorska organizacija*] or 'the locus of control' [*lokus kontrole*]) was unacceptable and 42 per cent said that the SKJ should be only one of several political parties.[18] What is particularly intriguing is the fact that only 25 per cent of the activists in the SSOJ were at the same time members of the Party. In 1982, a study on the involvement of the youth in the political system, noted that 'one can conclude that a huge number of young people is to be found outside of the active participation in the structure of the political system'.[19] This turned out to be the beginning of an irreversible process. In

1989 the percentage of those who declared that they were members of self-management bodies in 1985–86 dropped from 20 per cent to 7 per cent, while the percentage of those who said they would not like to be members increased from 33 per cent to 56 per cent.

However, the discontent with the functioning of the system and with the political elite did not imply an outright refusal of the Yugoslav model of socialism. In the 1989 survey, more than half of the respondents (53 per cent) declared their acceptance of socialism as a theory, while socialism in practice (i.e. as implemented in Yugoslavia) was not acceptable to 41 per cent of the respondents.[20] As it was observed, 'Despite seven or eight years of increasing economic crisis, there are no immediate signs of total loss of confidence in the system. But there is a growing sense of disillusionment'.[21] The following testimony by Zemira Alajbegović (born 1958), one of the leading members of the FV 112/15 theatre group and the Borghesia band, famous for its video art and multimedia performances, is illustrative of this:

> There is an inherent contradiction: on the one hand, it was normal to criticise a system which was fossilised, it ran out of ideas, and was endlessly repeating certain phrases – we portrayed that well in our videos, for example. On the other hand, it was very important for us and our activism and we believed in the socialist postulates of art and culture for the masses, in the fact that it's not necessary to go either in some sort of a bourgeois art or towards a consumerist model which we now live. That's why we were basing our work on the Russian activist art. That was a utopian project. It seems to me that back then we were all utopians – not only us in FV, but all of us believed that things can change only for the better. In that situation one didn't think that once socialism is transformed into capitalism, capitalism will be here to stay [laughs]. So, on the one hand, one was critical towards the socialist system, the project, but on the other hand we genuinely believed in some of those ideas.

Senad Pećanin similarly underlined that their activism was not inspired by an anti-socialist outlook:

> We were not anti-communist, especially not anti-anti-fascist. No, no. We were socialised in that spirit and anti-fascism was never put under question. On the contrary. What we found unthinkable was censorship. The regime, freedom of expression, a multi-party system – why wouldn't that be possible?

Beside an apparent discontent with the state of affairs in society and with the functioning of the political system, it is striking that nearly half of the respondents in the 1986 survey said that social change could be achieved in an institutional way (see Table 7). However, 42.9 per cent reported that they had not thought about the issue, which echoed concerns about the 'depolitisation' of the youth.

Table 7 Modes of realisation of social change

'Social change can be achieved above all through ...'	%
Working within the institutions of the socio-political system (SKJ, SSRNJ, SSO, etc.)	40.9
Working outside of the institutions	10.2
Working against the institutions	4.1
I haven't thought about it	42.9
No response	1.8

Source: Srđan Vrcan, 'Suvremena omladina i društvene promjene', in *Položaj, svest i ponašanje mlade generacije Jugoslavije*, p. 212.

A new sense of Yugoslav self-identification understood in non-national, but, rather, in broader cultural or civic terms, and often synthetic and inclusive in nature, was a dominant generational marker. The rapid decline in membership in the Party and the decline in support for 'really existing' self-management, on the one hand, and the acceptance of the Yugoslav framework, on the other, informed this new generational 'sense of citizenship'. Many wanted a decoupling of dogmatic socialism and cultural Yugoslavism and believed that such a move was viable. In essence, the generational critique which targeted the inherited norms and values of an older generation and the functioning of the political system they had built conveyed the need for new forms of political legitimacy and the reinventiion and democratisation of Yugoslav socialism and the Yugoslav state.

Under Tito's shadow: rethinking youth rituals

A significant part of the budget of the SSOJ was dedicated to the organisation of a number of traditional youth events – commemorative, competitive and cultural. 25 May –Youth Day – was considered the main event which carried the most symbolic weight, commemorating the legacy of the liberation struggle and Tito's leadership, and celebrating the achievements and the role of the youth in Yugoslav society. Competitive events such as the 'Festival of labour of the youth of Yugoslavia' [*Festival rada omladine Jugoslavije*][22] were designed both to foster a competitive spirit and endorse the doctrine of self-management. A large portion of youth took part in a range of cultural and art festivals in cinematography, theatre, literature, music and science that were – at least in an institutional sense – devoid of politics. The second most important youth event for the SSOJ, which embodied these commemorative, competitive and cultural dimensions, was the so-called 'voluntary work action' [*omladinska radna akcija – ORA*]. Young brigadiers were introduced to the practices of self-management as the actions were organised as small self-managing enterprises, but also preserved certain elements of the revolutionary past (the headquarters, the commanders of the brigade and the action, etc.). An excerpt from a report on the 'Neretva '87' work action sums up their role:

> at 'Neretva' young people from different national, social and age strata took part. The mass participation and this [diverse] structure allowed the spread and development of the legacy of the socialist revolution, development and nurturing of brotherhood and unity of the nations and nationalities, strengthening of friendship and solidarity, the creative spirit and enthusiasm.[23]

However, as of the late 1970s, the youth voluntary actions had lost almost all connection to their post-war ideological moorings and progressively came to represent and embody 'a youth tourist culture'[24] – where youngsters were indifferent to the ideological content and saw it as an opportunity for affordable travel. What remained one of their main features throughout the socialist era was their supranational dimension, i.e. their role as spaces where youngsters with different ethnic and social backgrounds could socialise, get to know each other and explore the country. Dragan Kremer recounted his experience of going to a summer voluntary camp and remembered the cultural

Figure 5 Youth celebration of the Macedonian anti-fascist uprising and fortieth anniversary of the Youth Voluntary Action 'Mavrovo', 1988

shock of encountering peers who could not have had a more different lifestyle than his:

> The first time I went to a work camp I met a guy who was two years my senior and who was a miner by profession, from Aleksinac. What did I know until then about miners? That a miner is the guy from the banknote, that miners are in the history textbooks, and sometimes in the news when an accident occurs. But a miner was never represented as a twenty-two-year-old guy. You meet this guy and he turns out to be very nice, funny … Probably I would have never met him.

With time, the majority of participants came to be secondary school students and youth from less well-off families. For instance, of the 789 participants at the youth work action 'Neretva '87' in Bosnia-Herzegovina, 442 were pupils, 257 were young workers and only 32 were university students.[25] As funds became scarce in the midst of the economic crisis, the whole concept began to be reconsidered. Yet, the so-called 'federal youth work actions' [*Savezna Omladinska Radna Akcija – SORA*] gathered a larger number of participants even in the second half of the 1980s, when their popularity generally began to decline. As an illustration, at the federal work action 'Youth railway Tuzla-Zvornik' in 1987 there were more than 3,100 participants in 73 brigades,[26] while only in Macedonia 4,348 work actions with 431,822 participants were organised between 1982 and 1986.[27]

Dragan Kremer's testimony captures very effectively the social divisions among the youth, and the role of these events as platforms for pan-Yugoslav youth encounters. The memory of these events is almost always underpinned by subjective retrospective statements, in this case that no matter how futile and unattractive they might have seemed at the time, they had a utilitarian value in having taught teenagers and young adults practical work skills and habits:

> I am sure that I am among the few who have gone several times to a youth work action – to the shock of many of my friends. But, my reasoning was – I would spend as much of my summer holidays as I can far away from my parents. There were maybe three other people from our high-school who went as well. But we found out where the signing up takes place … and you encountered a completely different circle of young people from the secondary vocational schools … It wasn't about an exclusivist attitude – 'I don't want to hang out with people like that' – simply, the majority of the kids from your street, from your primary school went to a gymnasium, in the city centre … And then you meet those young people whom you had heard about from the stories of your parents when they'd say to you: 'You know, there are children who can't go to the seaside for holidays, their parents don't have the money'. And you realise that [the work action] is their only opportunity for summer travel. At the work action itself there was an additional, wider circle of people you met.

You saw people from some places you've never been to, people you've never had a chance to meet before ... When you went to the army, you met yet other people who lived in your country, belonged to the same generation, but were significantly different and you would have never come across them unless you came to the army or you travelled a lot ... It was rare for gymnasium kids to go to work actions, it was almost looked upon with contempt – like, that was only for those who have nothing better to do. It was great for me – first I went with my parents [to the seaside], then at my grand-parents', and finally at a work action – four additional weeks without the parents over your head. Plus, it turned out to be fun and not hard at all – that was abundant/rich socialism, it wasn't work that would kill you ... I realised it was actually very useful, as I learned what it means to dig a two-metre trench with a shovel ... you simply see what you can do with your own two hands, something which proved helpful in the most critical moments of my life – in times of political pressures, etc. [I realised] I don't have to be always a journalist, I can do other things, even physical work ... it's not beneath me. I'd rather do that than to compromise myself, my attitudes and views.

By the end of the decade, through its commissions for voluntary work the SSOJ was attempting to modernise the concept of youth voluntary work. International volunteering camps with specific foci on ecology or archaeology, for instance, youth scientific research camps and opportunities for volunteering abroad came to supplement the classical model of the 'youth work action'. For example, in 1988 the SSMM committed to organising, beside the classic highway work action 'Skopje '89', a youth scientific research camp 'Youth '89', two international youth camps on ecology and applied art and four Yugoslav youth work camps.[28] Thus, the vocabulary had changed as well: in addition to the traditional 'youth work action' [младинска работна акција], 'international/ Yugoslav youth work camps' [меѓународни/југословенски младински работни кампови] were referred to and were included in the program. This implied reinvention of the concept of youth volunteering, as the Slovenian and the Vojvodinan SSOs in 1987 and the Macedonian in 1988, introduced the possibility of travelling abroad to take part in international youth volunteering camps. The newly conceptualised 'youth work camps' in Macedonia were meant to gather smaller number of volunteers (between ten and thirty-five), both from Yugoslavia and abroad, to be self-financed and to do away with some of the features of the old forms of volunteering, such as salaried members at the work action headquarters and the construction of a separate settlement for the volunteers.[29]

Similarly, the overall critique of the celebration of 25 May was essentially based on an attempt to modernise youth events by ridding them of classical and excessive Yugoslav socialist iconography and of the post-war cult of Tito, as well as to allow greater diversity of cultural expression. The voices within the youth realm which first engaged publicly in a more substantial critique of the Youth Day celebrations appeared in the Slovenian youth magazine *Mladina* in June 1983, where, in an article entitled 'Human or Deity' [*Človek ali božanstvo*] the author questioned its meaning and relevance.[30] In a similar text the same year in the Slovenian daily *Delo* the author concluded that the imagery at the Belgrade stadium represented 'the climax of socialist kitsch'.[31] However, this did not mean that there was a uniform attitude among the youth. The 1986 *JUPIO* study included questions on the Youth Day celebration, the forms of which reveal that even official analysts were concerned that these commemorations had lost their power through being considered out of date. The answers revealed discrepancies between the Slovene and the rest of the Yugoslav youth; yet, at the same time, these showed significant overlaps. Namely, while only 18.8 per cent of the Slovenian respondents declared that 'the celebration is good as it is', 47.2 per cent of the other Yugoslav respondents did so. Almost the same number of respondents agreed that 'There should be some modifications': 30.4 per cent of the young Slovenes and 28.5 per cent of the remaining Yugoslavs. The view that 'It is outdated and it should be completely changed' was expressed by 17.4 per cent of the Slovenian youth and 8.1 per cent of the Yugoslav, while 22.9 per cent Slovenes versus 5.7 per cent Yugoslavs said that 'We don't need that type of celebrations'. Almost an identical percentage – 10.4 per cent (Slovene) and 10.6 per cent (Yugoslav) – did not have an opinion or were not interested.[32] These statistics point to the emergence of several camps in the debate around the Youth relay, as well as to the fact that there was not a clear division line between those who argued for its abolishment and those in favour of its preservation. In Slovenia, the division ran along old youth institutional lines: it was the Ljubljana University branch of the SSOJ which argued for abolishing the event, while the 'reformist' stance was advanced by the Republic's branch of the SSOJ. Although the university branch put forward legitimate arguments concerning the cost of the entire event and its disputed symbolic meaning, the referendum it organised in December 1986 at Ljubljana University had a relatively low turnout of 43 per cent, out of which 92.4 per cent voted against the Youth relay.[33] The idea that change was necessary was upheld by almost all and was a central part of the debate within the youth sphere in the middle of the decade. Disagreements revolved around exactly what form that change should take.

Although there was a shared sentiment that the inherited models of youth commemoration had to change, not all branches of the SSOJ were equally vocal on the matter. Senad Avdić reflected on the 1987 local Youth Day celebration in the Bosnian town of Zenica:

> I don't know what role I played there – politician, manager, what not. I told [the director of the event] – 'You have to modernise it entirely'. What purpose using bodies for saying yet again that we love comrade Tito? ... So, I told the

Figure 6 Army cadets at 25 May celebration, Belgrade, 1981

director that it is very important that those patriotic songs disappear … and, believe it or not, we brought Pankrti in Zenica who sang [he sings] 'Bandiera rossa la trionfera' … We also brought Plavi orkestar, Zabranjeno pušenje, and the 'Surrealists' and it was also broadcast live … It was equally important for those bands [to take part in the event], as it was important for the youth organisation … Until then it was some yuck pop, folk singers that were performing at the youth voluntary camps. I said – why, why some folk singer would get the money instead of Zabranjeno pušenje, Elvis J. Kurtović? … We were making fun of the Youth relay events where for the one thousandth time you had [pop singer] Zdravko Čolić, you know, 'Godine su prošle pune muka' [laughs], I mean, ridiculous … The whole idea was passé. Bowing to a dead man, that was all stupid … But, apparently it had to take time, it couldn't happen overnight. Eventually, it resolved itself. Many things were tested [through the Youth relay], in the political, social sense. *Mladina*, for instance, was not one, but two steps ahead of what we would do later … The Slovenian organisation made a farce, a caricature out of the relay.

The debate on the traditional celebration of the Youth Day reached its climax in 1987 with the so-called 'poster affair'. This example illustrates the ever growing tensions between the desire to create a more diverse Youth Day and continuous efforts from the centre in order to preserve a degree of control and unity. Following a rotation principle, it was the turn of the ZSMS to organise the main event, as well as to select a poster and a design for the baton. The winning poster was signed by the *Novi kolektivizem* [New collectivism] graphic design studio (Dejan Knez, Miran Mohar, Darko Pokorn, Roman Uranjek), which was part of the NSK (*Neue Slovenische Kunst*) network. The poster represented a male figure holding the Yugoslav flag in one and a torch-like baton in the other hand. However, the whole matter did not explode into controversy until 28 February 1987, when the Belgrade daily *Politika* revealed the original precedent of the poster – a 1936 Nazi painting by Richard Klein entitled *The Third Reich*, in which the symbols were merely replaced. Once revealed and announced, it was interpreted that the artists were making an equivalence of Nazism and Yugoslav socialism. This caused a heated public debate, becoming the topic which animated the media, the social and the political sphere in the months that followed. Igor Vidmar was on the committee which had the task to select the poster:

> They assigned me a place on the board which was to decide about the poster design. The others were designers, architects, artists, etc. I was the only 'insider', so to say. I was shown both the final product and the original – the Nazi poster, and it happened right here, in Café Union, because they didn't have any offices. I sensed that there would be trouble. But, I said: OK. The idea is good, the argumentation is coherent and precise, it's also theoretically valid, so – hey, who am I now to start raising some fears? But, then, it happened what happened. You know what happened.
> L.S.: *Was there a consensus?*
> Yes, everybody was on the side of Laibach, there was no polemic.

The ZSMS found itself under double pressure: both from the Slovenian Party which expected it to condemn the *Novi Kolektivizem* design studio and distance itself from the matter, and from the social movements and the alternative scene which wanted to see it defend the principle of freedom of artistic expression. The Slovenian Youth League took a rather neutral stand and eventually distanced itself from the concept, claiming it was not aware of the original motive, subsequently attracting criticism from all sides.[34] An internal document reveals the sense of being torn between its role as a formal socio-political organisation and its increasingly diversifying 'base'.[35] The document stressed that their space for negotiation at federal level was seriously restrained by the 'poster affair'. It also reveals the in-between position of every republican branch of the SSOJ, the Slovenian in particular, that had to negotiate both with the federal level and its own republican branches. The document concluded that 'we understand the Youth relay as an element of connecting the Yugoslav young and their symbolic expression of commitment to self-management, democracy and progress. A different way of celebrating the Youth Day could be a result of a consensual decision in the [federal] conference of the SSOJ, a consensus which must be marked by patience and the willingness of everyone involved'.[36]

Nonetheless, as Alexei Monroe argues, 'The new designs were a major factor in ZSMS's reinvention of its image and its identification with alternative culture, and the opening up of a generational and cultural conflict in Slovenia'.[37] The NK design studio issued a *Proclamation!* in the form of a poster, explaining the principles of a political poster and their 'retro method', by claiming that 'the creative processes of reversed perspective, metaphors, hyperboles, time and space warp, unite and link everything that mankind has squeezed from its veins until now. Content and form are only tools which combine themes and symbols into dynamicism, tension, excitement and drama'.[38] The scope of the debate was at that point enlarged to include questions about the undemocratic principles imposed upon artists and the limited freedom of (artistic) expression. However, in February 1988 the public prosecutor of Ljubljana dropped the case against the authors of the poster, quoting the notion of artistic expression.[39]

As it has been pointed above, the Yugoslav youth sphere was not univocal on the issue of the Youth relay. On the surface, the debate was indeed about the relevance of old myths, the place and role of Tito's figure after his death and the outdated format of an event which started to appear out of pace with contemporary youth trends. However, essentially, the sensitivity and the longevity of the debate were due to the fact that it raised the question of the entire Yugoslav socialist project as it was imagined forty years earlier. Precisely because the event embodied all of the values socialist Yugoslavism stood for – brotherhood and unity, self-management, Titoism, the revolutionary legacy of the Second World War – any voice or initiative for its abolishment inevitably inferred a more substantial contestation of the political framework and the essence of the Yugoslav state. The controversial poster was replaced by a new one which featured a green leaf on a red background with a cut-out part in the shape of a red star. In hindsight, the empty, missing red star anticipated the end of the Youth Day celebration and the beginning of the end of Yugoslavia.

The official message delivered every year on the occasion of the Youth Day – *Poruka Štafete mladosti* [Message of the Youth relay] in 1987 echoed the sense that something was irretrievably lost. It had a requiem-like appeal:

> We are at future's threshold and it depends on us what it will be like. We grew up with the crisis, witnessing its every turn. Our first social experiences after the primer and the partisan stories were the inherited debt, the divisions, the endless lists at the employment agencies … From individuals insecure in themselves and in society, we became a generation uncertain of its own future and of the future of the society. Now, when it is needed to defend Yugoslavia, brotherhood and unity, self-management and this Baton of ours, we often feel powerless, stuck in other people's mistakes and in our own doubts. Where are the signposts? We refuse to always repeat that we are strongest when it is the hardest and thus console ourselves with the past. The victory which we hold

dearest is the upcoming one. We want to get involved in history. To support the Revolution means – building it! To be in favour of self-management means – developing it! We cannot afford anymore to be a generation which shrugs its shoulders. We are proud of having our own critical way of re-thinking the socialist world and our self-managing reality. The future won't blame us for that. Do not blame us either – you, who are still hesitating whether to listen to our voice. Are we storming the sky? Of course, the sky is conquered with onslaught![40]

Yet, as it has been discussed above, for a significant part of the youth and of the Yugoslav public the event indeed had symbolic weight and still appeared relevant. That same year the mainstream media still reported on the Youth Day celebration in the conventional way, while representatives of the Yugoslav Army branch of the SSOJ were received by the federal Secretary of Defence, Branko Mamula. He congratulated all the soldiers and young officers on their holiday and urged them to make 'Yugoslav socialist patriotism' grow and develop.[41] For a large portion of the youth which was not directly involved in the debates, it was hard to imagine that the Youth relay was anything more than a museum artefact.

Namely, on 26 January 1988, eight years after the federal jury for the celebration of 25 May concluded that there was a surprisingly small interest in submitting scenario proposals for the central stadium event, after three rounds of voting, with 83 votes 'for' and 6 'against' the federal leadership of the youth organisation decided to abolish the classical youth relay race and lay what some called the 'baton of absurdity' to rest. This was a major decision which was (rather unusually for this period) reached consensually, and which above all represented a definite break with a significant part of the socialist Yugoslav heritage and political values. Although the event was most fervently and persistently critiqued by Slovenian youth, it was in fact the regional SSO of Vojvodina which formally submitted the proposal for its abolition in October 1987. Their original initiative was entitled 'Concept for the celebration of the Day of Youth 1988' and foresaw a celebration without a relay race. According to the established practice, the initiative was then forwarded to all levels of the SSOJ for discussion and feedback. The opinions were highly divided, especially in Vojvodina and Croatia, while in Serbia, Macedonia, Kosovo and Bosnia-Herzegovina the youth (or the youth leadership which sent feedback on the proposal, like in the case of Kosovo) was predominantly in favour of preserving the event. The SSOJ army branch was, perhaps unsurprisingly, its most outspoken defender and the most 'orthodox' in its views.[42] On the day of the vote, of the twelve present members of the presidency of the 'Conference' of the SSOJ, eight were in favour of the Vojvodinian proposal. However, it was the 'Conference' and not its presidency which by the 'Statute' of the SSOJ was the highest organ allowed to take such decisions. The first two rounds of the vote did not reach the required majority of seventy-seven delegates. After 'a long debate full of pathetic calls for unity and demands for the "minority" to join the "majority"',[43] the 'Conference' approved the proposal of a Youth Day celebration without a baton and a relay race. The Slovenian delegates already raised the question of the format of the final stadium event, which that year, without the baton, was the last. Although the decision did not reflect a unanimously shared sentiment among the Yugoslav youth, it was seen as necessary in preventing further disagreements, arguments and erosion and denigration of the baton and what it stood for. There was a sense that it had to be 'saved from ourselves' and that it left an empty space, a need for a search for a new symbol: 'What is the new symbol? Those who claim that we don't have one and that the abolishment of the Baton is a rejection of the last value framework around which there was a quasi-consensus, are right ... It is difficult to promote this as a BIG AND HISTORICAL DECISION, when it is much closer to a sad necessity.'[44] This turned out to be one of the rare consensually taken major decisions in the realm of youth politics and institutional youth culture. Dejan Jović put it this way:

> In essence, it was a huge hassle for the youth organisation, because it had to put up with the organisation of the event. So, the Youth League here did not have many regrets when it all came to an end ... The baton and the voluntary work actions were the only two things where the Youth League had to demonstrate certain organisational skills – failure was not allowed. At one moment it all became too complicated and they didn't complain.

Although the majority of my interviewees referred to the Youth relay race in a negative way, the fact remains that a significant part of the youth saw it as an elite decision which was taken without wider consultations. What everyone agreed on was that the event had to be subject to change, although many did not wish to see it abolished outright. Nataša Sukič (born 1962) was among the founders of the first Slovenian lesbian group/movement. Her testimony conveys the awareness that the old, inherited ritualistic event no longer made sense. In her account there is also a retrospective reflection that these events nevertheless embodied some positive values which have since been lost:

> When you're young and rebellious, you joke about those things. What can I say? In primary school we even took part in a 25 May celebration and we were very proud of our outfit ... and we were very disappointed that we didn't go to Belgrade so that Tito can see our performance. That's my first memory of it. In high school, naturally, you are critical of all of that, you laugh at it, you rebel, but you would, anyhow, in any system. When I look at it now, I look with nostalgia. Yes, it looks as if one big dictator had his own ritual, but it was really something which was connecting people. The work brigades as well – people

were making friends, hanging out together. It was great. And they even managed to do something useful for all of us, for the common good – I don't see
what is wrong with that. Solidarity was something normal back then. Today
I think people have no clue what solidarity means. The concept of solidarity
today is [extinct] like dinosaurs. People don't know what it means theoretically,
let alone in practice.

The spectre of Nazism: contention, provocation and historical memory

New, subtle forms of anti-regime critique shaped by generational divides were
also emerging within the new music scenes. This section focuses on the re-
articulation of the anti-fascist legacy through certain case studies that scandalised
the Yugoslav public at the time. It is without doubt that one cannot trace a common voice through which these youngsters conveyed their artistic or journalistic
practices and sensibilities. Although I would be hesitant to put the heteroglossic
youth cultures and politics of the 1980s under the umbrella of a 'youth movement', it is tenable that 'The pan-Yugoslav youth movement's critique was aimed
at exactly the structures, ideology and mentality represented by conservatives in
the ruling party organisations'.[45]

Nowhere was the generational critique more apparent than in artistic products, where a new cohort of artists challenged some of the central aspects of
the value system of the first post-war Yugoslav generation. One of the major
transgressive trends in the sphere of young artistic production in the 1980s
was the attempt to break symbolically with some of the taboos of post-Second
World War Yugoslav society. To be more specific, they were questioning the
symbols of the state which had been portrayed as sacred and were contesting
mainstream memory of Nazism, wartime occupation and German culture.
While there were many cases of appropriating the symbols of the state or of
socialism – most notably the Yugoslav flag and the hammer and the sickle for
artistic/installation purposes,[46] reviving the traumas of the Nazi occupation
through clear references to German language/culture or the Nazi ideology
itself was something which, before the 1980s, had been clearly outside of the
boundaries of possible public expression. Writing in 1987, philosopher Mladen
Dolar identified the renewed need to employ certain fascist symbols among
part of the younger generation as 'a *call for a historical memory* not based on
the continuous reproduction of an unreflected trauma', and located it in the
fact that what had been transmitted through generations was not 'primarily a
knowledge of fascism nor an ability to analyse it, but above all certain patterns
of affective reaction to the trauma'.[47]

'Laibach are the first group to invade the ultra-posh Queen Elisabeth Hall
with a backdrop of hammers, sickles and swastikas, and the first Yugoslavians
to impersonate Freddie Mercury. They harangue Cabaret Voltaire for being

pathetically frivolous and hold Britain in thinly-veiled contempt', read a 1987 *New Musical Express* article.[48] The author pinpointed Laibach's originality in the fact that they 'resolve the contradiction of "painting the star over the swastika" within their Kunst'. Indeed, Laibach, one of the rare bands which did not come from a capital city, but from the small industrial/mining town of Trbovlje in Slovenia, were the first who managed to destabilise the consensus on the political memory of the Nazi occupation of Yugoslavia. In the eyes of the authorities, the band epitomised controversy. With their name coming from the German name for the Slovenian capital Ljubljana, reminiscent of the German occupation years during the Second World War, from the very beginning the band was destined to be perceived as a stunning provocation to the political and the social order. Banned from using the name 'Laibach' and hence forbidden to perform under that name from 1983 until 1987, Laibach was an unprecedented artistic and musical phenomenon in late socialist Yugoslavia, part of the wider NSK (*Neue Slovenische Kunst*) network.[49] From their establishment in 1980 the band assumed an ambiguous reflective and performative standpoint. Their aesthetics escaped precise categorisation, essentially reflecting the relationship between art and politics, and ' "rendering audible" of the hidden codes and internal contradictions of a series of artistic, musical, political, linguistic, and historical "regimes" '.[50] What Alexei Yurchak refers to as a 'mimetic critique of ideology' seems to be the closest to an accurate label for their work. Indeed, this way of formulating critique implied the use of a 'secondary discourse in the form of the primary ideological discourse'.[51] As Robert Botteri observed: 'I always saw them as having the same function as *Mladina* – the opening, the sensitisation of a certain space. They were a mirror of the society, showing things which the society wanted to hide from itself, they revealed the totalitarian image of the society which the society didn't want to see for itself.' Yurchak's notion and Botteri's observation are both reflected in Laibach's song 'Država' [State] which reproduced official state rhetoric by repeating 'Oblast je pri nas ljudska' [Authority here belongs to the people][52] and also featured original excerpts from one of Tito's most well-known speeches on the importance of brotherhood and unity: 'We spilt a sea of blood for the brotherhood and unity of our peoples and we are not going to allow anyone to touch, to uproot from inside or to destroy in any way brotherhood and unity.'

Their eclectic use of Nazi and communist/Yugoslav iconography, shocking video performances, political speeches, frequently provoked reactions not only at home, but also abroad. At the end of 1987 they found themselves at the centre of a controversy regarding what were construed as anti-Semitic comments during a press conference at the Transmusicales Festival in France, when the band blamed the non-showing of their videos in the United States on the influence of the country's Jewish lobby.[53] Journalists asked the band's spokesperson whether the way they dressed and presented themselves on stage did not smack of fascism and whether they were worried about attracting a fascist following considering some members in the audience were saluting in time to 'Life is Life'. Typically elusive, when, finally, confronted with a direct question about what they felt about the death of millions of people in Auschwitz, Ivan Novak replied: 'What do I feel? Well it's definitely not a good idea. But it's not a good idea that the death of millions of people in the third world is also basically being produced by certain economies, also the British government.'[54] Unsurprisingly perhaps, Novak used an argument that seemed as if plucked from official Yugoslav foreign policy discourse in the heyday of decolonisation and solidarity with the anti-imperialist cause. As it has been argued by Monroe, Laibach's aesthetics, like self-management, carried out some sort of demystification of its inherent ideological contradictions, covering ideology with a layer of its own reality. Without the Yugoslav context, Monroe argues, Laibach would have surely acquired a very different form.[55] Indeed, the principle of 'over-identification'[56] with the prevalent discourse and political ideology is visible in their 1982 'Ten Edicts of the Convention', which read:

(1) Laibach works in a team (collective spirit) modelled after industrial production and totalitarianism, which signifies: it is not the individual that speaks, but the organisation. Our work is industrial and our language political ...

(3) Every art is subjected to political manipulation ... except that which speaks with the language of this manipulation itself. To speak with a political expression means to reveal and admit the omnipresence of politics ... Ideology is the locus of authentic social consciousness.[57]

The lifting of the ban, however, was not solely decided by the authorities. In fact, it was the ZSMS that decided to support it and advance an official demand for it at its 12th congress in 1986. The fact that Laibach resorted to the youth organisation and received support from a body which was part of the official institutional political framework yet again throws light on the complex interplay of what was considered to be alternative and institutional. Igor Vidmar worked with Laibach and highlighted the role of the youth organisation in this case:

Laibach was the next big scandal. The youth organisation behaved a bit better, but, still, they were very uncertain about what it meant, they were scared. By the mid-1980s, there was a crisis in Yugoslavia and it was clear that things would be changing ... The youth organisation was opening up, they realised there would be some changes and they wanted to be part of that. Basically, quite a bit of careerism and opportunism. However, there were some authentic new, young people who wanted things to liberalise. So, in '86 they supported the legalisation of the use of the Laibach name, which was forbidden after a scandal in Zagreb in '83. But the ban happened in Slovenia, because Laibach were Slovenian, the republics had their jurisdiction and they couldn't be sanctioned in Croatia.

Slovenian band Borghesia, known for their video art in the 1980s, used similar artistic devices for framing their own version of political art.[58] The title video for the VHS cassette 'Tako mladi' [So young] featured marching Nazi soldiers, with excerpts from Leni Riefenstahl's *Triumph of the Will*, while many of their videos used excerpts from political speeches, documentary scenes and montage to articulate visually a critique targeting the Yugoslav political system. Their 1983 video entitled 'Socialism' features one phrase – 'Socialism in the world is gradually becoming a prevailing force' – pronounced by an old Yugoslav politician, the endless repetition of which is stretched to its limits, bordering on absurdity, towards the end of the two-minute video.[59] Zemira Alajbegović stressed that Borghesia and Laibach represented two different artistic concepts and approaches, yet she underlined the 'solidarity' which existed among the different factions at the young Slovenian alternative scene when it came to their 'common enemy' embodied in dogmatic socialism:

> We all felt a sort of solidarity, because we all had a common enemy, which was that socialist regime we were surrounded by. At that point perhaps it was less repressive, but it was equally boring and omnipresent ... There were opposing views, we sometimes had conflicts, but there was a sense of general solidarity and we all felt part of the Ljubljana subcultural scene ...
>
> We could all feel, it was in the air, that the regime was not as repressive anymore, and probably the regime itself no longer believed in all those socialist empty phrases – as passionately as it once did ...
>
> The [socialist] iconography was very powerful, it was ideal both for theatre and video. We used it a lot, we joked with it, with the partisans and that revolutionary poetry. It was ideal for video art, with those kilometers of recordings and speeches. It's a very powerful iconography. Not all iconography is as well arranged, disciplined and straightforward as the socialist and the communist iconography. So, it was an excellent material to work with [laughs].

The fact that the early punk wave and both Laibach and Borghesia came from Slovenia contributed to a widespread popular perception that the most northern republic was a hotbed of revisionist and hence anti-Yugoslav tendencies. However, in early 1987 the Yugoslav public and media were overtaken by another youth-related scandal with a Nazi overtone which did not come from Slovenia – the Sarajevo 'Nazi party' at the home of now famous Serbian writer Isidora Bjelica (born 1967). Organised as the host's birthday party in December 1986, it gathered people who were considered to be part of the young aspiring cultural elite of Sarajevo. Some of the nineteen- and twenty-year-olds wore Nazi uniforms and finger food decorated with mayonnaise swastikas was served.[60] The Sarajevo Party city branch accused the youngsters of siding with the Slovenian youth which requested abolishment of the Youth Day celebration: 'In that (fascistic) decor the idea of sending written support to the group of the university youth in Ljubljana was pondered, [the group] which organised the incident-provoking event demanding the abolishment of Tito's Baton and the introduction of civilian military service. They even talked about organising public demonstrations in Sarajevo as a sign of support for this "initiative".[61] Amid a wave of accusations, part of the youth press claimed that

> For those [generations] who come, the swastika does not have the same meaning like for the previous generations, i.e. it has a lesser significance. If it wasn't banned and seen as a taboo, the swastika would have no useful value for the young angry individual who is protesting and breaking the bans. Thus, he is not using it as a symbol which in itself reflects and affirms a political idea, but as a sign of moving away from the societal [trends of] symbolisation, as a signifier of a simple act of refusal.[62]

Unlike Laibach's acts, which were public, this one-off incident which included the display of Nazi symbols took place in a private space, but nonetheless sparked an attack by the mainstream media and a series of acts of public discrediting of the invlolved, which was vigorously condemned in the youth press. One journalist posed the rhetorical question of how long these youngsters will have to repeat 'that unfortunate [phrase]: "I am not a fascist"'.[63] What is striking is the link with the Slovenian youth which was implied by the Sarajevo Party branch as a means to launch an attack on the teenagers by associating them with the 'counter-revolutionary' Slovenes. More importantly, this hints at a connection, a sense of camaraderie and shared ideas and values which is overlooked in historical accounts that tend to focus on the Slovenian context as the liberal northern republic and leave out the southern Yugoslav regions as bastions of dogmatic Party rule. The majority of my interviewees from Bosnia-Herzegovina and Macedonia mentioned that they held the Slovenian youth initiatives in high regard and looked up to them with a sense of admiration, trying to copy or transplant some of those ideas. Senad Pećanin recalled the link with the Slovenian youth circles around *Mladina* and NSK in his testimony:

> At the time of the debates about the Youth relay, I was a secretary of the 'University Conference' of the Youth League in Sarajevo … I also organised a public roundtable discussion in [youth venue] CDA. I invited [Robert] Botteri, the editor of *Mladina*, Tone Anderlič was president of the youth organisation, Igor Vidmar from *Neue Slovenische Kunst*. We came up with an occasion – 4 April, the Day of Students. Actually 4 April was the day of students of Belgrade University, it has nothing to do with Sarajevo, but nonetheless, I spread the word that it's Student Day, no one asked me anything. We put up posters around and the City Committee of the Communist League jumped out and insisted we cancel the event. We refused. I said – 'No! You can ban it, but I'll announce that it was banned'. They demanded that we cancel it ourselves. I refused, so

on the day the hall was packed. I was still a young, inexperienced journalist and I was looking around for one of the more senior colleagues to chair the event – no one accepted, no one dared. I found that bizarre, I couldn't understand why, so I thought – OK, I'll do it. That was in 1988. There were many people from the state security agency inside … The themes were the Youth relay, multi-party system, the slogan 'Slovenija, moja dežela' [Slovenia, my homeland], freedom of expression, Article 133, civil military service. Then, Saša Hemon [writer Aleksandar Hemon] and I made an interview with [Igor] Vidmar, we broadcast it along with some Laibach music and that was a reason for me and Hemon to get a three-month suspension from the Radio, while Boro lost some 30 per cent from his salary.

It is apparent that there existed a consensus among the urban, educated activist youth all over Yugoslavia in that they tended to view the official rituals, the frozen historical narratives of the anti-fascist struggle, or the Youth relay celebrations as superfluous or as unnecessary exaggerations. Although their acts of critiquing the form and the unchanged discourse used to publicly endorse Yugoslav socialism were for the most part interpreted as direct attacks on the core values of the state, their alleged anti-Yugoslavism was often a media construct or a result of the often exaggerated fears of an older generation.

New music trends in the 1980s also sparked fear, controversy and debate in broader society over the development of contemporary youth. Punk not only managed to scandalise Yugoslav society; it also incited lengthy debates which transcended the initial narrow focus of punk music as a cultural form and grew to incorporate other key issues considered to be sensitive and off-limits. The late 1970s saw the emergence of the new punk youth sub-culture, initially completely outside of the institutional youth sphere, then evolving on the margins and eventually becoming a legitimate fragment in the late socialist mosaic of youth cultures. While punk youth in the USSR existed at the margins as an informal sub-culture, Yugoslav punk rock bands imbued the adopted 'form' with Yugoslav content, had their albums released by major state record labels, and gained visibility abroad when *New Music Express* and *Melody Maker* published articles on the Yugoslav scene and its up-and-coming bands. From an exclusively sub-cultural phenomenon in the late 1970s, punk quickly reached the agendas of meetings at the SSOJ. When, in 1982 at the 11th federal congress of the SSOJ in Belgrade, a member of the Slovene delegation reacted against the negative connotations associated with punk that arose during a discussion within the Commission for culture, members of the Yugoslav Army delegation reacted. A young army officer's reaction to the statement that punk was not against the system, but against the anomalies of the system, summed up one the most prominent lines of division among youth:

I am obliged, in the name of the coal miners' children, who do not have the time to eat because they dig coal for our new wavers, punkers and other idlers to keep warm; we applauded a discussion which is out of place. Please, let's be politically conscious and united since we made an oath to our beloved comrade Tito, that we will never, under no circumstances abandon his path. I am not educated enough to express myself in foreign words, but I only know that I would give my life for brotherhood and unity, for the defense and development of our beloved non-aligned socialist Yugoslavia.[64]

The exchange provides an excellent illustration of the type of political, class and lifestyle gaps and fragmentations which existed between people of the same generation and members of the same youth organisation. Even official youth studies acknowledged the fact that class-based differences among the young are the fundamental cause of the youth's heterogeneity and of an intra-generational conflict.[65] The 1986 youth survey confirmed this in what it detected as 'a certain cultural de-homogenisation of the Yugoslav youth'[66] or even 'polarisation'[67] among those who generally had a positive attitude towards the adults, the society, their future and the future of the state, versus those who held a critical, even negative, outlook. This also exposes a core aspect of this generation's media and cultural elite's self-perception and identity: an urban outlook, i.e. strong identification with one of the bigger Yugoslav cities.

Originally coined to describe punk in the British context, the assertion that 'Punk was a response to the power of social consent'[68] seems highly applicable in the Yugoslav context, as institutional/socialist Yugoslavism began to be contested at the porous boundaries between institutional and alternative youth politics and culture. Srđan Gojković (Gile) connected the socio-political atmosphere of the initial post-Tito period with the emergence of punk and new wave and curiously related the reality of their well-off middle-class background with 'the fake prosperity in socialist Yugoslavia':

Yes, [the music] was directed against the system, but only in the sense that it was about some kids who wanted a different way of life which of course did not coincide with that self-managing socialism ... That socio-political moment is very interesting. We as a band were formed during that vacuum period, when the level of concentration of some censors decreased, some people got tired ... It was the end of Tito's rule and his life and they probably dealt with other more serious problems than with us. So, we managed to slip through a crack ... And when that crack had split to such an extent [laughs], it couldn't be mended ... I think it was a philosophy of some kids who were actually the children of that middle class which existed in the fake prosperity in socialist Yugoslavia, in the period of the 1960s and the 1970s when we were growing up.

As it has been observed, 'Punk obscenities ... were justified as testing the boundaries of what society defined as socially acceptable. In this sense punk was

Figure 7 Young Sex Pistols fan, Novi rock festival, Ljubljana, 1984

deemed unusually political for the rock genre in terms of its lyric themes, song structures, subcultural style and aesthetic of boredom in mass society'.[69] This echoes Gregor Tomc's way of explaining 'the political' in their music and overall outlook:

> Absolutely, we [in Pankrti] were political. Using politics was the easiest way to shock. When in 1977 you say 'Comrades, we don't believe you' – I mean, nobody said that before. Of course, we were doing this partly because we were bored by these people, no one was taking the Communist Party seriously. For me at the time it was like looking at Indian chieftains, Indian tribes. They were

completely irrelevant. So, you don't talk seriously about that. But, you use them to provoke, you really want to annoy people. That's the easiest way to do it. If you sing about love, nobody is going to notice that. I think we were political in another sense, not in the sense that we had ideas about changing society – we had no ideas about that. But in the sense that we said – we don't care about this. I'm not interested in your socialist self-management. Do it for yourself, I'm doing my own thing. That was a very political thing to say, because, again, no one said that before. Everyone was pretending to be part of the system. We said – we don't want to be part of the system. So, this was very political. When I was writing – I'm not anti-Nazi, I'm not anti-anti-Nazi, I'm not anything, people didn't understand that. 'What is this, is he a Nazi?' I was just saying I don't care about any ideology, you know. And this was provocative. I think people understood it well, this was a political statement. But it was not a political statement in the sense that we had any positive goals. To be a punk, you had to be indifferent towards everything. That was the attitude – I don't give a f*** about anything. But, saying that in a communist country was political.

It was rightfully argued that 'the political relevance and impact of art … was also dependent on the political critique it engendered, and even on its prohibition'.[70] Although initially perceived and portrayed in the media as an insult to socialist morality, as recalled in Tomc's testimony, punk rock bands did not have an explicit political agenda. The desire to shock, to appear different through wit and irony and to attempt to destabilise and hence question the overpowering 'social consent' was what shaped the polysemic poetics of late Yugoslav youth culture. In addition, the importance of material conditions and socio-political context for the appearance of the new music scenes in late socialist Yugoslavia cannot be over-emphasised. Like in the British context where 'cheap rent, good book stores, squats and record shops'[71] and 'the long decline of the 1970s'[72] played an important role in the proliferation of punk, similar social circumstances shaped the new Yugoslav music scenes. Srđan Gojković (Gile) referred to this aspect when talking about the accessibility of the youth venues in his testimony:

> At the beginning everything was for free, all the bands were playing for free …That is why that nest was formed where we as kids could idle away without having to spend money – you would show up at SKC, you could stay there for hours and no one would chase you if you didn't buy a drink. People who were similar to you came there and different ideas started to boil.

Punk rock bands eventually became part of mainstream youth culture, or what could be referred to as a form of 'subversive pop art'.[73] Although their records appeared and sold in significant quantities and received public recognition – both in the youth press and by awards established by the youth organisation, their music was often labeled as 'šund', i.e. kitsch or of little or no real artistic value. A commission for music records in each republic's Committee for Education and Culture made the selections, which in practical terms meant that the records labeled as 'šund' were not exempt of VAT, thus being more expensive and consequently selling less.

One event that took place immediately after the death of Tito and managed to scandalise the Yugoslav public at the beginning of the new decade was the so-called 'Nazi-punk affair'. One year after the death of Tito, in a state of general insecurity and apprehension of hostile activities coming from outside and from within, the Yugoslav state did not hesitate to suppress any sign of 'counter-revolutionary', anti-socialist or anti-Yugoslav activity. The Nazi-punk affair, designated as a manifestation of 'political paranoia',[74] helped release from the Yugoslav Pandora's box what were considered the two principal historical demons – nationalism and fascism. In the media and in the Slovene Party heated debates were sparked by the trial and imprisonment of members of the '4R' band, whose name allegedly alluded to the Fourth Reich. The debate was initiated by a newspaper article in a Ljubljana daily entitled 'Kdo riše kljukaste križe?' [Who draws swastikas?]. The article carried a photograph of an English punk adorned with Nazi insignia and the author of the article, Zlatko Šetinc, was attacked by the Slovene youth media and members of the alternative scene for making a link between punk, on the one hand, and juvenile delinquency and Nazism, on the other. In his letter to the newspaper, Igor Vidmar wrote at length about British punk, the 'Anti-Nazi League' and the 'Rock Against Racism' campaign.[75] In December 1981 the Slovenian Secretary for Interior Affairs Tomaž Ertl told the Belgrade press that 'Above all it is necessary to stress that we think and we know that not all punks are neo-Nazis. It is really only about one small group, in fact individuals'.[76] The three members of the 4R band were held in custody for three months and two were accused on the basis of Article 133. The trial, however, did not commence until 1984 and the charges against the two were dropped due to lack of evidence.[77] Eventually, the debates moved within the framework of the SSO and popular youth culture, up until the 1986 'fascist birthday party' and the 1987 'Poster Affair' scandal which again reinvigorated wider public debates on youth and Nazism.

Gregor Tomc reiterated the existence of a 'moral crisis' and a 'moral panic' on the part of society which was prone to perceive the new youth alternative scene around punk not as a real, but rather as 'a symbolic threat'. Interestingly, he reflected on the relative impotence of the 'federal level' and the importance of 'personal taste'. As has been argued, 'punks had established their own scene exactly along the boundary which sharply separated their own and the previous generations' musical preferences … They were not confronting "totalitarian" socialism per se, but the "old guard", without offering any alternative political programme, except to reject the state power and to advocate human rights'.[78]

It was completely fabricated. There was absolutely nothing to it. It was a typical example of a moral crisis … And people later went to court and were found innocent. But, anyway, this moral panic was picked up by the media, blown out of proportion and after that I think the punk scene in Ljubljana was never the same. Up until then we always had problems, but somehow you had the feeling that the state was acting towards the punk subculture as a symbolic threat. They weren't really taking us as a real threat to the political system. After that, people had serious problems. And it all had to do with the fact that the Party leader of Slovenia France Popit decided that there was enough of punk. Before that it was really tolerated. After that you still had concerts, but it was very hard to rediscover that spontaneity – the places where you could meet, associate freely, and so on. People started to be afraid, because you would never know when the police would pick you up. … All the graffiti writers were arrested, for example. It was like a police state at that time. So, from then on, the whole scene became more … sort of artistic, you know. There was not so much of that spontaneity and the fun.

The federal level was very dissatisfied with how the Slovenian level was dealing with it. I don't know about this, but there had to be pressures. But, the pressure came from the Slovenian level, because the federal level could do nothing in Slovenia. It was Popit. Basically, Popit was a big fan of our country music, you know. So, he hated rock 'n' roll. And he especially hated punk [laughs]. So, that had something to do with it as well. I think it was also a question of personal taste.

In response to the events, in April 1981 the Slovenian Youth League organised a roundtable discussion entitled 'Some actual questions concerning the cultural politics of the ZSMS and the youth activity in the sphere of culture'. Young participants from the youth music circles such as 'Radio Študent' journalists Igor Vidmar and Samo Hribar argued for a change in the public attitude towards punk rock, i.e. demanding that it is accepted as part of popular culture and not as an excess or a political project. Pursuing repressive measures against the punk rock youth, they argued, would expose the weaknesses of the youth organisation and the entire society, which in that way 'a priori launches a conflict with its own members using the power argument'.[79] In 1984 Radio Študent organised another public discussion entitled 'Fascism at the Ljubljana alternative scene'.[80] The debate generally revolved around questions about the way in which punk was presented in the mainstream media – as a cradle of anarchism and Nazism, which was strongly refuted by people who were closely related with the scene and were attached to the youth organisation through its publications, magazines, cultural centres, etc. Igor Vidmar in his radio show *Rock Fronta* in November 1981 problematised the public stigmatisation of punk and attempted to defend it publicly by saying that his colleagues in Radio Študent and himself have on so many occasions thus far emphasised the anti-Nazi and anti-racist content of British punk, while in the lyrics of the domestic bands or the behaviour of the fans there is no trace of Nazism or nationalism. This did not save Vidmar from spending thirty days in prison in 1982 for wearing 'Nazi punks fuck off' and 'Crazy governments' badges. Although by the end of 1981 a consensus was reached within the Slovenian Youth League that punk rock was a legitimate stream of youth popular music and that the sensationalist disqualifying media reports linking it to nationalism were unfounded, throughout the decade young musicians continued to encounter obstacles, mostly related to lyrics that were seen as problematic. Although the new music scenes around punk rock could certainly not qualify as youth mainstream/pop culture, they enjoyed striking visibility and presence in the youth media which significantly surpassed their popularity and numerical relevance. Nevertheless, having the youth media as their allies and as platforms where they could promote their work and concert activity, they left a significant imprint on 1980s youth culture.

In conclusion, the reiteration of socialist slogans appeared anachronistic to a generation which witnessed their pure rhetorical, performative use and hence used them to challenge the official socialist discourse through various cultural forms. With the mainstream media and the political establishment often on the opposing side, the young resorted to acts of (self-)justification and distancing themselves from an alleged espousal of the Nazi ideology. Pečanin's testimony in this sense reads as a summary:

> What mattered for us was the sense of freedom [*osjećaj slobode*]. We took great pleasure in smashing whatever was considered to be a taboo. Making jokes about Tito, everything that was forbidden – we really enjoyed that. Everything that was official politics, communism … But not in the way that we detested communism or we had some big ideology behind what we were doing – we just felt the need to do it and we considered freedom of speech as the most normal thing: someone's right to express their opinion which doesn't represent a call to violence, it has nothing to do with fascism, hatred, nationalism – why not? It seemed perfectly normal to us, generationally speaking. We could in no way understand or accept that it was not allowed to speak out. That was our basic motif and we enjoyed it.

Throughout the 1980s the youth sphere witnessed a number of debates concerning the future of the inherited socialist framework of values and commemorative practices and the ways Tito's legacy should be carried forward following his death. The critique which generally stemmed from the youth cultural realm sought to rethink the performative and the discursive dimension through which the different levels of the Yugoslav post-war consensus were manifested. Although frequently reproached for an alleged appropriation of far right ideologies, the actors themselves defended their 'acts' as manifestations of freedom of expression. Although openly targeting the form of the inherited youth rituals and the socialist rhetoric which began to appear anachronistic in the context of a multi-level crisis, the different cultural acts cannot be reduced to a straight-forward contestation of Yugoslav socialism. Rather, they challenged the norms and discourse of an older generation, essentially seeking to reinvent socialism and youth culture through new cultural tendencies and through the state's youth institutions.

Notes

1 As cited in Aleš Erjavec, 'Neue Slowenische Kunst – new Slovenian art: Slovenia, Yugoslavia, self-management, and the 1980s', in Aleš Erjavec (ed.), *Postmodernism and the Postsocialist Condition: Politicized Art under Late Socialism* (Berkeley, Los Angeles and London: University of California Press, 2003), p. 144.

2 Archive of Yugoslavia, Belgrade (hereafter AY), *Savez Socijalističke Omladine Jugoslavije* SSOJ 114, folder 235, 'ZAPISNIK sa sednice žirija Saveznog odbora Dana mladosti za Konkurs scenarija završne priredbe Dana mladosti '80', 15 January 1980.

3 Open Society Archive, digital archive (hereafter OSA), Slobodan Stankovic, 'Tito and his personality cult reduced to human proportions', *Radio Free Europe* Background Report 309, 11 November 1981.

4 Stephen Clissold, 'Review: *Novi prilozi za biografiju Josipa Broza Tita* by Vladimir Dedijer', *The Slavonic and East European Review* 60:4 (1982), 632–4, p. 633.

5 OSA, Slobodan Stankovic, 'Tito and his personality cult reduced to human proportions'.

6 OSA, Zdenko Antic, 'Yugoslav officials criticize Tito's personality cult', *Radio Free Europe* Background Report 144, 24 June 1983.

7 Mladen Babun, 'Dan mladosti 1984: hoćemo teret na svoja leđa', *Polet* 267 (1 June 1984), pp. 12–13.

8 Nebojša Vladisavljević, 'Institutional power and the rise of Milošević', *Nationalities Papers* 32:1 (2004), 183–205.

9 V. P. Gagnon, 'Yugoslavia in 1989 and after', *Nationalities Papers* 38:1 (2010), 23–39, p. 35.

10 The results for the other republics were as follows: Slovenia (51.8 per cent + 5.6 per cent + 0.2 per cent = 57.6 per cent); Montenegro (40.9 per cent + 0.4 per cent + 0 per cent = 41.3 per cent); Vojvodina (40.0 per cent + 1.3 per cent + 0 per cent = 41.3 per cent); Croatia (33.3 per cent + 1.9 per cent + 0.1 per cent = 35.5 per cent); Serbia proper (34.7 per cent + 0.7 per cent + 0 per cent = 35.4 per cent). Sergej Flere, 'Odnos mladih prema etnosu', in Srđan Vrcan *et al.*, *Položaj, svest i ponašanje mlade generacije Jugoslavije* (Beograd: Centar za istraživačku, dokumentacionu i izdavačku delatnost Konferencije SSOJ/Zagreb: Institut za društvena istraživanja Sveučilišta, 1986), pp. 131–49.

11 The *JUPIO* study noted a tendency of valuing individual (as opposed to cultural/ethno-religious) traits when choosing a marriage partner or a friend: moral values (80.5 per cent), understanding of life (62 per cent), intelligence and sense of humour (61.8 per cent) mattered the most, while religion (19.5 per cent) and social origins (16.7 per cent) were at the bottom of the list, confirming a tendency of

'modernisation of the value system'. Furio Radin, 'Vrijednosti jugoslavenske omladine', in Vrcan *et al.*, *Položaj, svest i ponašanje*, pp. 63–4.
Similarly, 88.7 per cent of the respondents said they agreed with the statement that 'the biggest value of the youth is that the young are not slaves to habits and patterns, but are capable of establishing and developing new relations'. Mirjana Ule, 'Odnos omladine prema mladosti, odraslosti i budućnosti', in Vrcan *et al.*, *Položaj, svest i ponašanje*, p. 109.

12 Sergej Flere, 'Odnos mladih prema etnosu', in Vrcan *et al.*, *Položaj, svest i ponašanje*, pp. 147–9.

13 The preparedness to engage for the interests of Yugoslavia as a whole was above the average among respondents from Montenegro (66 per cent), Bosnia-Herzegovina (65 per cent), Kosovo (60 per cent) and Serbia proper (59 per cent). Although the percentage of the Slovene respondents who expressed 'very high' preparedness for the interests of Yugoslavia as a whole was lowest – 17 per cent, when combined with those who expressed 'average' (31 per cent) and 'high' interest (18 per cent) it came up to 66 per cent. Mirjana Vasović, 'Percepcija društvenih sukoba', in Srećko Mihailović *et al.*, *Deca krize: Omladina Jugoslavije krajem osamdesetih* (Beograd: Institut društvenih nauka/Centar za politikološka istraživanja i javno mnenje, 1990), pp. 68–9.

14 *Ibid.*

15 Ljiljana Baćević, 'Nacionalna svest omladine', in Mihailović *et al.*, *Deca krize*, pp. 147–72.

16 Srećko Mihailović, 'Zbrka u glavi i strah u srcu: omladina Jugoslavije krajem osamdesetih', in Mihailović *et al.*, *Deca krize*, p. 282.

17 Jordan Aleksić, 'Mlada generacija i Savez komunista Jugoslavije', in Vrcan *et al.*, *Položaj, svest i ponašanje*, p. 190.

18 Mihailović, 'Zbrka u glavi i strah u srcu', pp. 239–40/280.
The *JUPIO* report in the chapter on 'The young generation and the League of Communists of Yugoslavia' outlined similar tendencies:

  1. The membership of the young in the SKJ is in a noticeable and continuous decline.
  2. The motivation for membership deviates in a conformist-pragmatic direction.
  3. The identification with the actions of the SKJ is weakening.

19 Dubravka Velat, 'Omladina u političkom sistemu', in *Mlada generacija, danas društveni položaj, uloga i perspektive mlade generacije Jugoslavije* (Belgrade: NIRO Mladost/Predsedništvo Konferencije SSOJ, 1982), p. 54.

20 Mihailović, 'Zbrka u glavi i strah u srcu', p. 280.

21 Harold Lydall, *Yugoslavia in Crisis* (Oxford: Clarendon Press, 1989), p. 217.

22 Other events which were organised at federal level and embodied some of the core political values of Yugoslav socialism were the 'Championship of knowledge Tito-revolution-peace' [*Šampionat znanja Tito-revolucija-mir*], the youth march 'On Tito's paths of the revolution' [*Titovim stazama revolucije*], the 'Week of youth solidarity' [*Nedelja omladinske solidarnosti*] organised on the occasion of 21 March, the International Day for the Elimination of Racial Discrimination. The cultural event 'The youth of Sutjeska' [*Mladost Sutjeske*] gathered young artists from all over the country at the place of the infamous Second World War Sutjeska battle. The most famous and widely accepted event which the SSOJ organised traditionally

every year was the youth festival in the Vojvodinian town of Subotica [*Festival 'Omladina'-Subotica*] which gathered young pop and rock bands and musicians.

23 Archive of Bosnia and Herzegovina, Sarajevo (hereafter ABH), *RK SSOBIH*, box 124, 'Izvještaj o ostvarenim radnim i društvenim aktivnostima na ORA "Neretva '87"', Mostar', Septembre 1987.

24 Dragan Popović, 'Youth labor action (*Omladinska radna akcija, ORA*) as ideological holiday-making', in Hannes Grandits and Karin Taylor (eds), *Yugoslavia's Sunny Side: A History of Tourism in Socialism (1950s–1980s)* (Budapest and New York: Central European University Press, 2010), p. 283.

25 ABH, 'Izvještaj o ostvarenim radnim i društvenim aktivnostima'.

26 ABH, *RK SSOBIH*, box 124, 'Bilten br. 1, ORA Omladinska pruga Tuzla-Zvornik, Zvornik', May 1988.

27 *XII конгрес на Сојузот на социјалистичка младина на Македонија* (Скопје/Кочани: Републичка конференција на ССММ/Младост, 1986), p. 83.

28 Archive of Macedonia, Skopje (hereafter AM), *Републичка конференција на ССММ*, box number 1/1989, 'Информација за текот и степенот на подготвеност на формата и облиците на доброволните младински активности за 1989 година'.

29 AM, *РК на ССММ*, box 1/1989, 'Правци на развој на формите на доброволните младински активности во СР Македонија во 1989 година'.

30 Igor Mekina and Silvo Zapečnik, 'Somrak štafete', in *Kompendij za bivše in bodoče politike* (Ljubljana: ZSMS, 1989), pp. 105–6.

31 *Ibid.*

32 Mirjana Ule, *Mladina in ideologija* (Ljubljana: Delavska enotnost, 1988).

33 *Ibid.*, p. 109.

34 See: Blaž Vurnik, *Med Marxom in Punkom* (Ljubljana: Modrijan, 2005).

35 Archive of Slovenia, Ljubljana (hereafter AS), *RK ZSMS 1974–1990*, AS 538, technical unit 387, 'Poročilo o štafeti (material za razpravo)'.

36 *Ibid.*

37 Alexei Monroe, *Interrogation Machine: Laibach and NSK* (Cambridge, MA: MIT Press, 2005), p. 110.

38 'Plakatna afera', http://slovenska-pomlad.si/1?id=199&aofs=3 (last accessed 28 April 2016).

39 *Ibid.*

40 'Poruka Štafete mladosti '87', Museum of the History of Yugoslavia, Belgrade (permanent exhibition).

41 'Јединствени симбол', *BORBA* (25 May 1987), p. 1.

42 Borislav Vasić, 'Dosije "Mladosti": Spas od žalosne nužnosti. Štafeta: simbol kojeg više nema', *Mladost* 59 (8–21 February 1988), pp. 25–8.

43 *Ibid.*, p. 28.

44 *Ibid.*

45 Gagnon, 'Yugoslavia in 1989 and after', p. 35.

46 Sven Stilinović's (born 1956) installation *Flag* from 1985 consisting of densely arranged razor blades, which 'turn the iconography of the most important state symbol into a field of pain'. See: www.avantgarde-museum.com/en/museum/collection/authors/sven-stilinovic~pe4572/ (last accessed 23 September 2016).

47 Mladen Dolar, 'Psychoanalysis in power: On fascism, Marxism and the poster scandal', in Zdenka Badovinac, Eda Čufer and Anthony Gardner (eds), *NSK from*

Kapital to Capital: An Event of the Final Decade of Yugoslavia (Cambridge, MA: MIT Press, 2015), pp. 170–1.

48 Biba Kopf, 'Laibach and think of England', *New Musical Express* (4 April 1987), pp. 24/51.

49 Apart from Laibach, the network was composed of a group of graphic artists Irwin, the Theatre of the Sisters of Scipio Nasica and the Red Pilot Cosmokinetic Theatre and the design group New Collectivism. The initial core was formed in 1984, with artistic eclecticism and the historical/early Soviet avant-garde as a shared platform. Cross-referencing at Yugoslav level, especially between the Irwin artists and other Yugoslav art scenes included drawing upon the works of Dragoljub Raša Todosijević (whose seminal 1977 performance was titled 'Was ist Kunst?') and Goran Đorđević from the Belgrade conceptual art scene of the 1970s.

50 Monroe, *Interrogation Machine*, p. 7.

51 Erjavec, 'Introduction', p. 10.

52 Laibach was not the only collective resorting to these discursive strategies. The song 'Maljčiki' by Belgrade-based new wave band Idoli [Idols] and especially the video for it released in 1981 featured socialist realist iconography, verses in an improvised Russian and a plot which presented an enthusiastic proletarian as a factory worker. The St. Petersburg band Pop Mekhanika staged concerts in the 1980s dressed as a military band and often passed for an official Soviet orchestra. The lyrics of 'State' by Laibach read:

'The state is responsible for / The protecting / Elevation / And exploitation of the forest / The state is responsible for / The physical education of the people / Particularly of youth / In order to raise standards of national health / Labour / And defence potentials / It is becoming more and more lenient / All freedom is allowed / Authority / Here belongs to / The people!'

53 Jack Barron, 'Laibach in Auschwitz storm', *New Musical Express* (2 January 1988), p. 4.

54 *Ibid.*

55 Alexei Monroe, 'Laibach: Made in Iugoslávia', in Fernando Oliva and Marcelo Rezende (eds), *Comunismo da forma* (São Paulo: Alameda Casa Editorial, 2007).

56 Slavoj Žižek, 'Why are Laibach and NSK not fascists?' in *NSK from Kapital to Capital: An Event of the Final Decade of Yugoslavia*, pp. 202–4. See also: Slavoj Žižek, *The Plague of Fantasies* (London: Verso, 2009); Zdenka Badovinac, 'An exhibition about the NSK commons', in *NSK from Kapital to Capital: An Event of the Final Decade of Yugoslavia*, pp. xxxvi–xlii; Alexei Yurchak, 'Mimetic critique of ideology: Laibach and Avia', http://chtodelat.org/b8-newspapers/12–51/mimetic-critique-of-ideology-laibach-and-avia/ (last accessed 28 April 2016).

57 Erjavec, 'Neue Slowenische Kunst', p. 147.

58 They started off as a theatre group in 1980 first under the name 'Theater Group' and later as FV 112/15. Some of their productions until the group disbanded in 1983 included: 'The Big May Show – How Nice It Is to Be Young in Our Country', 'Nothing Should Surprise Us' and 'Who Turned Out the Light?' See: Neven Korda *et al.*, *FV – Alternative Scene of the Eighties* (Ljubljana: International Centre of Graphic Arts, 2008).

59 Video available at: www.e-arhiv.org/diva/index.php?opt=work&id=385 (last accessed 23 September 2016).

60 Senad Avdić, 'Krakasti od kečapa', *Polet* 360 (30 January 1987), pp. 6–7.

61 David Tasić, '(Relativno) dugi marš', *Polet* 360 (30 January 1987), p. 6.

62 Jasna Babić, 'Đavolji dodir', *Polet* 360 (30 January 1987), p. 7.

63 Tasić, '(Relativno) dugi marš'.

64 '11 kongres ZSM Jugoslavije', in *Punk je bil prej: 25 let punka pod Slovenci* (Ljubljana: Cankarjeva založba, 2002), p. 169.

65 Jordan Aleksić, 'Omladina: indikatori i funkcije', in *Omladina Beograda: statistika i istraživanja* (Beograd: Marksistički centar organizacije SK u Beogradu, 1983), p. 13.

66 Vlasta Ilišin, 'Interesiranja i slobodno vrijeme mladih', in Vrcan *et al.*, *Položaj, svest i ponašanje*, p. 129.

67 Mirjana Ule, 'Odnos omladine prema mladosti', in Vrcan *et al.*, *Položaj, svest i ponašanje*, p. 113. On social inequalities/class in Yugoslavia, see: Rory Archer, 'Social inequalities and the study of Yugoslavia's dissolution', in Rory Archer, Armina Galijas and Florian Bieber (eds), *Debating the Dissolution of Yugoslavia* (London: Ashgate, 2014), pp. 135–51.

68 David Pottie, 'The politics of meaning in punk rock', *Problématique* 3 (1993), 1–21, p. 15.

69 *Ibid.*, p. 6.

70 Erjavec, 'Introduction', in *Postmodernism and the Postsocialist Condition*, p. 47.

71 Pottie, 'The politics of meaning in punk rock', p.10.

72 Jon Savage, *England's Dreaming: The Sex Pistols and Punk Rock* (London: Faber & Faber, 2005), p. 110.

73 Pottie, 'The politics of meaning in punk rock', p. 10.

74 Gregor Tomc, 'Škandal v rdečem baru', in *Punk je bil prej*, p. 86.

75 Igor Vidmar, 'Dead Kennedys: "Kdor je fašist, ni punk – kdor je punk, ni fašist", Nedeljski dnevnik, 29.11.1981', in *Punk pod Slovenci*, pp. 235–7.

76 Stevan Zec, 'Uspon i pad Četvrtog rajha', Ilustrovana politika, 1.12.1981, in *Punk pod Slovenci*, pp. 237–40.

77 See: Gregor Tomc, 'Spori in spopadi druge Slovenije', in *Punk pod Slovenci*, pp. 9–27.

78 Rajko Muršič, 'Punk anthropology: From a study of a local Slovene alternative rock scene towards partisan scholarship', in Laszlo Kűrti and Peter Skalnik (eds), *Postsocialist Europe: Anthropological Perspectives from Home* (New York and Oxford: Berghahn Books, 2009), pp. 188–206.

79 'Kulturni plenum ZSMS', in *Punk pod Slovenci*, pp. 190–3.

80 Zoran Medved, 'Slovenačka alternativna scena – fašizam u Jugoslaviji', *NON-List mladih Srbije* 498 (11 November 1984), p. 37.

3

'The phantom of liberty': new youth activism

Gdanjsk osamdesete, kad je jesen rekla ne
Gdanjsk osamdesete, držali smo palčeve
Rudari, studenti, brodogradilište svi mi
Gdanjsk osamdesete uzazvrele tvornice
Dvaput se ne šalju tenkovi na radnike
Nisu se usudili pobijedili smo svi mi
Poljska u mome srcu ...[1]

'Poljska u mome srcu', Azra (1981)

The SSOJ was not simply an arena where a younger generation critiqued an older order and value system – it was also a space where new political languages and forms of youth activism developed. This indeed stands in contrast to the institutional youth sphere in many other European socialist countries, where these organisations no longer generated new forms of political expression and where environmentalist or peace groups emerged outside of the formal youth structures.[2] In Yugoslavia, many youth actors still believed in the capacity of the institutional youth sphere to be an incubator for new types of politics, and sought to shape a specifically Yugoslav youth political realm where new 'social movements' emerging from the bottom up could be integrated into the SSOJ. This echoed the findings of the 1980 UNESCO report on youth about 'an issue-oriented style of youth action'.[3] It also revealed, as I shall explore below, a tendency to look to Western Europe for new forms of politics in evolving 'social movements', rather than within the Eastern Bloc. Illustratively, Slovenian sociologist Tomaž Mastnak (born 1953) argued that:

> We should not try to repeat what Solidarity tried – and failed – to do. We should try to invent new forms of democratic activity appropriate to our particular situation... Inventing the single issue-oriented political campaigns common in Western European democracies would be a very good start ... we lack

a democratic tradition and popularly shared memories of a strong and independent civil society. Issue-oriented campaigns – involving women, opponents
of nuclear power, gays, pacifists and others – are crucial for filling this gap, and
for producing a democratic culture in Yugoslavia.[4]

This chapter addresses how new areas for political expression opened up
around issues of peace, anti-militarism, environmentalism, nuclear disarmament and sexuality and how the League of Socialist Youth brought these
issues into its orbit. Linking this with a generational sense of 'Europeanness',
the chapter maps the emergence of social and political issues which older
generations had not previously defined as arenas of political contestation.
Divergent issues such as military service and sexuality illustrate both the
broadening out of political language in late socialism, the ways in which they
nested within the SSOJ, and how a new generation shifted the boundaries of
the political. Late socialist Yugoslav society witnessed the proliferation of a
youth arena of civil initiatives and activist citizenship which, although fragmented and often discordant, eventually found shelter and support within
parts of the existing youth infrastructure. Although they carried the seeds
of the processes of socio-political reformation and democratisation which
were already underway, for the most part they were significantly embedded within the dominant political/socialist rhetoric – in particular within
Edvard Kardelj's notion of the 'pluralism of self-managing interests'. One of
Yugoslavia's principal theoreticians and legalists, in his book *Roads of Development of the Socialist Self-Management Political System* [*Pravci razvoja političkog sistema
socijalističkog samoupravljanja*] he argued that:

> this does not mean that we are or should be hostile to every form of democratic
> political pluralism. On the contrary, because of the multitude of interests in
> society arising from class, economic, political, social, and other considerations
> in the life, work, and creativity of people, it is clear that there can be neither
> democracy nor human freedom if man is not able to enjoy free expression of
> his interests and his ideas, of his aspirations and creative views.[5]

Appropriating this political language, in its 1986 official congress materials the
SSOJ argued that it was necessary to accommodate the new movements and their
demands within the youth organisation: 'It is impossible to realise the affirmation
of the idea of pluralism and democratic "youth politics" … without the acknowledgement of the right of independent existence of the social movements … the
SSO should create space for the work of the feminist, the peace, the ecological
movements, as well as for the other progressive movements among the youth.'[6]
Moreover, the 1986 draft documents for the federal youth congress stated that
'If the youth organisation does not take up the challenge which the new social
movements are offering, it will suffer grave consequences, it will close itself up and

renounce the essential struggle to become mass and front organisation'.[7] Hashim Rexhepi, president of the SSOJ at the time, upheld this vision the following year in an interview for the daily *Borba* by stressing that 'We want the [new social] movements to become an integral part of the SSO. After all, socialism, too, is a movement'.[8] In that same 'congress' year, the ZSMS at its 12th (so-called Krško) congress, put forward slogans such as: 'Let's legalise the new social movements', 'Let's democratise political culture', 'For an independent and responsible Youth League', 'For workers' democracy', 'For pluralism of self-managing interests', 'For the word not to be an offence'.[9] The 1989 youth survey confirmed that the level of approval/support for the new social movements had generally increased, despite the fact that it remained highest among the Slovenian youth (71 per cent), the 'Yugoslavs' from Croatia (64 per cent) and the 'Yugoslavs' outside of Croatia and Bosnia-Herzegovina (58 per cent).[10] However, the level of support across the different 'social groups' was almost the same (e.g. among students in the different federal units) and it differed among national groups (e.g. 37 per cent of Kosovo Albanians versus only 13 per cent of Albanians outside of Kosovo).

The goal of this chapter is not to account for the broader frame of Yugoslav socialist civil society, nor for the entirety of 'acts of citizenship' related to the new social movements. Its aim is to offer a closer observation of the process of the nesting of a range of youth 'acts' within the wide framework of the SSOJ, turning parts of the youth infrastructure into new sites of struggle and constantly testing and stretching its boundaries. Some of the issues raised by youth activists combined and echoed both the 'inner', that is Yugoslav-specific contestations of the socio-political framework and 'outer' challenges resulting from developments at international level, i.e. demands and initiatives which did not possess a specifically Yugoslav outlook, but had a trans-national or global identity. These included youth initiatives regarding different political and institutional matters such as the abolishment of the death penalty,[11] de-militarisation, conscientious objection, anti-nuclear and ecological claims, feminism and the rights of sexual minorities. The chapter addresses several of a range of issues where these new forms of activism were articulated. First, it maps what was referred to in the Introduction as the second generational pillar, which relates to this generation's own distinct sense of Europeanness which mirrored in many ways Yugoslavia's peculiar geopolitical positioning in the context of the Cold War. Then it reflects on the ways the myth of (gender) equality was challenged by youth activists within a social ambience of proliferation of various feminist, lesbian and gay groups within the youth organisation and its media outposts. Finally, it engages with the narratives of anti-militarism, the conscientious objection initiatives and petitions that all the while challenging one of the major pillars of Yugoslav socialism – the Yugoslav People's Army and its stature in the political and public life, found ways to reach institutional forums and incite public debates.

Facing East, looking West: new transnational identities

The new social movements that were to challenge the official political values and language within the SSOJ framed their issue-oriented acts in response to the specific Yugoslav context. Nevertheless, many of them in fact were inspired by similar campaigns and groups from outside the country. The late socialist period, in particular after 1975 and the Helsinki Accords where Yugoslavia played a prominent role, saw the establishment of a transnational European network of actors and groups voicing various demands concerning civil liberties, environmental and anti-nuclear anxieties in the aftermath of the Chernobyl disaster.[12] As it was pointed above, the Yugoslav urban youth attentively followed the events in Poland at the beginning of the decade, and in particular those from Slovenia forged links with some of the Central/Eastern European groups which converged around issue-oriented campaigns such as conscientious objection and nuclear disarmament.[13]

The relative openness of Yugoslavia, alongside its noted presence at the international sports arena and its remarkable cultural scene which fed into a sense of superiority, contributed to this generation's sense of internationalism/ Europeanness, to the widening of their horizons, expectations, references and lines of identification. There has been little work on what Europeanness meant in socialist Yugoslavia, or indeed how individuals understood Europe and Europeanness and how their lived experiences were moulded into a wider European frame. The latter of the two major youth surveys from the 1980s revealed certain attitudes of the young towards the European Community of the time – in particular in the context of support for a potential accession. For instance, 59 per cent chose the sense of European belonging as 'important'. This was second in rank under the sense of Yugoslav belonging, which was ranked as 'important' by 73 per cent of the respondents.[14] Asked about the changes in the economic system, the youth in this last survey declared preferences for a market economy ('like the one in the West'), private property and an accession to the European Economic Community: for 64 per cent of the respondents joining the European common market was a preferential option. Yet, pinning down the sense of Europeanness could be best achieved 'from below' through oral history testimonies. Hence, the individual recollections analysed below offer a useful perspective on this generation's understanding of transnationalism, internationalism and Europeanness.

Not strictly belonging to the Eastern European world under Soviet domination, and having the opportunity to travel freely across the continent and interact both with the East and the West, was crucial in instilling a different sense of trans-national/European belonging. To Igor Vidmar, as someone who worked for a long time in Radio Študent and was personally involved in the

Slovenian alternative cultural scene, the link with Britain, for instance, was a reciprocal one:

> We in Radio Študent were subscribed to *New Musical Express, Melody Maker, Sounds*, and we travelled there – myself for the first time in 1974, then in 1979, etc … It was also the other way around – the first article on Slovenian punk was in *Melody Maker* by Chris Bohn in 1980 or so.

Vidmar was Chris Bohn's guide and intepreter when Bohn visited Yugoslavia at the beginning of 1980, a visit which was summarised in a two-page article entitled 'Non-aligned punk'.[15] This was one of the first articles to correctly position the country and its youth in geopolitical terms – throughout the 1970s both *New Musical Express* and *Melody Maker* persistently referred to Yugoslavia as 'behind the Iron Curtain', which provoked angry reactions by some of their Yugoslav readers. 'As a regular reader of NME I feel insulted by the way your write about Yugoslavia in your issues of May 3 and May 17', wrote a reader from Zagreb in 1975.

> In your 'Teazers' column you worry about 'How will the Communist Bloc take to British pub rock when Kilburn And The High Roads tour Yugoslavia and Poland in August.' Now try to get this: Yugoslavia does not belong to any bloc, so you better don't try to make jokes about something that may be irrelevant to you, but is of principal meaning for Yugoslav people … This is not fair toward your Yugoslav readers and many other rock fans in our country. The same singles, albums, groups and singers that top the Pop Polls in Britain are very popular in Yugoslavia, too … So you see, there is no sense in considering Yugoslavia so inferior.[16]

Writing in 1978, a certain Tomash Domicelj from Ljubljana similarly complained in the *Melody Maker* that he was 'fed up with reading again and again about Yugoslavia being behind the Iron Curtain. We are, if anything, on the border of that Curtain, which MM staff and other British people involved in the music business should know by now. Remember 1948, when we told Stalin off? If not, ask some historians about that'.[17]

Indeed, the geopolitical positioning of Yugoslavia had significant impact on the way the youth conceptualised and articulated its self-identification and sense of belonging in wider European/global terms. As it was observed in the late 1980s, 'The right to travel is defined as a fundamental attribute of being a Yugoslav by many Yugoslavs, especially, but not only, in Slovenia and Croatia'.[18] Vlatko Stefanovski's testimony underlined this awareness of being neither East nor West, but also taking a certain pride in the fact that Yugoslavia was not part of the Eastern Bloc. Indeed, 'Yugoslavia's peculiar position with regard to the Cold War divide in Europe had thus allowed Western-supported retrospective self-positionings of superiority towards those who had been considered "really Eastern" Europeans (i.e. citizens of Warsaw Pact states)'.[19] A sense of superiority towards the countries of the Eastern Bloc is common place in many personal narratives. In this case it serves as an example of how it worked to feed into the sense of dignity, pride and relative Yugoslav patriotism:

> As young people we were very, very lucky to live precisely in-between two principles, two blocs ... and we were the 'best of two worlds', I would say, because we had a pretty stable social system which, I think that, after all, functioned very well. We enjoyed enough freedom, as well as civil and human rights. By human rights I understand the right to food, the right to health-care and the right to education. All social strata enjoyed these rights ... Each and every one could reach high academic status and titles. The more that period becomes distant, the more I look upon it with a justified nostalgia as I look now how the Western world crumbles down, and the Eastern world is wondering ...
>
> In 1988 we went on a one month tour to the USSR. It was an exhausting tour because there was not enough food, there were no restaurants. There were only some little shops with vodka and sausages or cigarettes in front of which there was a one hundred metre line ... When we came back I kissed the runaway, if you can believe it [...]
>
> I had a cultural shock when I first arrived in London after a three-day train journey, I arrived at Victoria Station. And I saw this Mecca of rock 'n' roll ... I was totally blown away when I first saw London. I was going to concerts every night, to the clubs – to the iconic Marquee Club, the 100 Club, London Astoria – every night there were excellent concerts by top musicians and top bands ... On the other hand, there were charter flights from Belgrade to London almost every day and we could fly pretty cheap to London, we used to buy equipment, guitars, amplifiers, clothes. We used to come back home inspired by what we had seen, we lived our dream.

This excerpt paints a contrasting image where a young Yugoslav is fully mobile on the international scene of divided Europe, welcomed to perform and travel both in the East and the West, but thoroughly enchanted only by the West – which eventually led to a rather widespread tendency which allowed them to 'see themselves as the West to the Soviet bloc's East'.[20] In Stefanovski's testimony London is *the* topos of reference for this generation, as most of the interviewees who spoke about travelling, or indeed about their work/activism did not fail to mention London or Britain.

Neven Korda (born 1956) was a member of the band Borghesia and the FV group. Echoing Mastnak, he reflected on another level of distancing from the acts of dissidence and opposition in the countries of the Eastern Bloc:

> For me, that rebellion of theirs against the Soviet Union, and the way I saw Lech Walesa – it was reactionary ... I said to myself – Well, if I have to choose, then the Soviet Union is better [laughs] than their type of Christianity, nineteenth-century type of traditionalism ... The Czechs, too. They were more ... sort of

bourgeois. We didn't cherish that vision of going back to some type of bourgeois democracy. We looked forward.

An excerpt from Slovenian writer Aleš Debeljak's (1961–2016) book links the
narratives of distinct Yugoslav political and cultural identity, cosmopolitanism
and mobility in the West to a new generational consciousness:

> Throughout the time I was growing up – the late 1970s and early '80s – I shared
> with my peers the easy feeling that we didn't have it bad at all. We were dif-
> ferent from our counterparts in the Soviet empire's East European satellites
> by way of the nonaligned politics of Tito, the great guru of the 'third way',
> who discovered the trick of playing West and East off each other so that both
> sides would generously contribute money to build his Potemkin villages of self-
> management. But those were issues of high diplomacy that for a long time we
> neither understood nor cared about. Our interests lay elsewhere.
>
> Most of all, we wanted to know in what European town Oscar Peterson
> would be playing next summer and when John Fowles's newest book would
> hit the bookstores in nearby Trieste, Vienna, or Munich, if not Ljubljana. We
> traveled widely and unhindered, both within Yugoslavia and abroad. We made
> pilgrimages to jazz and rock concerts as far afield as Moers, Florence, and
> Montreux. We believed that mass culture gave us more in common with youth
> in London than with our parents. In their novels and literary reviews, our older
> colleagues had told unsettling stories of suffering in the clutches of Titoism,
> of the communist regime's brutality, but we understood these then as a far-
> removed allegory that no longer defined us in any significant way.[21]

There is a cynical distancing at three levels in this excerpt: from 'our counterparts in the Soviet empire's East European satellites', from 'our parents'
and from the older generations' denunciatory stories about Titoism and communism. At the same time, there is a tension between the acknowledgement
(and an implicit appraisal) of the fruits of Yugoslav 'high diplomacy' on the one
hand and the remark referring to the 'Potemkin villages of self-management',
on the other. The ability to travel 'widely and unhindered' is yet again emphasised, along with the proximity in cultural preferences, tastes and worldviews
with 'the youth in London'.

For a different segment of the youth, however, Western Europe embodied
another set of values and opportunities. For those who became active in the peace
or sexual minorities groups, visits to Western European countries appeared to
be a decisive experience. Marko Hren (born 1959) was at the helm of the peace
movement in Slovenia in the 1980s. He self-identifies as a pacifist whose initial
interest lay with the New Age movement and he claims he drew his ethical code
from the Buddhist teachings on non-violence: 'My inspiration for engagement
was radical pacifism and my motivation was fuelled by international pacifist

movements – War Resisters International, London-based. I met them sometime in 1974 in Switzerland.'[22]

Nataša Sukič was among the founders of the lesbian activist core in Slovenia and is still actively involved in the International Lesbian, Gay, Bisexual, Trans and Intersex Association (ILGA Europe). Her testimony reflects the importance of the trans-national aspect, i.e. the exposure to similar events unfolding in Western European countries, as well as the pan-Yugoslav, anti-nationalist dimension of the Yugoslav feminist movement:

> Everything started in the 1980s within the framework of the new social movements and alternative cultures, which were quite prominent in Ljubljana. They were all – how shall I put it? – interconnected and had an impact on our own [lesbian] activism. Especially the video art and Borghesia influenced us significantly, because they questioned the media representations of sexuality and for the first time sexuality began to gravitate in the social space as a political question … Borghesia's videos were totally radical for that time and they certainly had an influence on us. Later came the MAGNUS [gay] festivals, the feminist movement, the peace movement – it was very vibrant and it was only a matter of time for the lesbian movement to get established. First I was part of the feminist group and later when I went to Holland and for the first time saw a pride parade that left a huge impression on me. I thought – if they can have it all, why couldn't we? So, I met Suzana Tratnik and together we founded the group [LL – Lesbian Lilith] – that's how it all began.

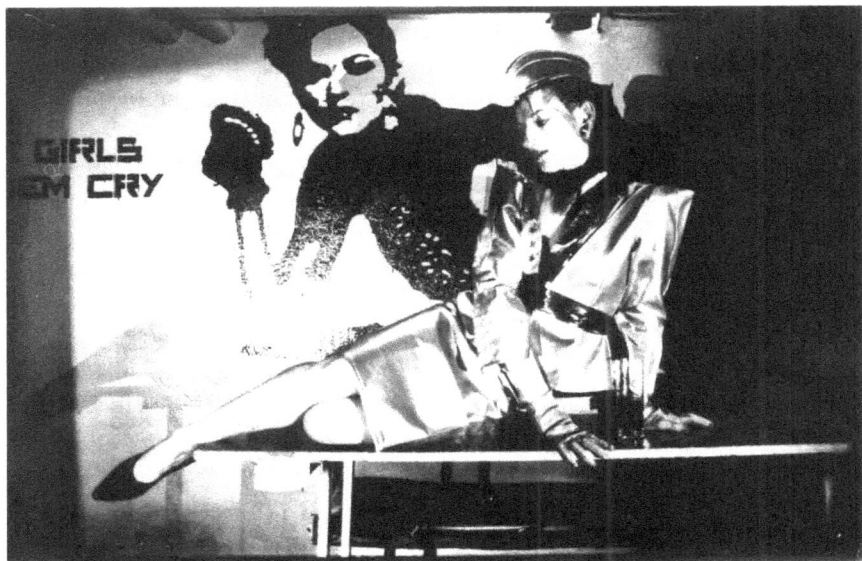

Figure 8 Borghesia performance *Young Prisoners*, 1984

Western Europe was the space which the small lesbian activist core appropri-ated as a reference point and a source of inspiration for their activism and where they travelled and liaised with fellow activists. Before the foundation of LL, they co-operated closely with the group of gay activists 'Magnus' and had contacts and meetings with activists from the Vienna-based 'Homosexuelle Initiative' (HOSI). LL became part of ILGA as of 1987, got involved with the Interna-tional Lesbian Information Service (ILIS) and took part in many international events that year: from a semi-legal gathering in Budapest in November under ILGA's patronage, to the 'Gay and Lesbian Pride' in the Netherlands in June, and at the 'Lesbenwoche' in Berlin in October. In August 1988, after having become an independent 'lesbian section LL' under the umbrella of ŠKUC, they organized an 'international lesbian camp' on the Croatian island of Rab which gathered activists from both Yugoslavia and Western Europe (Italy, Germany, England, Ireland, Austria, Portugal, the Netherlands).[23]

As the socio-political situation started to deteriorate in the late 1980s, one could observe a rise of a self-ironical, self-critical discourse and a bitterness caused by the onslaught of nationalist euphoria and its contribution to the increasingly negative perceptions of Yugoslavia abroad. For example, in October 1988 the London reporter for *Polet*, the youth weekly magazine of the SSO of Croatia, reported among other things on an article in the *Guardian* which described an atmos-phere in Yugoslavia where foreign journalists were being attacked (quoting an inci-dent of a Reuters journalist being beaten up by the police at a rally in Titograd, Montenegro's capital) and concluded: 'Yugoslavia is these days a typical example of Balkan backwardness, of repressed, basic nationalist instincts which furthermore cor-rode the otherwise corroded union – at a time when Europe is forging economic and other alliances in order to make its population richer, more content, happier.'[24] As Yugoslavia drifted away from a peaceful solution of its political crisis at the end of the decade, a growing sense of alienation from the European space and the European values was detectable in the youth media. This was then carried forward in political and media discourse to the post-Yugoslav era – most prominently in Slovenia and Croatia – as a way of distancing from the Yugoslav space and the Yugoslav past.[25]

The possibilities of mobility across the European continent and the expe-riences of travel both in the East and in the West put this generation of young Yugoslavs in a unique position of exposure to the two sides of the Cold War. A sense of solidarity with the East emerged at crucial points such as the military dictatorship in Poland, for instance; yet, it was coupled with a sense of superior-ity toward the Eastern Bloc countries and with a sense of belonging to the cul-tural realm of Western Europe. Indeed, it was non-state socialist Europe which acted as a source of inspiration both with regard to culture and new forms of activism, as social movements from the West were crucial in shaping expecta-tions of what could be possible under Yugoslav socialism.

Gender (in)equality and sexuality

Yugoslav feminism and the subsequent gay and lesbian movement of the 1980s were significantly impacted by Western European theoretical and activist developments. Predominantly composed of intellectuals and hence well acquainted with international academic feminism,[26] an older cohort of Yugoslav feminists who were involved in the public debates with the political elites in the 1970s and organised the international conference 'Comrade woman' at the Student Cultural Centre in Belgrade in 1978,[27] formed the core of a pan-Yugoslav network of feminists whose theoretical and subsequent activist engagements played a decisive role in the intellectual and academic identities of the younger generation. Although most of the concrete problems which preoccupied the feminists and the young gay and lesbian activists were primarily rooted within the Yugoslav reality, they were for the most part eclectic and international in their theoretical expertise and their attention was almost exclusively directed beyond narrow national confines. For instance, some of the participants at the first Yugoslav meeting of feminists [*Prvi jugoslovenski susret feministkinja*] that took place in 1987 in Ljubljana insisted on the importance of the notion of solidarity and quoted positive examples of dealing with family rape and violence from Peru, Nicaragua, Britain and Canada.[28] In a similar vein, the demands of the Magnus section of gay activists from Ljubljana presented at the festival of the new social movements in the Slovenian town of Nova Gorica in August 1986 reflect comparable manifestations of transnational solidarity: not only did they demand, among other things, the removal of the legal provisions which criminalised homosexuality in Serbia, Bosnia and Herzegovina, Macedonia and Kosovo,[29] they also insisted that the Yugoslav government lodged a note of protest with the governments of states which discriminate and imprison homosexuals, such as Romania, the USSR, Cuba and Iran.[30]

With the exception of the women's groups within the sociological associations of Croatia and Slovenia [*Sekcija Žena i društvo pri Sociološkom društvu Hrvatske* and *Ženska sekcija pri Sociološkom društvu Slovenije*], all the other groups which gathered feminist and gay activists found an institutional shelter within the youth infrastructure: the women's section 'Lilith' formed at the ŠKUC in April 1985 hosted the lesbian group 'LL' [*Lezbična Lilit*] until it became an independent group under ŠKUC's umbrella in 1988; the Belgrade-based feminist group 'Women and society' [*Žene i društvo*] which sprung from a series of public round-tables at the Student Cultural Centre (SKC) in 1982 continued to hold its meetings there; while the feminist group 'Trešnjevka' was founded in 1987 as the division for women's social activity at the League of Socialist Youth municipal Zagreb branch 'Trešnjevka' [*Sekcija za društvenu aktivnost žena OK SSO Trešnjevka*]. It was the women's group within the youth organisation in Trešnjevka that initiated the first telephone line for women and children victims of violence. The institutional umbrella of the youth sphere provided activists with a sense of distance from the realm of official politics: 'We do not want to define ourselves a priori theoretically or institutionally, what we want is a free space for development.'[31] Some of the texts reveal the ambiguous relationship which existed between the activists and the institutions of the system – at the same time denouncing them and their approach to the 'unprivileged groups' and victims of violence and suggesting different ways of improving women's and children's positions through co-operating with the institutions of the state: 'The cooperation with the relevant institutions (in social work, health, justice, legislative, police, etc.) is particularly important and therefore we will dedicate special attention to it.'[32] Although they did not receive institutional funding and the work was done by volunteers, the line was supported in terms of space and logistics by the SSO branch of Trešnjevka municipality and the city of Zagreb and the activists insisted on the principle of solidarity, which was normally upheld as one of the official postulates of Yugoslav self-management:

> The institutions protect the patriarchal order by trying to make the individual adjust to his/her role. The institutions have this attitude towards all individuals who experience problems (the unemployed, the ill, those receiving social benefits ...) ... The SOS telephone line is something different: it is autonomous from institutional influence and possesses its own *raison d'être* ... Institutional changes are indispensable, above all in the preliminary contacts of the officials with the victims of violence with the aim of preventing further victimisation. We are thinking about cooperation with the SIZ [Self-managing interest community] for employment.[33]

This not only sheds light on the complex relationship which existed between activists who had found shelter in a *de facto* institutional space and the official politics and institutions of the state, it also demonstrates that although their activism embodied something that was novel and alternative when compared to the official political discourse and established social practices, having chosen a semi-institutional setting they inevitably had to engage with the state and challenge it on these issues from within. These new groups themselves later acted as infrastructural umbrellas. Thus, in 1989 'Lila' – the first lesbian initiative in Croatia – was launched as a subgroup of the Trešnjevka Women's section, 'encouraged by the organising of lesbians worldwide, particularly in Slovenia'.[34] Most of its members were aged between twenty-five and thirty-five and the gay and lesbian activists in Slovenia were looked upon and often recalled as a positive example to be followed. As was observed in a youth press article, 'Progressive ideas were always initially encountering fertile ground in Slovenia ... Today, when we all publicly declare in favour of democracy and pluralism, the Lila Initiative should present a form of concrete action that will receive understanding and support on the part of society'.[35]

The trend of accommodating new youth initiatives and groups within the framework of the SSOJ became especially pronounced after 1986, when the SSOJ first tacitly and later openly endorsed the inclusion of these new groups within the institutional youth sphere. In her testimony, Sukič underlined the importance of the student and the youth organisation, the 'huge support' the activists received and the opening up and liberalisation, which, in her view, does not comply with the post-Yugoslav arguments that seek to stress the dictatorial nature of the system:

> ŠKUC had a very strong tradition since 1972 and a very progressive student scene and it came naturally that it provided space for the new social movements – the feminist, the gay and later the lesbian … I could not think of any more natural space for all of them than ŠKUC.
>
> We cooperated a lot with the peace movement, with the League of Socialist Youth of Slovenia, who gave us huge support and I think they even issued a declaration saying they support the politicisation of the homosexual question … I say, those were really open times. Today I can't believe how people can get easily manipulated … in terms of saying that those were terrible times, that it was a one-party dictatorship, I don't know what … What dictatorship, please? OK, maybe it was in the immediate post-war period, but from the 1970s onwards – certainly it wasn't. I mean … and in the 1980s – of course not!

The existence of a rather open youth infrastructure that appeared welcoming to new forms of art and activism was also crucial for the development of a conflated feminist/lesbian circle of activists. Indeed, it was the 'peripheral' parts of the youth infrastructure, such as the youth press and the cultural venues, that contributed the most to the raising of their visibility in the public sphere. For instance, while LL still acted as part of the feminist/women's group Lilith, a range of their activities were hosted by ŠKUC in 1986 – from presentations on the lesbian scenes in Berlin and London to exhibitions and performances such as Austrian Krista Beinstein's exhibition *Obszöne Frauen* [Obscene Women]. Later, ŠKUC Gallery would also host the 'Week of lesbian film' in December 1988.[36] A crucial moment for the lesbian movement not only in Slovenia, but also in Yugoslavia was the appearance of a special annex to the youth weekly *Mladina* in October 1987 entitled 'Ljubimo ženske' [We love women/Let's love women], which featured anthropological and psychological articles on homosexuality, alongside the programmatic goals of the ILIS, a call from Amnesty International for the reporting of cases of imprisonment based on sexual orientation, an excerpt from the book *Our Bodies, Ourselves* and the 'public inauguration' (or what some of the activists referred to as 'the coming out') of the LL group. It outlined their program and invited those interested to get in touch via the group's official address and telephone number. Speaking as a representative of the women activists from Belgrade at the first Yugoslav meeting of feminists in Ljubljana, Lepa Mladenović spoke about her excitement upon seeing the *Mladina* supplement: 'When we saw the supplement in *Mladina*, which we didn't know was being prepared, we were very impressed. Of course, the coming into existence of the first lesbian group in Yugoslavia for us is a historical event which we celebrate … What some of us [in Belgrade] dreamed of and wished for was realised by our comrades from Ljubljana and we were really impressed/enthused.'[37]

From all the new social movements which found nesting ground within the youth infrastructure, the feminist and lesbian movements were the ones which had framed their activism within a Yugoslav framework, beyond the confines of the federal units. Referring to Yugoslav feminism[38] of the 1980s as 'a small beacon of opposition to nationalism', Jill Benderly rightly argued that 'Womens' solidarity above and beyond national identity made feminism a fairly unique social movement in the period when most other movements had, to varying degrees, become nationalized by 1991'.[39] Sukič's testimony lends legitimacy to this argument. Although the Slovenian gay/lesbian scene was the most prominent and recognisable in Yugoslavia, they remained open for co-operation and forging of trans-republican ties:

> Ours was the first lesbian group in Eastern Europe, not only in Yugoslavia. We established connections in the Yugoslav context through the feminist movement, through Lepa Mladenović, for example. The first Yugoslav feminist festival took place in Ljubljana. During the festival Suzana and I presented this initiative. Soon afterwards, there was a similar lesbian-gay initiative in Croatia. We were always in communication with the rest of the Yugoslav space … Even today we are well connected, recently maybe even more.

Hence, Ljubljana seemed as a logical choice for a host city of the first Yugoslav meeting of feminists that took place in December 1987. The conclusions of the meeting reflect the initial conflation of the lesbian and the feminist cause:

> We, the women who gathered at the first Yugoslav meeting of feminists that took place in Ljubljana from 11–13 December 1987, conclude:
>
> > That all feminist initiatives and groups in Yugoslavia are legitimate and legal.
> > That we call upon women to join the existing feminist groups or to establish their own.
> > That violence against women is widely spread in our country: marital and extra-marital rape, physical abuse of women and children, sexual

blackmailing and many more. We agreed that we will work on organised help and self-help for the women victims of violence through
the S.O.S. telephone lines, counseling, shelters, etc. We demand that
the relevant institutions join these actions because so far they haven't
responded adequately to this problem.

We demand that ... lesbianism becomes publicly visible; we invite all lesbians to establish their own groups throughout Yugoslavia; we intend to
organise the first Yugoslav lesbian festival. We demand a constitutional
amendment that will guarantee the equality of all women and men
regardless of their sexual orientation. [...]

The Yugoslav feminist meetings become one of the modes of our common
actions and exchange.[40]

One of the issues raised at the Ljubljana Yugoslav feminist meeting was that
of elitism. This example is illustrative of the Yugoslav-specific traits of some of
the debates. Lydia Sklevicky (born 1952), a feminist from Zagreb, recounted an
event where a lesbian couple of highly educated and socially well-established
lesbian friends – a poet and a historian of art – 'who could afford to carry the
stigma of lesbianism' because 'they were in a way part of the social elite', did
not show solidarity for a lesbian from a less privileged background who worked
as a typist. She raised the question of whether they as feminist activists have
managed to raise awareness about the class question: 'We are not reaching to
other women who are less privileged and who do not have enough free time
to be raising awareness about their problems.'[41] This demonstrates a certain
degree of self-awareness about the actual degree of 'elitism' among the feminist
activists which, after all, was distinct from the perceived elitism of those women
who worked for the official women's institution – the 'Conference for the social
activity of women' [*Konferencija za društvenu aktivnost žena*] within the Socialist Alliance of Working People.

Indeed, socialist theory and in this case the issue of class, were important
in forging activist identities. As 'benevolent dissidents'[42] in late socialism, they
were involved in debates over socialist theory and practice, recognising that the
legal framework (family law, the right to abortion, etc.)[43] provided women with
full emancipation, but which in reality did not amount to full equality. Indeed,
'The feminist movement in Yugoslavia did not, of course, speak of overthrowing
socialism, but it did speak of the need to overthrow patriarchy and of the failure
of socialism to do so'.[44] Patriarchy was seen to embody not only the causes for
the unequal treatment of women, but also of all other groups, alternative life-
styles and individuals who were discriminated by virtue of being different: 'What
feminism is against is patriarchy and its system of values based on violence and
disrespect for human rights, it is against all who sustain that system regardless of

their gender … Homosexuality is an alternative lifestyle which is equally valid and legitimate as heterosexuality … Patriarchy does not allow any alternative.'[45]

Theoretically eclectic and international in their outlook, feminist and lesbian/gay activism was nevertheless significantly defined by its rootedness in the Yugoslav context. Institutionally sheltered by parts of the youth organisation, these groups and initiatives gained visibility and voice through the youth press and the youth cultural venues. This position allowed them to distance themselves from the sphere of official politics and forge alternative identities and demands; yet, it also provided them with enough leverage to channel their critique more effectively and challenge the state from within.

Peace and anti-militarism

As in many parts of socialist Europe and the developed world, the 1980s saw the emergence, or in some cases, the reinvigoration of peace and anti-militarist activism. Yugoslavia was no exception: here, these initiatives mainly focussed on conscientious objection/civilian service, although other issues such as the public control of the army and arms sales abroad were also addressed. What set Yugoslavia apart, especially compared to other state socialist countries, was the fact that the youth organisation was still seen by a majority of activists as the forum for articulating these demands. Moreover, these new debates, especially those that concerned conscientious objection, used the language of Yugoslav socialism. For example, documents from the 1980s show that the initiators of the conscientious objection initiative were still prepared to couch their activism in the language of socialist self-management, convinced as they were in the capacity for state institutions – who might respond to such language – to be the carriers of change. They tried to demonstrate that conscientious objection was part of a democratic society, that it is connected with Marx's understanding of human society and human freedom and argued that such a position does not stand in opposition to the concept of 'general people's defence and social self-protection' [*opštenarodna odbrana i društvena samozaštita*].[46]

The 1980 UNESCO report on youth foresaw trends in peace and anti-nuclear/environmental activism, claiming that 'They [the young] protest against threats to the environment and against so-called progress …They also are troubled by the resources and knowledge squandered on a highly destructive arms race. This ecological awareness is of an utmost importance … the crucial factor of ecological issues is not properly speaking ecological … so much as political'.[47] Indeed, anti-nuclear/environmental activism became especially prominent in Yugoslavia in the aftermath of the Chernobyl disaster.[48] As it was noted at the time, 'Yugoslavia is the only East European state nation where protests after Chernobyl have been continuously massive ... Yugoslavia's peace and ecology protest is probably the best example of the way in which independent protest is infused into existing officially-established organisations or agencies, in the process making them less dependent on the state'.[49] In the youth realm, the 1986 federal youth congress was the platform where nuclear power and the issue of civilian military service became the subjects of vigorous debate. While both the (anti-)nuclear and the military service debate were significantly informed by similar initiatives and developments in Western Europe and in the Eastern Bloc,[50] they had specificities conditioned by the Yugoslav context. The congress of the SSOJ had a specific session dedicated to the new social movements and it was said that 'this is a time when new social actors appear on the social and the political scene ... which are embodiment of a critique of the classical social movements and political institutions'.[51] Despite the numerous disagreements, the congress accepted the initiative to ask for a more precise formulation of the contentious 'Article 133' and almost unanimously upheld the anti-nuclear argument,[52] enhanced by the Chernobyl nuclear disaster that took place in April that year. The congress adopted a resolution demanding moratorium on the international tenders for nuclear technology Yugoslavia had initiated, termination of all activities for construction of nuclear plants and public presentation of what had been invested thus far.[53] Accompanied by the delegates' applause, Žarko Bokanović, one of the congress delegates, even handed out a bunch of anti-nuclear badges to the congress guests seated in the first row, among who was the president of the Party Presidium Vidoje Žarković. After the Yugoslav federal government had declared support for a moratorium on the construction of nuclear power plants in 1987, in June 1989 the Yugoslav federal assembly passed a law banning future constructions of nuclear power plants or facilities for processing or storing nuclear waste.[54] At the end of 1989, the anti-nuclear movement was rightfully labelled 'the last all-Yugoslav movement'.[55]

One of the new groups that followed a vaguely defined 'green' politics and upheld the demands of the Slovenian peace groups was 'Svarun' from Zagreb. Dejan Jović recalled the difficulties they faced while trying to incorporate them under the institutional umbrella of the SSOJ:

> *Svarun* from Zagreb was the first group of greens constituted in Croatia, a group which gathered the peace and the green movements. They wanted to join the League of Socialist Youth, but, of course, the dogmatic elements in the youth organisation said – 'No way'. But I was very much in favour of that. I said – 'Excellent, if we are a pluralistic organisation, let's welcome them'. I was in the minority in that respect, but they found an open door at the city level, in the youth organisation in Zagreb, they were allowed to use some space and were closely working with the student organisation and *Studentski List*.

More importantly, it was not only activist youth who used the institutional youth sphere for channelling their initiatives and demands. The SSOJ was the realm where the professional young army officers and the recruits had a chance to interact with the 'ordinary' youth and the representatives of the new social movements, i.e. with those who began to question the set-up of the military sphere in the country. Milan Lišanin (born 1960) was a young army officer who was schooled at the Sarajevo military high school and began his military career in 1979 in Postojna, Slovenia. He took part in the 1986 federal youth congress, where most of the amendments and proposals regarding conscientious objection put forward by the delegates from the ZSMS caused fierce debates and a consensus could not be reached. As Lišanin recalled:

> As an active member of the youth at the time I participated at the last, twelfth congress of the League of Socialist Youth of Yugoslavia in Belgrade … There it was already obvious that there are different camps … As far as I remember, it was Slovenia which was sticking out and all the delegates who were discussing … but you could already see that something needed to be defended. At that point I could not even conceive of the idea that what happened could ever happen. It would not even cross my mind. Not only back then, but even in 1990, up until the moment the end was really there.

In addition to the SSOJ, the youth and the army principally overlapped in three realms: the obligatory conscription, the military education system and the compulsory military education for all students as part of the doctrine of 'general people's defence and social self-protection'. Lišanin reflected on the close-knit relationship the army had with the local community, in particular with the youth:

> The secondary military school in Sarajevo actively co-operated with the other secondary schools in the city[56] … The co-operation of the cadets of the military schools with the local youth was very dynamic. Likewise, in Slovenia, since I worked at the reconnaissance unit, we co-operated with the scouts from the town, we organised technical shows … functions, quizzes … The police youth was also involved, even though later we were in conflict, while we were 'normal' we used to co-operate … Also, when the Postojna youth used to organise an excursion to, say, Plitvice Lakes, to the town of Jajce – 'On the Paths of the Revolution', we accompanied them. There was co-operation in the field. That co-operation existed everywhere. Later … it was different.

Undoubtedly, all of the projects and events of interaction between the army and the local youth were not equally successful and did not target the youth which held firm beliefs and who perceived the army through its most senior figures, rather than through their military coevals.[57] For instance, at 24 per cent, the percentage of young officers who were members of the Party was relatively small, compared to 31 per cent of the overall officer corps and 33 per cent of the civilian employees in the JNA.[58] These overlaps were indeed ignored at the time and are overlooked in scholarly literature nowadays, leading to a restricted view of youth culture and activism.

The Slovenian branch of the SSOJ was the most vocal on this matter – which in itself reinforces the argument of the importance of the decentralised nature of the institutional youth sphere. In 1987 the ZSMS and its Ljubljana University branch initiated several round table discussions with the aim of reforming/abolishing the compulsory military classes in secondary schools and at university level. Referring specifically to the education of pre-school and primary school children which included frequent encounters with military content, a 1989 issue of *Mladina* asked if it was not the time 'to put an end to the terror of the Revolution against the children?'[59] Without trying to undermine the argument which posits Slovenia at the forefront of these debates, it is indispensable to paint a more nuanced picture and consider facts which somewhat undermine the already taken for granted anti-JNA/anti-Yugoslav tendencies among the Slovenian youth. At the end of 1986, an internal document emphasised that the claim that the attitude of the Slovenian youth towards the army is negative is unfounded, since one can't equalise a critical attitude with a negative one. The document quoted a survey where 86 per cent of secondary school pupils said that a strong army was needed in order to preserve peace and confirmed that the number of Slovenian applicants to the military educational institutions was not decreasing, on the contrary.[60]

The unique role of the Yugoslav People's Army as a 'politically important factor' and one of the principal pillars of socialist Yugoslavia indeed contributed to its image as 'Yugoslavia's ninth province'.[61] Nevertheless, at the beginning of the 1980s the army still enjoyed a rather positive reputation in public life and in the youth media. A 1982 article entitled 'Some strange army' underlined the unconventional, social/community oriented role of the JNA:

> Seven thousand kilometres of roads. Seven hundred kilometres of railway lines. Five thousand flats a year. Three hundred thousand [trained] cooks a year. Four hundred thousand [trained] drivers a year. This is only a small part of the gift by the JNA to our society. While in some parts of this crazy planet the army 'convinces' its people that they haven't chosen the best road towards a better future, another army takes part in film and series shoots. While in some parts of this planet divided into blocs the army leaves the barracks in order to demonstrate its 'great concern' for its people, the same army from the first sentence leaves the barracks only when it needs to save its people from natural disasters.[62]

The realm of the obligatory military service was a diverse space that gathered youngsters from all strata and all parts of Yugoslav society, and it was what

Figure 9 Young army recruits in training, Skopje, 1980

provided the peace groups with their most powerful argument – the right to conscientious objection. Article 172 of the federal Constitution from 1974 stipulated that the 'Defence of the state shall be inviolable and inalienable right and the highest duty and honour of every citizen' and the evasion of the call for the military service was criminalised.[63] Hence, a refusal to respond to conscription entailed imprisonment and military service was strictly confined to the JNA.

Although the army was perceived and critiqued by peace activists as one homogenous, unanimous body that was conservative and unwilling to compromise, in reality, a slow process of negotiation and change was underway, as individuals who refused to carry arms were appointed to serve their military duty in parts of the JNA where carrying of arms was not required. Simo Spaskovski testified to the existence of a rather informal practice of accommodating individual cases of refusal of carrying arms:

> In 1979, as lieutenant of the Yugoslav People's Army, I was the commander of the platoon in the logistics educational battalion in Skopje. Despite the training for logistical duties, the soldiers also had to undergo combat training, which means they were given weapons. That year for the first time I had a soldier in my platoon who was a professional musician, who did not want to carry a weapon, did not want to be trained in shooting, but was willing to perform all

other tasks. In that situation, since there was no legislation, I got approval from my battalion commander that the soldier can serve without arms. So, he was deployed in the 'Military Club' to be in charge of the cultural and entertainment programs for the troops … So, this practice existed before being legally regulated.[64]

Activist Marko Hren also confirmed that he was allowed to serve the army without a weapon. Yet, his testimony also serves as an example of the often subjective criticism towards the officers seen as inferior – significantly conditioned by the subsequent armed conflicts and the role of the JNA in the Yugoslav dissolution:

> I did serve the army and I did not want to carry weapons, so I was working in culture. I was in the cultural department, I was playing in a band and I was organising cultural events.
> L.S.: *This was allowed because you objected?*
> I don't know. Now when I had an insight in the intelligence service archive, I saw they were following me before the military [service]. They immediately asked me if I would translate for them the papers I received from War Resisters International. So, I did. So, I think they had a plan. They wanted to know what our intentions are. They allowed me actually to be there without really being a soldier … And they continued following me.
> L.S.: *Was it a negative experience, would you say?*
> Being in the military for me was a decisive experience. I faced a ship of fools.
> L.S.: *Where did you serve?*
> In Belgrade. In the elite barracks. I was in the headquarters as a co-ordinator of news, for example. I did different things for the general staff. I was for example at the manoeuvres of the heavy artillery and I really saw that this is a pathological institution. People recruited in the headquarters were from the poor areas of Serbia and they were crazy … completely disorganised.

Indeed, conscription was not embraced enthusiastically by many from the cultural realm – on the contrary. The absolute majority of my interviewees – in particular those from the cultural milieus – expressed strong views on the futility of conscription and generally described it as an absolute waste of time. Zoran Predin underlined the often-quoted description of the JNA as the 'cemetery' for Yugoslav rock bands and 'the darkest side' of the country – through the prism of its subsequent role in the Yugoslav dissolution wars:

> The JNA was a cemetery for Yugoslav bands. The JNA destroyed so many good bands. It was the darkest side of the former Yugoslavia. If the politicians were smart enough to decrease the influence of the army in time, probably history would have turned out to be different. What should have been the forgery of brotherhood and unity, turned into the very opposite. The command cadres were more or less of Serb origin. I served the army in 1981 in Zagreb, after Tito's death – they were pretty nervous. I was sent to the anti-terrorist division.

Today all of that makes me laugh. After a couple of months I decided I've had enough, so I initiated an action which ended up with a diagnosis of *psychoneurosis nuclearis*, they let me go and I never came back. The entire Yugoslav project had the potential to survive only if it was democratised – at the right time, in the right manner. But it's easy to be smart now.

Senad Avdić, although formally a member of the Bosnian branch of the SSO, did not hesitate in describing the army as a 'stupid, inert, sluggish, dogmatic structure which was defending something that no one was attacking, as it turned out at the end, and was attacking something that no one defended':

L.S.: *What was your experience in the JNA?*
Ever so beautiful! [laughs] It was one repressive mechanism … An absurdly wasted year that I spent in Prishtina. 1986–87. They were preparing us for something without you knowing for what. The entire society in the mid-1980s entered a state of an unrelenting atrophy.

Although the debates on the role of the military and the right to conscientious objection reached their climax towards the end of the decade, there is a much broader story to be told regarding the issues of military conscription and the perception of the JNA among the youth in the 1980s, which begins well before the often quoted events. Namely, in December 1983 the federal assembly, through an expedited procedure, approved the amendments to the law on military service. The amendment foresaw a continuous fifteen-month period of military service for students replacing the previous system of 12+3 (likewise introduced through amendments in 1980). The presidency of the SSOJ lodged a request against the mode of approval through an expedited procedure, while the presidency of the ZSMS sent 'substantive comments' and conclusions from the public debate they organised. Both of these requests were ignored and the ZSMS put the blame on the Slovenian delegates at federal level who did not raise the question and hence did not properly represent their 'base'.[65] The perception of the ZSMS as more progressive and hence exceptional and different from the other Yugoslav branches was omnipresent among the interviewees and accepted as a well-established fact in the scholarly literature. While it cannot be denied that the ZSMS was more outspoken on these issues, it is also worth pointing out that there were cases, such as this one, when the federal youth organisation took the same line and upheld the demands of its Slovenian branch. In all of its written communication and complaints from the second half of 1983 sent to different political bodies regarding the lack of institutional debate on the law amendments and the 'expedited procedure' for their approval, the ZSMS referred to the fact that this 'is also the position of the Presidency of the League of Socialist Youth of Yugoslavia'.[66] The demand by the SSOJ that the law be amended in a regular procedure after all the open questions are resolved was

even supported by the JNA delegate to the SSOJ.[67] The different local organisations of the ZSMS forwarded their official conclusions and opinions on the
proposed amendments. The arguments which in this case came from the official youth bodies and were signed by the local youth functionaries have striking
resemblances to the later demands and to the language used by the activists
of the 'peace movement'. For example, a letter signed by the secretary of the
municipal conference of the ZSMS in Ilirska Bistrica stated the following: 'As a
humanist society we must strive to reduce the amount of weapons and to fight
for peace. That is why we advocate the reduction of the military service …
which would be particularly effective and would imply a reduction in the cost of
the JNA[68] which apparently consumes huge resources that in the contemporary
difficult economic situation could be spent more wisely.'[69] The Koper branch of
the ZSMS stated that 'It is very encouraging that the youth can have a debate
about these amendments today, which was not possible in the years 1980 and
1981, a right which we have guaranteed by the Constitution'.[70]

Although there was a widespread consensus that the fifteen-month obligatory military service should be replaced by a twelve-month period, most of the
letters from the regional ZSMS branches openly stated that a longer period
does not in itself guarantee an effective army and well-trained youth, and that,
on the contrary, there should be continuous exposure to military knowledge
and training. One could argue that this was a strategically framed argument
which in no way reflected the genuine attitudes of its authors, since it stands
in stark contrast with the contentious argumentation against the law in question. This echoes Paul Betts' claim with regard to the context of the GDR that
'People were good at exploiting the system using socialist civil rights language
to extract concessions from state authorities'.[71] On the other hand, it is equally
arguable that at this point in time the concept of national defence, the JNA
and Yugoslav self-management were still not subject of severe criticism, nor
were they discredited in the public eye to the same extent as in the late 1980s.
There is a telling parallel to be drawn between the East German 'peace movement' initiated in 1981, which was 'the campaign for a community "peace
service" as a real alternative to military service … Whilst protesters of all
kinds had to expect possible and sometimes severe punishment, the group's
rejection of militarism did not necessarily mean that they rejected the GDR
and all it stood for'.[72]

In October 1986 the presidency of the Republican Conference of the ZSMS
drafted 'theses' regarding the initiative about an alternative (civil) military
service for the upcoming discussion within the Commission for General People's Defence and Social Self-Protection at the Republican Conference of the
SSRNJ. Interestingly, although the document advanced demands and propositions which were in opposition to some of the core postulates of the Yugoslav

socialist defence system, it posited the initiative within the mainstream discursive framework:

> We are aware that safety is one of the fundamental values of every society. We are also aware that we have to fight for freedom over and over again and that it is not won forever and never again jeopardised ... We do not find the present way of dealing with the conscientious objectors (repetitive sentencing) appropriate and in accordance with socialist humanism as one of the fundamental orientations of our society ... Our conception of ONO and DS is based upon the individual as a decisive factor in our defense capabilities. Our opinion is that we must not give up in advance any category of the population (in this case the objectors), nor turn them into potential enemies of the system (usually the objectors are very loyal citizens) ... The [Second World War] liberation front of the Slovenian people included all kinds of people in its ranks who were ready to fight for the freedom of the people ... There were those among the partisans who never carried arms. But they carried the wounded ... thus the society and more specifically the JNA would make an exceptionally positive political move by recognising the right to conscientious objection ... Complaints about repression against the objectors would no longer be possible, while the society would have more benefit from them ... The sense that they are beneficial to society and that the society has not given up on them in advance would be important. An appropriate solution to the problem of conscientious objection would increase the reputation of socialist self-management worldwide.[73]

Indeed, 'Activists' vocabularies of protests are shaped and limited by ostensibly non-cultural political, economic and legal structures'.[74] In this case, the youth bodies were impelled to frame unconventional political demands using the institutional vocabulary of Yugoslav socialism. In 1986 the federal youth magazine *Mladost* published a 'dossier', i.e. a longer analysis on the initiative for civilian military service, where the argumentation similarly drew upon Marx, Kardelj, Yugoslavia's doctrine of mass participation in the system of all-people's defence and the formal dedication to the pursuit of peaceful conflict-resolution in international relations.[75] It also called for democratic resolution of such conflicts, strengthening of democratic instutional mechanisms and doing away with 'authoritarian-repressive forms of decision-making'. Similarly, an internal document about the new social movements in Slovenia and in Yugoslavia noted that:

> The Yugoslav attitudes about the demands the movements advance and which were presented at the youth congresses, belong to two extremes: that those are the real concerns of the contemporary times, to those that see them as an outright penetration of liberalism and counter-revolutionary attitudes ... In Slovenia we have publicly expressed our opinion in certain [institutional] spaces that the movements raise questions which are also questions [relevant]

for socialist self-management and that because of that their interests are an integral part of the pluralism of self-managing interests, and which in this way can gain prominence within the Socialist Alliance as a front of progressive forces. In this framework the movements would have to respect the rules of the game and eventually succumb to the will of the majority. Having said this, we can't ignore the fact that within these movements there are individuals or groups close to the positions of the bourgeois right, as well as that there were attempts of abusing the spontaneous movements for anti-socialist or anti-communist aims (certain slogans during the protests, certain articles in *Mladina*).[76]

The document further noted that within the Yugoslav People's Army circles there were different views on the matter and that there were signs of readiness to accept conscientious objection for religious reasons, but only if conscripts remained within the military. Although the official line of the army on the matter was well-known, this didn't prevent the process of consultation and negotiation to continue. For instance, in May 1986 the federal Defence Secretary met with representatives of the ZSMS to discuss the issue.[77] Robert Botteri similarly recalled his participation at a round-table discussion they initiated with the army, where military representatives who took part agreed that reform was necessary, but, later, when the official reports were published, it was on a completely different note: 'They had to write that they don't agree with us.' A year later, at its twenty-fourth session in July 1987, the presidency of the ZSMS adopted several conclusions pertaining to the conscientious objection initiative. In an official correspondence addressed to the Federal Secretariat for National Defence, it requested that the Secretariat provides information on the progress of the initiative (commenced in December 1985 within the SFRY presidency) for the annulment of the recurring court cases and verdicts against the conscientious objectors.[78] The letter also requested information on a particular individual – theatre director and member of the NSK network Dragan Živadinov, noting that since he was a public figure and all kinds of speculative information was circulating in the public, this 'could unnecessarily dishonour or damage the reputation of the JNA'.

These examples demonstrate how the formal youth structures chose a pragmatic, yet tactful, approach in order to articulate the demands and concerns coming from their 'base' or indeed from without its narrower membership body and to navigate and pave the space between the youth discontents and activists and the higher political/institutional realm. Not surprisingly, in order to add more argumentative weight, activists also referred to Resolution E/CN.4/RES/1987/46 of the United Nations Commission on Human Rights, which recommended 'to States with a system of compulsory military service, where such provision has not already been made, that they consider introducing various forms of alternative service for conscientious objectors which are compatible with the reasons for conscientious objection, bearing in mind the experience of some States in this respect, and that they refrain from subjecting such persons to imprisonment'.[79] The fact that Yugoslavia was among the fourteen countries which abstained from the vote (and not one of the two which voted against) lends legitimacy to the argument that in the second half of the 1980s the Yugoslav state and its army were already in the process of changing their policy on the potential venues for accommodating the different demands for civil military service. Hren's testimony echoes these developments. He emphasised that the peace activists were 'legalists' and confirmed their interaction with the different political organs and institutions of the system:

> Our interlocutors were institutions, both federal and republican ... We were in these terms legalists ... We were a human rights movement. Conscientious objection was a human right in the understanding of the UN. So, we were legalist. We have the UN, which is the supreme framework for human rights and Yugoslavia was not following ... The moment we came into conflict with the Yugoslav regime was the moment when Slovenian policy-makers, starting with the ZSMS, supported our ideas, and the Yugoslav [federal level] didn't.

The first battle was won when in December 1985 a decision by the federal presidency provided legal basis for the avoidance of repetitive prison sentences for conscientious objectors in a way that upon their second call they would be deployed in the army without an obligation to carry arms.[80] In August 1986 the decision was incorporated within the military legal system.[81] This did not satisfy the demands of the peace activists, as essentially it did not decriminalise conscientious objection. As a 1987 Helsinki Watch report noted: 'In short, in Yugoslavia, as in Poland, the tactic will probably continue to be one of accommodating protesters but not fully institutionalising and legalising conscientious objection and alternative service.'[82] However, in April 1989 the federal parliament adopted amendments to the 1985 law on the military service duty to accommodate those refusing to carry arms due to religious beliefs: 'The soldier who refuses to receive arms due to religious beliefs serves the military duty term without arms for the period of 24 months.'[83] Considering the fact that the regular military service was twelve months, this amendment was also generally seen as unsatisfactory, in particular because it did not foresee the option of a service outside of the military. Marko Hren labelled it 'an attempt to mislead public opinion'.[84] Nevertheless, this legal change indeed decriminalised conscientious objection and demonstrated that even within the army – seen as a bastion of political conservatism – there were processes of reform underway which ran counter to some of the core doctrines it embodied.

The event that sealed the possibility of any further negotiations with the army, cemented the anti-Yugoslav image of Slovenia and effectively paved the way for Slovenia's secession from Yugoslavia, was the so-called JBTZ affair, or 'the trial of the four'.[85] It has been hailed as the milestone event leading to Slovenian independence and the single most important event of the 'Slovenian spring'. Following the arrest of the four on 31 May 1988 on suspicion of disclosure of military secrets, the ensuing trial at the military court in Ljubljana sparked mass protests, shook the Yugoslav political scene to the core and led to a relative homogenisation of the Slovenian public. The 'Committee for the defence of Janez Janša', which was later renamed as the 'Committee for the defence of human rights', came to represent all oppositional voices – the main points of contestation being that civilians were tried at a military court and the trial was conducted in Serbo-Croatian language. However, the indictment was not in breach of the existing legal and constitutional framework. Article 221 from the 1974 federal Constitution stipulated that criminal offences committed by military personnel and certain criminal offences committed by other persons relating to the national defence and security of the country, as well as other legal matters relating to disputes in connection with the service in the Yugoslav People's Army will be decided upon by military court. The indictment was based on Article 224 of the federal penal code: 'Whoever without authority communicates, confers or otherwise makes accessible to another information which constitutes a military secret, or whoever compiles such information with a view to convey it to an unauthorised person, shall be punished by imprisonment for a term exceeding three months but not exceeding five years.'[86] The trial came as a convenient occasion to fuse the different types of anti-regime critique, as the protests were not so much about the defence of Janša or the other three in particular. Indeed, they presented an opportunity to articulate a deeper and more serious type of critique of the entire existing state, political and legal order. This event could also be considered 'the point of no return' where an anti-regime, but pro-Yugoslav sentiment was irreversibly dissipating and losing any Yugoslav content that was left, and where all hopes for the democratisation of Yugoslavia began to wither away. Although the 'opposition', including *Mladina*, became openly and unanimously antagonistic to the army and the politics of the Serbian Party, reflecting back on the event occurs through a different lens, as Robert Botteri's testimony shows:

> Janša used to write for *Mladina*, he even ended up in prison because of *Mladina*, which was some kind of repression against *Mladina* … In that phase of the struggle for democratisation we were on the same side. Later, when he turned into a nationalist and a professional politician, we quickly parted ways … Especially because even before the war, in 1990, we proposed that Slovenia unilaterally de-militarises and thus sets an example for everyone in Yugoslavia – 'Look, we stand for a society without an army, we call upon you to do the same and solve this peacefully'. But, Janša sabotaged that action, they labelled us

'traitors' and they chose a war. Later he turned into the politician who uses all means just to stay in power.

The role of the army in the Yugoslav political system, in society and in public life was first put under scrutiny in the official youth media in Slovenia, while the ZSMS decided to uphold the initiatives for conscientious objection of a relatively small group of peace activists and hence incite an all-Yugoslav debate. As one of the 'socio-political organisations', it initially framed the demands within the vocabulary of Yugoslav socialist self-management. The debate on nuclear disarmament was similarly taken up by the SSOJ and produced greater consensus at federal level. As the decade wore on, the socialist rhetoric was dissipating and the differences in the political and public arena deepened, but at the same time there was an increasing awareness within the political and the army leadership that some of the demands put forward by the youth organisation should be accommodated. To refer back to Isin's definition of 'acts of citizenship', these initiatives sheltered by the different branches of the SSOJ managed to transform the established forms/modes of being political through re-creating and using parts of the youth infrastructure as legitimate, institutional sites and channels of struggle, requiring the state to respond and engage.

Despite the fact that the federal youth organisation did not explicitly endorse all of the initiatives stemming from the new social movements, it did provide spaces for some of them and increased the visibility of their demands in the public space. While the youth bodies were borrowing from the state vocabulary in order to frame and articulate their initiatives and demands more successfully, the institutions of late socialist Yugoslavia were reluctantly, but slowly consenting to the various calls for democratisation and doing away with certain taboos and subjects which so far had not been considered as legitimate arenas for political expression. The appropriation of some of the socialist/self-management values and vocabulary both by the youth organisation and by the activists themselves reflected an implicit support for some of the postulates of Yugoslav socialism – above all the concepts of solidarity, equality and emancipation. The way they framed their 'acts of citizenship' and articulated their demands conflated their particular identity as stemming from the Yugoslav context, with a transnational/international realm which served both as a personal inspiration and a platform for meaningful exchange and interaction. Thus, Helsinki Watch was right in drawing a line of distinction between the young activists sheltered by the youth organisation and the more visible nationalist dissidents, when it observed that 'the young people infused the official organisations with their enthusiasm, to "keep the system going, but, at the same time, to change it for the better" – thus by-passing the route of repression and preoccupation with personal defense that became the lot of Yugoslavia's civil rights and nationalist dissidents'.[87]

Notes

1 'Gdansk 1980, when the autumn said no / Gdansk 1980, we kept our fingers crossed / Miners, students, shipyard, all of us / Gdansk 1980, boiling factories / You don't send twice tanks against the workers / They didn't dare, we won, all of us / Poland in my heart ...' (from the song 'Poland in my heart').

2 See: Padraic Kenny, *A Carnival of Revolution: Central Europe 1989* (Princeton: Princeton University Press, 2003).

3 *Youth Prospects in the 1980s: Synthesis Report Presented to the General Conference of UNESCO at its Twenty-First Session* (Paris: UNESCO, 1980), p. 23.

4 'Yugoslavia', in *From Below – Independent Peace and Environmental Movements in Eastern Europe and the USSR* (New York: Helsinki Watch Report 1987), p. 186. Not only Solidarity and the events in Poland provoked a widespread media attention, they were also the subject of several publications, among which: Vladimir Lay (ed.), *Društveni pokreti i politički sistem u Poljskoj 1956–1981* (Beograd: Institut društvenih nauka, 1985); Biserka Rajčić (ed.), *Poljsko pitanje: članci, eseji, polemike* (Beograd: Radionica SIC, 1985); Dana Mesner and Stane Andolšek, *Solidarność v poljski krizi: 1980–1982* (Ljubljana: Republiška konferenca ZSMS/Univerzitetna konferenca ZSMS, 1985). For an analysis of the reaction to Solidarity in Western Europe, see: Idesbald Goddeeris, *Solidarity with Solidarity: Western European Trade Unions and the Polish Crisis, 1980–1982* (Plymouth: Lexington Books, 2010).

5 As cited in: Slobodan Stanković, *The End of the Tito Era: Yugoslavia's Dilemmas* (Stanford: Hoover Institution Press, 1981), p. 33.

6 *Predlog dokumenti dvanaestog kongresa Saveza socijalističke omladine Jugoslavije, Beograd 12–14 juna 1986* (Beograd: Konferencija SSOJ/Službeni list SFRJ, 1986), p. 93.

7 *Ibid.*

8 Mirko Mlakar, 'SSO ipak nije siv', *Borba* (17–18 January 1987), pp. 2–3.

9 Archive of Slovenia, Ljubljana (hereafter AS), *RK ZSMS 1974–1990*, AS 538, technical unit 383, '12 kongres ZSMS, Krško'.

10 Srećko Mihailović, 'Ka novoj političnosti: mnenje omladine o novim društvenim pokretima', in Srećko Mihailović *et al.*, *Deca krize: Omladina Jugoslavije krajem osamdesetih* (Beograd: Institut društvenih nauka/Centar za politikološka istraživanja i javno mnenje, 1990), p. 127.

11 In 1984 a petition for the abolition of the death penalty signed by 866 individuals was submitted to the federal assembly and published in *Mladina*. Thirty-nine death sentences were carried out in Yugoslavia between 1970 and 1979. See: *Yugoslavia: Prisoners of Conscience* (London: Amnesty International Publications, 1985), p. 87.

12 For a transnational approach in studying the grassroot social movements in Central Europe, see: Gerd-Rainer Horn and Padraic Kenny (eds), *Transnational Moments of Change: Europe 1945, 1968, 1989* (Lanham: Rowman & Littlefield, 2004); Kenny, *A Carnival of Revolution*; David Featherstone, *Solidarity: Hidden Histories and Geographies of Internationalism* (London and New York: Zed Books, 2012).

13 Marko Hren maintained links with the War Resisters' International office in London. See: Marko Hren, 'The Slovenian peace movement: An insider's account', in Bojan Bilić and Vesna Janković (eds), *Resisting the Evil: [Post] Yugoslav Anti-War Contention* (Baden Baden: NOMOS, 2012), pp. 63–83.

14 Mihailović *et al.*, *Deca krize*, p. 282.

15 Chris Bohn, 'Non-aligned punk', *Melody Maker* (22 March 1980), pp. 24–5.

16 J. Siftar, Zagreb, Yugoslavia, 'Serbo-Croats rule – ok?', *New Musical Express* (14 June 1975), p. 42.

17 'Raising the curtain', *Melody Maker* (18 February 1978), p. 14.

18 William Zimmerman, *Open Borders, Nonalignment, and the Political Evolution of Yugoslavia* (Princeton: Princeton University Press, 1987), p. 70.

19 Stef Jansen, 'After the red passport: Towards an anthropology of the everyday geopolitics of entrapment in the EU's "immediate outside"', *Journal of the Royal Anthropological Institute* 15:4 (2009), 815–32, p. 828.

20 Wendy Bracewell, 'Adventures in the marketplace: Yugoslav travel writing and tourism in the 1950s-1960s', in Anne E. Gorsuch and Diane P. Koenker (eds), *Turizm: The Russian and East European Tourist under Capitalism and Socialism* (Ithaca: Cornell University Press, 2006), p. 264.

21 Aleš Debeljak, *Twilight of the Idols: Recollections of a Lost Yugoslavia* (Buffalo: White Pine Press, 1994).

22 In Switzerland, youth groups with similar demands for de-militarisation, civil service, cuts in the military budget and non-violent forms of resistance managed to gather the minimum of 100,000 signatures required to secure a popular referendum on the issue of the abolition of the Swiss Army in April 1987. The initiative was rejected by popular vote both in 1987 and 1989. On the parallels between the Swiss and the Yugoslav defence policies, see: Pierre Maurer, 'Defence and foreign policy: Switzerland and Yugoslavia compared', in Marko Milivojević, John B. Allcock and Pierre Maurer (eds), *Yugoslavia's Security Dilemmas: Armed Forces, National Defence and Foreign Policy* (Oxford and New York: Berg Publishers, 1988), pp. 97–125.

23 Different individual activists have pointed to different European countries/cities as decisive in their socialisation as activists. For Mojca Dobnikar it was the encounter with Berlin that was decisive. See: 'Mojca Dobnikar: Ne bom dala miru, dokler ne bom imela Berlina v Ljubljani', in Suzana Tratnik and Nataša S. Segan (eds), *Zbornik o lezbičnem gibanju na Slovenskem 1984–1995* (Ljubljana: ŠKUC, 1995), pp. 100–4.

24 Gordana Milijašević, 'Domovina sa naslovne strane – što ovih dana o Jugoslaviji govore i pišu Englezi?', *Polet* 396 (14 October 1988), p. 13.

25 Slovenia was said to have 'asserted its Central European identity forcefully' when it rejected an invitation to the Balkan Summit in Crete in November 1997. See: Geoffrey Swain and Nigel Swain, *Eastern Europe since 1945* (London: Palgrave Macmillan, 2003), p. 243.

26 Dubravka Zarkov, 'Feminism and the disintegration of Yugoslavia: On the politics of gender and ethnicity', *Social Development Issues* 24:3 (2002), 59–68.

27 In October 1978, the Student Cultural Centre in Belgrade hosted the international conference entitled 'Comrade Woman: The Woman's Question: A New Approach?' [*Drugarica žena. Žensko pitanje: novi pristup?*], which explored the issue of inequality and challenged the myth of gender equality in socialist self-management. The attendance of feminists from France, Italy, Britain, West Germany, Poland and Hungary made it a unique initiative of second-wave feminism in Eastern Europe. See: Chiara Bonfiglioli, ' "Social equality is not enough,

we want pleasure!"': Italian feminists in Belgrade for the 1978 "Comrade woman" conference', *ProFemina* (2011), 116–22.

28 Staša Zajović *et al.*, 'Ženske akcije sad i ovde', *Student* 25–26 (25 December 1987), p. 8.

29 Slovenia, Croatia, Montenegro and Vojvodina decriminalised homosexual rela-tionships in 1977. The different Republics' penal codes had different wordings and age limits – for instance, in Slovenia the age of fourteen was taken as the minimum age of consent, while in Croatia it was eighteen. See: Dean Vuletić, 'Gay i lezbijska povijest Hrvatske od Drugog svjetskog rata do 1990', *Gordogan* 1:45 (2003), 104–23. For comparison, homosexuality in England was decriminalised by the Sexual Offences Act 1967 (both men had to have attained the age of twenty-one), while in Scotland it was decriminalised in 1980 and in Northern Ireland in 1982.
    In the realm of popular culture, Croatian rock band Prljavo kazalište [Dirty theatre] released the first gay-themed song 'Some boys' [*Neki dječaci*] in 1979, followed by Belgrade new wave band Idoli [Idols] in 1980 and their widely popular song 'I rarely see you with girls' [*Retko te viđam sa devojkama*]. Serbian pop rock artist Oliver Mandić introduced the drag look and cross-dressing through his show on Belgrade Radio-Television 'Belgrade at night', which won the 1981 Rose d'Or award for entertainment television. Croatian band Xenia released the lesbian-themed song 'My girl-friend' [*Moja prijateljica*] in 1983, while Slovenian Borghesia experimented with explicit references to homosexuality in their video art.

30 'Festival Magnus', http://slovenska-pomlad.si/1?id=168 (last accessed 28 April 2016); see also: Sanja Kajinić, 'Dismantling the geotemporality of Europeanization: The first European festival of lesbian and gay film was Yugoslav', *Southeastern Europe* 40 (2016), 13–31.

31 Jasenka Kodrnja and Katarina Vidović, 'SOS telefon za žene i djecu žrtve nasilja', *Žena* 46 (1988), 68–77, p. 69.

32 *Ibid.*, p. 74.

33 *Ibid.*, pp. 76–7.

34 Sanja Sagasta, 'State of the art: Lesbian movements in former Yugoslavia', *The European Journal of Women's Studies* 8:3 (2001), 357–72.

35 Nataša Lalić, 'Totalno relativni spol, *Polet* 422 (26 January 1990), p. 30.

36 The festival of gay and lesbian film began in 1984 and became a traditional annual event, with the exception of 1987 when it was banned after a launch of media alle-gations that it was in fact an international congress of homosexuals. The full list of films – predominantly from Western Europe and the United States, is available at: www.ljudmila.org/siqrd/fglf/20/20let.php (last accessed 23 September 2016).

37 'Predstavitev ženskih skupin v Ljubljani', in Tratnik and Segan, *Zbornik o lezbičnem gibanju*, p. 29.

38 A conference entitled 'The social position of women and the development of family in self-managing socialist society' was organised by the Party between the 18th and 20th of March 1976. Having provoked a polemic debate between the party hard-liners and the feminists, it is considered as the feminist 'coming out' in Yugoslavia.

39 Zarkov, 'Feminism and the disintegration of Yugoslavia'.

40 Lepa Mlađenović *et al.*, 'Ženske akcije sad i ovde', *Student* 25–26 (25 December 1987), p. 9.

41 'Predstavitev ženskih skupin v Ljubljani', in Tratnik and Segan, *Zbornik o lezbičnem gibanju*, p. 30.

42 Arguably, 'Since the state was not the primary addressee of their demands, because it enabled the institutionalisation of equality, feminists did not question the state apparatus. Socialist system, on the other hand, promised to work towards the full emancipation of the human being, and feminists saw themselves rather as the allies than the foes of that cause ... A self-managing socialist state was necessary, but not sufficient for the full emancipation of the human being, regardless of its gender.' See: Adrijana Zaharijević, 'Being an activist: feminist citizenship through transformations of Yugoslav and post-Yugoslav citizenship regimes', *CITSEE Working Paper Series 2013/28*.

43 Žarana Papić quotes the right to education, the right to work, the right to divorce and the right to abortion as 'essential women's human rights' which women enjoyed under socialism. She argues that by granting these rights, the male-dominated patriarchal socialist order worked actually to silence and disempower women. See: Žarana Papić, 'Bivša muškost i ženskost bivših građana bivše Jugoslavije', in A. Zaharijević, D. Duhaček and Z. Ivanović (eds), *Žarana Papić. Tekstovi 1977–2002* (Beograd: Centar za studije roda i politike, Rekonstrukcija ženski fond i Žene u crnom, 2012).

44 'Feminism in Yugoslavia', in Sabrina P. Ramet, *Social Currents in Eastern Europe: The Sources and Consequences of the Great Transformation* (Durham, NC: Duke Unviersity Press, 1995), p. 226.

45 Slađana Marković, 'Feminizam – alternative ili ne', *Student* 25–26 (25 December 1987), p. 8.

46 On the organisation of the Yugoslav defence system – the JNA, as well as the 'Territorial Defence', see: Marko Milivojević, John B. Allcock and Pierre Maurer (eds), *Yugoslavia's Security Dilemmas: Armed Forces, National Defence and Foreign Policy* (Oxford and New York: Berg Publishers, 1988); Zvezdan Marković, *Jugoslovanska ljudska armada (1945–1991)* (Ljubljana: Založba Defensor, 2007).

47 *Youth Prospects*, p. 36.

48 The debate revolved around issues of cost, environmental damage and prospective divisions of the country into Western and Eastern 'nuclear spheres'. On some of these debates, see: Open Society Archive, digital archive (hereafter OSA), Slobodan Stankovic, 'Nuclear energy: A political Pandora's box', *Radio Free Europe Situation Report*, 27 March 1986; Maurizio Olenik, 'Zelena ZSMS', in *Kompendij za bivše in bodoče politike* (Ljubljana: ZSMS, 1989), pp. 125–42.

49 'Yugoslavia', in *From Below*, pp. 191–3.

50 In the academic sphere, a Croatian university professor called for re-examination and a reversal of the decision for the construction of a nuclear power plant in Prevlaka, Croatia, quoting a range of international – American and Western European – scholars and sources that gave credibility to the anti-nuclear argument. See: Inge Perko-Šeparović, 'Alternativni interesi', *Politička misao* 23:1 (1986), 90–100.

51 Marijan Grakalić, 'Kako se dogodio kongres omladine Jugoslavije', *Polet* 352 (20 June 1986), p. 6.

52 The anti-nuclear sentiment was not a novel thing. In the late 1970s, parts of the Yugoslav music scene formulated a creative response to the global concerns related to nuclear threats and the Cold War. For instance, the bend *Atomsko Sklonište* [Nuclear Shelter] in the cover song of their 1978 album *Ne cvikaj, generacijo* sang: 'Što te panika hvata/Neće biti, neće biti trećeg svjetskog rata/Nećemo valjda biti mi ta nesretna generacija/Na kojoj će se izvršiti velika posljednja racija' [Why are you caught up in panic / There won't be a third world war / Hopefully we won't be that unlucky generation / That will suffer the last big raid]. Similar concerns were espoused by the early 1980s British punk scene, where groups from the second wave of punk gave proliferation to concerns of the youth ranging from police brutality, conscription and unemployment, to a looming nuclear crisis. As Worley notes, 'between 1980 and 1984, countless punk songs gave vent to rage at the prospect of war and/or revelled in the gory detail of the nuclear aftermath'. Matthew Worley, 'One nation under the bomb: The Cold War and British punk to 1984', *Journal for the Study of Radicalism* 5:2 (2011), 65–83, p. 77.

53 Maurizio Olenik, 'Zelena ZSMS', in *Kompendij za bivše in bodoče politike*, p. 127.

54 'Yugoslavia nuclear chronology', *Nuclear Threat Initiative*, www.nti.org/media/pdfs/yugoslavia_nuclear.pdf?_=1316466791 (last accessed 25 February, 2014).

55 Maurizio Olenik, 'Zelena ZSMS', in *Kompendij za bivše in bodoče politike*, p. 130.

56 Secondary military schools: School of Land Forces – Sarajevo [SVŠ KoV – Sarajevo], Music Secondary Military School [Muzička SVŠ – Sarajevo], Procurement Secondary Military School – Sarajevo [Intendantska SVŠ – Sarajevo], Technical Secondary Military School of Land Forces – Zagreb [TSVŠ KoV – Zagreb], Naval Technical Secondary Military School – Split [Mornaričko-tehnička SVŠ – Split], Medical Secondary Military School – Novi Sad [Sanitetska SVŠ – Novi Sad]; Military gymnasiums: Air Force High School 'Marshal Tito' – Mostar [Vazduhoplovna gimnazija], 'Brotherhood and Unity' – Belgrade, 'Ivo Lola Ribar' – Zagreb, 'Franc Rozman Stane' – Ljubljana; Military academies: Technical Military Academy of Land Forces – Zagreb, Military Academy of Land Forces – Belgrade, Air Force Technical Military Academy – Rajlovac, Air Force Military Academy – Zadar, Naval Military Academy – Split.

57 Simo Spaskovski (born 1954), a retired colonel, was a junior officer who began his professional service in 1978. He studied at the air force gymnasium in Mostar and recounted an organised visit to a lecture by a yoga guru who was touring Europe in the early 1970s, something that proved decisive for him – he has been practicing yoga ever since. He maintained that the JNA was pretty liberal in that sense, as they had a rock band in the gymnasium and people were free to have long hair. Indeed, although social, class and lifestyle divisions were real, there was also a sense of shared values, fashions and styles, regardless of whether one was a military school student or a young urban rock musician or peace activist.

58 See: Florian Bieber, 'The role of the Yugoslav People's Army in the dissolution of Yugoslavia: The army without a state?', in Jasna Dragović-Soso and Lenard J. Cohen (eds), *State Collapse in South-Eastern Europe: New Perspectives on Yugoslavia's Disintegration* (West Lafayette: Purdue University Press, 2007), pp. 301–32.

59 'Vzgoja oboroženega ljudstva', *Mladina* 14 (14 June 1989), p. 6. See also: Blaž Vurnik, *Med Marxom in Punkom* (Ljubljana: Modrijan, 2005).

60 AS 538, *RK ZSMS 1974–1990*, technical unit 391, 'Spontana družbena gibanja. Gradivo je interno', 3 November 1986. A classified military report produced by the Slovenian Secretariat for National Defence in August 1984 concluded that the military high school in Ljubljana and the Air Force High School in Mostar attract four-fifths of all Slovenian applicants. Considered to be the elite military educational institutions, the Air Force High School and the Air Force Academy were indeed the most competitive and the most attractive. AS 538, *RK ZSMS 1974–1990*, technical unit 364, 'Informacija o odzivu za vojaške šole v letu 1984', August 1984, p. 10.

61 Adam Roberts, 'Yugoslavia: The constitution and the succession', *The World Today* 34:4 (1978), 136–146, p. 145.

62 'Čudna neka vojska', *Mladost* 1268 (18 January 1982). The army was involved in a range of non-military activities, its social role and presence being rooted in the character of Yugoslav self-managing socialism. For instance, between 1945 and 1972 its engineering units built 3,400km of roads, 116 tunnels, 9,996m of bridges, on average 100km of water supply pipes per year, the army participated massively in rescue and reconstruction during floods and after earthquakes, and around one million conscripts got training certification for e.g. drivers, nurses, cooks during their army service. See: Radisav Ristić, 'Učešće JNA u izgradnji zemlje', *Jugoslovenski pregled* (April 1981), pp. 53–60.

63 Article 214 of the federal Penal Code read:

    (1)   Whoever, without justifiable cause, fails to report for military conscription, for the war assignment or reception of arms, or for the compulsory military service, military training or any other military duty at the appointed time, even though he has been summoned by an individual or general call-up, shall be fined or punished by imprisonment for a term not exceeding one year.

    (2)   Whoever has hidden himself in order to evade military conscription referred to in paragraph 1 of this article, even though he has been summoned by an individual or general call-up, shall be punished by imprisonment for a term exceeding three months but not exceeding five years.

    (3)   Whoever escapes abroad or without authority remains abroad with a view to evading the recruitment, statutory obligation as to military service, drill or any other military duty, shall be punished by imprisonment for a term exceeding one year but not exceeding 10 years.

64 Email correspondence, 19 November 2013.

65 AS 538, *Republiška konferenca Zveze socialistične mladine Slovenije, 1974–1990*, technical unit 364, 'Zadeva: ugotavljanje odgovornosti za nepravilnosti v postopku sprejemanja Zakona o spremembah in dopolnitvah Zakona o vojaški obveznosti', 9 February 1984.

66 *Ibid.*

67 AS 538, *RK ZSMS 1974–1990*, technical unit 364, 'Informacija o postopku sprejemanja zakona o spremembah in dopolnitvah Zakona o vojaški obveznosti', 10 January 1984.

68 The army's budget was reduced progressively from 1976. While for the period 1976–80 it was allocated 6.17 per cent of national income, it received only 5.39. Although in 1980 the new five-year plan foresaw a budget at 5.8 per cent, during

the first two years it reached 4.79. In addition, the JNA was reduced from 252,000 soldiers in 1981 to 210,000 at the end of 1986. Professionalisation of the military was undertaken with legal amendments in 1985 and the recruitment of professionals in 1987. See: James Gow, 'Legitimacy and the military: Yugoslav civil-military relations and some implications for defence', in Marko Milivojević, John B. Allcock and Pierre Maurer (eds), *Yugoslavia's Security Dilemmas: Armed Forces, National Defence and Foreign Policy* (Oxford and New York: Berg Publishers, 1988), pp. 60–94.

69 AS 538, *RK ZSMS 1974–1990*, technical unit 364, 'Občinska konferenca ZSMS Ilirska Bistrica, Razprava o "vojaški obveznosti"', 21 October 1983.

70 AS 538, *RK ZSMS 1974–1990*, technical unit 364, 'Stališća Komisije za SLO in DS pri OK ZSMS Koper'.

71 Paul Betts, *Within Walls: Private Life in the German Democratic Republic* (Oxford and New York: Oxford University Press, 2010), p. 186.

72 Anna Saunders, *Honecker's Children: Youth and Patriotism in East Germany, 1979–2002* (Manchester: Manchester University Press, 2011), p. 67.

73 AS 538, *RK ZSMS 1974–1990*, technical unit 364, 'Teze za razpravo: Ob pobudi za civilne službo', 20 October 1986.

74 Francesca Polletta, '"Free spaces" in collective action', *Theory and Society* 28 (1999), 1–38, p. 17.

75 Mirjana Križman, 'Civilna vojna služba: Prigovor savesti protiv naoružanog naroda', *Mladost* 23 (28 July–10 August 1986), pp. 25–8.

76 AS 538, *RK ZSMS 1974*–1990, technical unit 391, 'Spontana družbena gibanja. Gradivo je interno', 3 November 1986.

77 Vurnik, *Med Marxom in Punkom*.

78 AS 538, *RK ZSMS 1974*–1990, technical unit 391, 'Predsednik RK ZSMS Tone Andrelič, to Zvezni sekretarijat za ljudsko obrambo'.

79 UN Commission on Human Rights, *Conscientious objection to military service*, 10 March 1987, E/CN.4/RES/1987/46.

80 Marko Hren, 'Svoboda misli je sicer vsem zagotovljena, kar pa še ne pomeni, da je izražanje te misli tudi vedno dovoljeno', in *Kompendij za bivše in bodoče politike*, pp. 45–68.

81 Ivan Čečko, a Jehovah's Witness from the Slovenian town of Maribor who spent fifteen years in prison (in a series of repetitive sentencing) was released in November 1987. From 1972 until 1987, 152 individuals were sentenced for refusing to carry arms on religious grounds – most of them were Jehovah's Witnesses, Seventh-Day Adventists and Nazarenes. See: 'Yugoslavia', in *From Below*.

82 *Ibid.*, p. 203.

83 'Указ за прогласување на законот за измени и дополненија за законот за воената обврска', *Службен лист на Социјалистичка Федеративна Република Југославија* 26/1989 (21 април 1989); 'Pravilnik o vršenju vojne obaveze', *Službeni vojni list* 21/1991 (25 september 1991).

84 By 1990 the demand for conscientious objection and 'civilian military service' had transformed into a demand for de-militarisation and abolishment of the army: Zoran Oštrić, 'Marko Hren: Vojsku treba ukinuti', *Polet* 422 (26 January 1990), p. 13.

85 JBTZ stands for the surnames of the four indictees: journalist and former youth functionary (Janez) Janša, JNA sergeant major (Rajko) Borštner, *Mladina* journalist David Tasić and *Mladina* editor (Franci) Zavrl. Eventually, Janša and Zavrl were sentenced each to one-and-a-half years in prison, Tasić to five months and Borštner to four years.

86 *Yugoslavia: Criminal Code of the Socialist Federal Republic of Yugoslavia*, 1 July 1977, www. refworld.org/docid/3ae6b5fe0.html (last accessed 28 April 2014).

87 'Yugoslavia', in *From Below*, p. 195.

The eighty-eighters: the arena of youth politics and the break-up of Yugoslavia

Socijalizam sinova ne može
u svojoj konkretnoj viziji i oličenju biti
socijalizam očeva.[1]

Milan Kučan (1986)

'With the abolishment of the Youth Baton we lost an archaic ritualistic practice, but in return we obtained nothing. In other words, we obtained an empty space, within which democratic struggles could commence', concluded the young authors of an essay entitled 'The twilight of the youth baton'.[2] Indeed, the space which throughout the 1980s was cleared of what was perceived to be outdated Yugoslav socialist rubble by the various reformist youth and student initiatives, was only partially filled with new progressive and democratic content. The withering class/Marxist paradigm by the end of the 1980s was being replaced by an ethno-national one, while in the more dominant political and cultural arenas the different voices coming from within the youth sphere were outperformed or overshadowed and did not have the vigour to counter the ones coming from more senior actors. The radical political decentralisation of the state, which in the 1980s opened the way for the emergence of many pockets of opposition (liberal, socialist reformist, nationalist) was understood by some as the implementation of the Marxist notion of the withering away of the state,[3] which the Yugoslav political elites were committed to and upon which they sought to build unity after the Second World War. More crucially, however, as Dejan Jović convincingly argues, it was the progressive 'breakdown of the elite ideological consensus'[4] after 1974 that eventually brought the country to a collapse. It was in particular during the second half of the 1980s that the fractures along what has been referred to as Yugoslavia's 'natural cleavage lines'[5] started to become more exposed, during a period of intensified intra-party struggles and weakening federal institutional framework. Different actors began competing for the space which was gradually emptied of the doctrine of socialist self-management. In this context, with the exception of the youth leaderships in Serbia (proper) and Montenegro, the political youth realm realigned mainly around reformist and liberal ideas. Although, in hindsight, the dominance and superiority of ethnic politics and nationalist parties is often taken for granted and as a *fait accompli*, the state of affairs at the end of the 1980s was such that there were many potential venues for other outcomes of the crisis. A consensus that change and doing away with the old was necessary, albeit without a common platform about the content and the manner in which change was to be achieved, was a dominant discursive stream within the volatile late Yugoslav public sphere. At the same time, reformed communists and ardent nationalists were competing with a range of liberal and social-democratic platforms and actors, some guarding hope that they would be able to triumph at the federal elections that never materialised. In this context, it is important to re-emphasise the heterogeneity of the youth leaderships both at republican/provincial and at federal level and the fact that different individuals within the same presidency or 'Republic's Conference' of the SSOJ could hold disparate views.

While the early 1980s witnessed the growth of cultural and journalistic challenges to the institutional youth sphere, by the late 1980s, the entire set-up of the SSOJ was being challenged, primarily due to its takeover by a new generation of political activists whose political views converged around socially liberal concepts. Political cleavages among 'liberals' and 'conservatives' powerfully crystallised around 1988, creating divides that would become influential in shaping the politics of a post-Yugoslav era. These new elites would play pivotal roles in negotiating the changing role of the SSOJ, some trying to maintain a transrepublican organisation, some increasingly turning to republican-based units that foreshadowed the break-up of the country. This chapter seeks to add new perspectives to current narratives of youth and the dissolution of Yugoslavia, through the inclusion of republics other than Slovenia, and through bringing a new angle to late Yugoslav politics by uncovering an overlooked trans-republican convergence around progressive, loosely defined liberal values.

This chapter addresses the ways the youth organisation initially sought to reform and reinvent its role and mission and was later subsumed in, and divided by the wider Yugoslav political debates and developments in the country. Nevertheless, there was a range of shared values and beliefs across the SSOJ, as suggested by the fact that several of its branches were transformed into liberal political parties after 1989.[6] The events of 1988 (the 'anti-bureaucratic revolution', the abolishment of the Youth relay race, the 'trial of the four') are considered the most important tipping point in this context. In addition, it focuses on the debates over the future of the SSOJ and its eventual demise. The chapter seeks to analyse the outcomes of the debates which unfolded within the late socialist Yugoslav youth realm in the second half of the 1980s and some of the solutions which emerged and were proposed by different actors considering the future of the SSOJ. Essentially, it reflects upon the (lack of) consensus about the dilemma of how to modernise Yugoslav society and the sphere of institutional youth politics and culture. Initially, the youth organisation engaged with an internally generated debate on its reformation and with the question of self-abolishment of the youth organisation. This was accompanied by a marked shift in rhetoric and in the way reform was envisioned. This chapter also offers a perspective on the 1988 events 'from below', through the experiences of the political activists who worked for the SSOJ and/or happened to be in Belgrade during the political upheavals. 1988 accelerated the process of disintegration of the institutional youth sphere, through debates concerning its future and the future of the country on the eve of Yugoslavia's break-up. Finally, this chapter reflects upon the question of why this generation's sense of multilayered citizenship and vibrant activism failed to materialise into a viable pan-Yugoslav political alternative.

Attempts at reinventing institutional youth politics in the second half of the 1980s

A determination for change which, as late as 1986, had not stretched beyond the scope of the 'pluralism of self-managing interests', was transformed by 1988 into platforms, initiatives and demands which were almost entirely stripped of their original socialist shell. Members of the youth political elite initially argued for a more assertive role of the SSOJ, while later in the decade the central issue of contention and debate became the very redefinition of the role for the SSOJ. A shift away from the vocabulary of self-management and the pluralism of self-managing interests and towards a broad interest in human rights and freedoms, rule of law and political pluralism in the second half of the 1980s, unfolded both as a result of internally initiated debates within the SSOJ, but equally so in response to deepening political polarisation within the Yugoslav political scene. After 1987, these new political cleavages clearly affected different levels of the youth organisation. A national fracturing also saw greater divergence developing within the republican Youth Leagues, as what had once been a shared culture was gradually being lost.

1986 can be considered a pivotal moment for the SSOJ in this regard. It was the year of the 12th congress of the ZSMS – the so-called Krško congress, where members of the organisation pioneered a new vocabulary, new demands and forms of youth activism. The 'liberalisation' in Slovenia arguably coincided with the stepping down of conservative Party leader France Popit and the rise of a new younger leadership headed by Milan Kučan. It was Kučan who at the 27th session of the Central Committee of the SKJ in March 1986 said something which would become an often-quoted statement: 'The socialism of the sons, cannot be in its concrete vision and embodiement the socialism of the fathers ... Departing from what is already achieved, they search for materially and spiritually richer socialism, freer, more democratic and more humane. Every generation gives its own creative contribution.'[7] It was also the moment when the federal congress of the SSOJ for the first time abandoned mainstream socialist vocabulary and, in contrast to the report from its 1982 congress, produced a critical, analytical text outlining its position and mapping out the socio-political state of affairs. The period before and after the congresses was characterised by a partial fulfillment of the long-argued for change in the role of the youth organisation as a mere observer and passive participant in the system. Silvija Žugić-Rijavec, the only female president of the SSOJ in the 1980s, signalled this change and the subsequent reactions on behalf of the state and Party organs in her speech at the 27th session of the Central Committee of the federal Party, when she accused certain forces within the SKJ of acting in a 'paternalistic' manner not only towards the youth organisation, but also toward other socio-political organisations:

> As long as the youth organisation dealt only with different actions and demonstrations, apart from criticisms addressed to the League of Socialist Youth, there were no other problems. Since the XI congress and especially during the preparations for the XII congress, we emphasised the demand for democratisation of the relations within the youth organisation, for its vertical independence ... But, certain problems and conflicts have already appeared [because of that].[8]

Although the official discourse still revolved around the paradigm of responsible self-management, the formal report of the 1986 federal congress addressed certain concerns in a straightforward manner: 'The animosity which the young generation rightly feels towards the bureaucratised "all-political representatives" would soon be interpreted as a refusal of socialist self-management.'[9] The report abounds in calls to 'de-bureaucratise' the youth organisation and society and in attacks on the 'bureaucratic-technocratic ideology' and the 'youth bureaucracy'. Interestingly, the report begins with a quote by Edvard Kardelj, which reads as an attempt to relativise the superiority of socialism: 'Socialism cannot preserve the aureole of historical progressiveness only because it is called socialism in name, but only if it increasingly expands the dimensions of his [the working man's] freedom and democracy in society.'[10] Thus, the federal level of the SSOJ argued that new political forms were needed to keep the country up to date with contemporary technological developments: 'to the challenges and demands [encountered] at the point of transition into the era of informatics, microeletronics, robotics, i.e. the third scientific-technological revolution, [the socio-political organisations] responded with weapons from the past', or that 'in a system where decisions about the most important questions of social development are mainly made in two ways – through the state and the party, there is no space for the development of the youth organisation as an independent political subject'.[11] The congress programme also announced the incipient changes in the organisation and functioning of the SSOJ, by targeting the 'subjective forces [which] compile lists of societal changes without doing much to change themselves' and expressing a commitment towards 'radical change of the means of [our] struggle – the [youth] organisation itself'.[12] This commitment began to materialise with a marked change in the vocabulary of some of the official youth representatives – such as the already quoted statement by its president from 1987 that the inclusion of the new social movements is necessary, as well as the debate on the Youth relay which culminated in its abolishment in early 1988. The former was in line with the 1986 congress materials' call for the 'creation of space' within the youth organisation for the women's, the peace, the ecological and other 'progressive movements'. An attempt on the part of the federal leadership of the SSOJ to somehow reconcile and acknowledge the different grievances and visions is visible not only in the congress documents, but also in the subsequent attempts to strike a balance between those who sought radical change and those who argued for minimal change or the preservation of the existing norms and practices.

The different republican branches espoused 'change' within what was seen as a flexible institutional and political framework which had already undergone several constitutional changes and was susceptible to yet another reform. Yugoslav socialism had to be reformed, but not entirely abandoned. However, the way change was embraced and articulated differed significantly between Slovenia, for instance, and Macedonia or Serbia. Although certain individuals among the new Macedonian youth leadership who were elected at the 1986 congress of the SSMM would become vocal opponents of the regime and the status quo after 1988 and would shift their rhetoric and demands to match their Slovenian counterparts, the 1986 congress materials bear witness to an organisation which had not significantly departed from its previous congress framework. Although the congress was hailed as a congress of 'unity, action and change' and voiced most of the already established complaints such as youth unemployment, careerism, insufficient inclusion of the young in the delegate system and calls for effective 'de-bureacratisation', the congress stage was adorned with the slogan 'On Tito's path – in Tito's manner' [На титовиот пат титовски].[13] The Serbian SSO similarly organised its 1986 congress under the banner of 'change' [Мењајмо да нас не промене]. Zoran Anđelković, the president of the Serbian SSO, concluded his speech by reiterating how indispensable change was: 'This congress must be a congress of change ... Let's change the relationships within our organisation – let's make it more democratic, more open, more courageous ... Let's change those who oppose change.'[14] However, besides talking about the main problems facing the youth, he also referred to the 'forced emigration of Serbs and Montenegrins from Kosovo' as 'the biggest political problem in the country'.[15]

Thus, under the aegis of reform and change, 1986 saw the beginning of what would become an irreversible process of fragmentation of the SSOJ. The ZSMS launched more concrete demands which were articulated as slogans and printed on stickers on the occasion of its 1986 congress. Demanding democratisation of political culture, a more genuine worker's democracy and freedom of speech, it also hinted at the inherited, rigid forms from the past by outlining that 'we are not primarily interested in the "internal and the external" enemy, but in democratic self-managing decision-making which advances social development, because we want to live in the present that we will co-create'.[16] The concluding remarks of the speech of the president of the ZSMS read as a generational manifesto:

> For us there is no way back. A way back is a way to a slow, but certain death. It is a departure towards historical oblivion. We want to be a generation which decides and not only obeys. We want to be a generation of knowledge, new technology, flexible and effective economy, we want to be a generation of open culture and social imagination, a generation which is allowed to think with its own head and express those thoughts freely, a generation which is not and will not be satisfied with what had already been achieved; in brief, we want to be a generation of freedom and human dignity.[17]

Although the core of the 1986 congress programme of the ZSMS dealt with domestic issues, Zoran Thaler (born 1962), former ZSMS activist and later a member of the Liberal Party, Slovenian Minister of Foreign Affairs and a Member of the European Parliament, underlined the importance of the international context and in particular the political developments in Eastern Europe:

> L.S.: *How did ZSMS conceive of the 1986 platform?*
> I think one should consider the global context. Solidarity and the putsch on 13 December 1981 in Poland had a big impact upon me, my generation. I had just returned from the military and I remember well that during the first year at university I wore a Solidarity badge ... I organised an action of sending postcards to Jaruzelski ... We were also fascinated by the 1972 student movement. At that time the 'Library of revolutionary theory' [Knjižnica

revolucionarne teorije – KRT] appeared … There, a book was published on the student movement 1968–72 and it was a revelation for us … The main weapon was irony, sarcasm, cynicism … Krško [congress] was a litmus for the new time. It was also a resistance against the militarisation which developed after the 1981 Kosovo riots.

Some of the new political stances articulated by some members of the youth organisation in the late 1980s transcended the mainstream (conservative versus reformist/liberal) discourse. After 1986, as it was becoming clear that the ideological status quo was no longer tenable, different voices began to invade the political realm. Parts of the youth sphere demonstrated a relatively high degree of openness, creativity and imagination, as ideas ranged from democratic multiparty federalism, liberal democracy or hybrid variations of democratic socialism, as shown in this 1988 statement by Miha Kovač:

> We, in the circles around *Mladina* and the alternative movements, argue that you can have both economic and political democracy. We believe that self-management shoud remain as the institution of enterprise democracy, only the political bureaucracy should be removed from power – which could be accomplished by changes in the electoral system and by the creation of free trade unions, etc. … Our idea is to change this body (the Chamber of Socio-Political Organisations) into a democratic political assembly, without any leading role for the party. It would be elected directly, not on the basis of a classical multiparty system – which we think would be a regression – but on the basis of citizens organising themselves in various political movements expressing various interests.[18]

In the same interview Kovač asserted that the position of the Slovenian Party of not being interested in propagating democratisation for all Yugoslavia – a position which might lead to a confederation or establishment of independent states – is 'neither desired nor realistic'. This not only shows that the range of alternatives for filling the increasingly unstable and withering ideological space was immense, but also that this polyphony of political visions for the future of the institutional set-up could easily implode or turn into a cacophony. Against this background, the SSOJ increasingly became involved in wider societal issues and in new debates over rights and citizens. It progressively abandoned the older rhetoric of socialist self-management from 1988 onwards. In particular, certain branches became involved in rethinking the role of the citizen within socialism and drew on newly emerging political languages of human rights. One example was a decision of the SSOJ from 1988 to open up a public debate on the subject of 'The liberties, rights and duties of the man and citizen in the socio-political system of the SFRY'. The project was meant to 'bring to the surface a range of questions about the non-conflictual character of Yugoslav society', noting that the

'sanctioning of the duties in our, as in many other societies, is far more developed
than the respect and the advancement of human rights'.[19] The numerous affairs,
incidents and instances of popular unrest which occurred during 1987 and 1988
and required intervention by the police acted as the impetus for the youth organisation to use the occasion of the fortieth anniversary of the Universal Declaration of Human Rights for initiating the debate. The numerous strikes, protest
marches and interventions by the police were said to have raised an awareness
about citizens' rights, about their violation and 'the need for their development
and advancement in our country, which implied a rupture with the old way of
thinking about the once-and-for-all given and guaranteed rights and the perfec-
tion of the existing system and state of affairs'.[20] The presidency of the SSOJ
commissioned two young legal scholars – Goran Svilanović[21] (born 1963) and
Vojislav Stanimirović (born 1964) to write short summaries on the state of human
rights and freedoms in Yugoslav constitutional and criminal law and offer rec-
ommendations. The shorts texts they produced, where 'verbal crime' Article 133
and the freedom of thought and expression were pinpointed as needing urgent
attention and amending, were to serve as initial basis for a wider debate.

This particular example illustrates a crucial shift in the way the SSOJ envisioned its social and political role, as well as in the very form and content of its
politics and engagement both in the youth realm and in the wider public sphere.
The shift away from the dominant vocabulary of self-management/pluralism
of self-managing interests and a shift towards an interest in human rights and
freedoms were certainly not the result only of an internally generated debate.
It should be observed within the contemporary context of the various citizens'
initiatives and groups which converged around different demands framed in
the discourse of human rights.[22] Yet, as a formal institution and part of the
political system, the youth organisation acknowledged the existence of serious
human rights violations and by putting the burden of responsibility on the state
organs and discarding 'the old way of thinking' which saw the existing system
as perfect, it symbolically initiated the severing of ties with its long-time senior
political sibling.

1988: the point of no return

The period 1987–88 has been embedded in political histories, which tend to
focus on elite stories around the ascent of Slobodan Milošević, the rise of Serbian nationalism under the guise of what has been termed 'ethno-technocratic
populism'[23] and the internal splits within the Serbian Party. Mass workers'
protests which wrapped their discontent with the socio-economic situation
in the classical symbols of Yugoslav socialism, additional austerity measures,

protests of the Kosovo Serbs, the resignation of the Montenegrin leadership, the dismissal of the Kosovan-Albanian leadership, the 'yoghurt revolution' in Vojvodina, the 'trial of the four' in Ljubljana and the subsequent protests, were some of the events which posit 1988 in historical, but also in subjective, autobiographical terms as the turning point in recent Yugoslav history.[24] This section addresses an unexplored question of how this impacted on activists and the local youth realms. It seeks to bring to light the diversity of experiences and offer a perspective on the 1988 events 'from below'. Indeed, nearly all interviewees maintained that 1988 was the turning point and this was particularly prominent among those who happened to be based in Belgrade at the time. Moreover, the events of 1988 had real impact on the tone of debates within the youth sphere, as this moment shifted discourse, limited the scope of what was possible in terms of change and reform and forced the different republican Youth Leagues to take new positions.

The political crisis which began to throw Yugoslavia's existence into question brought the youth organisation and its media outlets into the debate. The events which were unfolding with an ever increasing speed initiated a process of fragmentation along republican lines, but also a convergence across national lines. The rifts became more visible as the 'anti-bureaucratic revolution' was gaining momentum and the debate on the constitutional changes which sought to restore the political and judicial powers of Serbia proper over its provinces was nearing its end. Different republican SSOs began to take divergent positions. The Serbian Youth League openly sided with the Serbian Party when in 1988 it launched a propaganda campaign in support of the Serbian constitutional amendments, calling on the young to vote at the referendum and to express support for the Republic's leaders.[25] Furthermore, it progressively appropriated the official political discourse on Kosovo – among other things advocating a new 'population politics which will lead to the decrease in birthrates'.[26] The decision of the Montenegrin youth officials to side with the protesters and join in their demands for the resignation of the old Montenegrin political leadership could be interpreted in a twofold manner: both in light of the previously upheld rhetoric on 'de-bureacratisation', and as a pragmatic choice in advancing their career prospects.[27] As a response to the act of aligning of the Serbian SSO with the politics of Slobodan Milošević and of the Serbian League of Communists, the SSO of Vojvodina launched its own set of materials, a document entitled 'For Yugoslavia – my country' [Za Jugoslaviju – moju domovinu]. The demands the material posed were more or less those which would later be upheld by the new liberal/reformist camp across the SSOJ: abolishment of the national economies and introduction of a market economy, opening up of Yugoslavia for foreign investment and inclusion in the European integration perspectives, consolidation of a system of rule of law, accountability of all political bodies, direct elections for political positions and a new short, concise and efficient constitution fit for a modern polity.[28]

These events could only aggravate the already fragile consensus which was built upon a loosely defined need for change. They also induced an atmosphere where it was difficult for individuals and the youth organisations to stay neutral. The polarisation at federal level between Serbia and Slovenia (primarily over Kosovo and the political restructuring of the federation) the following year further destabilised the political structure of which the youth organisation was part. The 'particular system of conflict regulation and social integration through devolution'[29] was called into question by Serbia's demands for re-centralisation and revision of the autonomy of the provinces. The federal level of the youth organisation could not stay immune to these and the accompanying debates. Moreover, an inherited consensus on curbing nationalist discourse – 'Yugoslav communism's strong antipathy to overt nationalist tactics'[30] – began to unravel.

This moment is mentioned as the central turning point in many biographies. It was often linked with changes in urban environment – especially in Belgrade. Risto Ivanov (born 1960) was delegated to the SSOJ in Belgrade from Macedonia during 1986–88. He reflected on one prominent division which ran along the lines of loyalty versus competence and the consensus which existed among 'the liberal camp':

> What is interesting, however, and might be relevant today is the fact that the more liberal camp was dominated by highly educated individuals who had some professional experience; on the other side, for example those who were advancing the politics in Serbia and Montenegro, did not have a university degree and entered politics as a token of loyalty, not competence. They were easier to control. So, even when there were arguments in the organisation, if it was for this other camp I call 'advantage of competence, not loyalty', it was possible to reach an agreement, there was a chance for agreement ... It became obvious that loyalty would trump competence and rationality. The seams began to break. At the end, everyone went where they came from. So, when you came back home [after your mandate], people could easily find fault and that wasn't pleasant at all. For example, people used to meet me on the street and say: 'What is it, you are plotting something with the Slovenes? You're trying to please them, eh?' That wasn't pleasant ...
>
> The idea at the time was to open up certain spaces and that competent individuals come to the fore. But, apparently, the working class paradigm was replaced with that of nationalism. One group was simply replaced by a different one where the same rules apply – loyalty, not competence. That's when the seams began to break and everyone retreated to their own national group – no connecting thread was left.

Rasim Kadić (born 1960) was delegated to the presidency of the SSOJ in Belgrade in 1986 as a full-time professional employee in the department for education and student standard. Kadić became the focus of media attention because he publicly labelled Mirko Ostojić – member of the presidency of the Socialist Alliance as 'a political advocate of Slobodan Milošević in Bosnia and Herzegovina'. He recalled the infamous 8th session of the Serbian Party's Central Committee which took place in September 1987:

> I remember very well when the 8th session of the Central Committee of the League of Communists of Serbia was taking place, there was a football match Yugoslavia-Italy. It was the first time that instead of watching the football game I watched the broadcast. Of course we were against Milošević, many of my friends in Serbia were also against that rigid form of nationalism backed by the JNA ... After Milošević won, I gathered everyone on the twenty-second floor, bought them coffee and told them – 'Guys, this is my farewell coffee, I'm going back to Bosnia because this is no longer my country' [...]
>
> The moment Milošević won was that point for me. The moment he won I was twenty-seven. I can't say I knew, but I could feel intuitively that it was the end. I could see it was simply something that can't be saved ... I could have gone for a second mandate in Belgrade, but I left it, I left a girl behind, a good salary, privileges, friends ... I almost did not notice that Yugoslavia disappeared. Because for me Yugoslavia was not a grand, abstract notion ... For me Yugoslavia was the friends, the people with whom I communicated and with whom I still communicate. So, in that sense, Yugoslavia did not disappear at all.

Ivanov's testimony echoes Kadić's and those of the other youth functionaries who worked at the SSOJ in Belgrade during the last years of the 1980s:

> As far as the break-up of Yugoslavia is concerned, I can say that the period I spent in Belgrade was the beginning [of the end of Yugoslavia].
>
> L.S.: *So, one could sense it?*
>
> Yes. It wasn't anticipated, but the key moment was when Dragiša Pavlović was removed from the position of President of the City Committee of the Party in Belgrade and from then on one could feel that the whole atmosphere began to change ... After that, everything changed. Namely, before that, Belgrade was a city that left you fascinated. Whoever went there, they felt 'European', welcome, the way of life, the communication ... It literally had the appeal of a world metropolis. Only few months later it became obvious that Belgrade is no longer hospitable to everyone. That was the key moment and it later reflected in the youth organisation and all other bodies.

A sense of being taken by surprise by the radical change in public discourse and in what was considered to be a social and political consensus thus far was so prominent precisely because the public display of nationalism – in particular of the two 'big nationalisms', the Serbian and the Croat – was actively discouraged in post-Second World War Yugoslavia and perceived as politically incorrect. Dejan Jović located a feeling of 'uneasiness' during those years: 'It's the end of the 1980s – 1986/87/88, when it all began feeling uneasy. [National belonging] began to matter. It was shocking for me to hear "Slobo Srbine, Srbija je uz tebe" [Slobo, you Serb, Serbia is behind you], that concept was completely unacceptable and frightening to me.'

A sense of 'shock' was echoed by interviewees with very different backgrounds. Simo Spaskovski, at the time a young JNA officer from Macedonia, talked about his own 'shock' when he first saw people adorned with 'chetnik' symbols on the streets of Belgrade when he visited the city on several occasions in 1988 and 1989 while attending lectures at the Command-staff academy of the Yugoslav Army. Miha Kovač, who was doing his army service in Serbia in 1987, similarly underlined that he was 'quite shocked' by the shifts in the Serbian media discourse. His testimony echoes the significance of the socio-political consensus which sought to stigmatise and ban public manifestations of nationalism through his conviction that anyone who espoused such views in public would be dismissed:

> I strongly disliked Milošević … I was serving the Yugoslav Army in 1987, when he was starting to rise. The army was boring for me. They knew that I am a dissident, they knew that I am coming from a good socialist family, so they didn't know exactly what to do with me. So, they put me in a warehouse, where I had to take care of Party flags and I was basically sleeping there. I spent a lot of time reading [Belgrade daily] *Politika*. I was quite shocked, you know. In the letters by the readers appeared letters which were extremely chauvinist and nationalistic. When I saw them, after a few weeks I said [to myself] – 'They will remove the editor of *Politika* in a few months' – because no decent Communist Party would allow something like that. But, then, the content of these letters started to move to the regular text in the paper. So, when I came back from the army I was much more aware than other Slovenians about what was going on in Serbia. My theory was that it was a fascist movement … But then, at a certain point I became very sceptical about people who were around [Slovenian journal] *Nova revija*, who claimed that we need national freedom first and democracy second … If you ask common people in Slovenia, they will say – 'Oh, our state, we were dreaming for a thousand years about this'. But this is bullshit … For a very long time Slovenians were dreaming not about independence, but about a more democratic Yugoslavia. The clue about the destruction of Yugoslavia is definitely in Belgrade. To put it very simply, Serbs made Yugoslavia and Serbs destroyed Yugoslavia.

Indeed, media reports and editorial politics became increasingly divergent and irreconcilable.[31] In a similar vein, Senad Avdić, the editor-in-chief of the federal youth magazine *Mladost* underlined the fragmentation of the media space. He recounted a trip to Kosovo during the *Stari trg* miners' strike in early 1989. He followed Stipe Šuvar into the mine and had a chance to speak to the miners. Avdić recalled the existence of completely disparate media reports on the events, claiming that the Serbian one in no way corresponded to what he had actually seen: 'You've got millions of details like that, which are not details, but big things ... It told you that some sort of madness had prevailed.'

The realm of the youth press was not immune to the radical changes and realignments across the political scene. Although the various youth magazines naturally differed in their approach, editorial style and the level of boldness and critique, the majority of them shared an openly critical attitude towards the increasingly aggressive politics of the Serbian Party headed by Milošević. In an issue of Bosnian *Naši dani*, the editorial board of the magazine published a letter addressed to Stipe Šuvar, at the time chair of the Party Presidium, demanding from him, from the presidency of the Party's Central Committee and the SKJ 'a decisive settling of scores with the anarcho-nationalist processes threatening to shatter us all into ashes' – alluding to the rise of Serbian nationalism and the mass rallies organised by the Serbian Party.[32] It was the youth media based on the territory of Serbia that came under increasing pressure in 1988 when the Serbian League of Communists began to purge local media of those who were not willing to compromise and adjust their editorial line. Petar Janjatović's testimony is illustrative of these context-specific developments and of the change in the manner of navigating the permitted boundaries of public critique after 1987:

> Even at the time when [Dragan] Kremer and I were working on the 'Rhythm of the heart', we instated that mode of talking about politics through rock 'n' roll. We also had a show on the second programme of Radio Belgrade that was called 'This is only rock 'n' roll'. We started it in 1987. When the entire madness with Milošević began, the focus was on the first programme of Radio Belgrade. The censors hardly ever listened to the second programme. We were spitting on [Vojislav] Šešelj, on Sloba [Milošević], we were playing Rambo [Amadeus], [the song by Croatian band Film] 'E moj druže beogradski', until they figured it out and threw us out. As I said before, through writing and talking about rock 'n' roll one can talk about anything. Especially when the times are screwed.

Print media were more visible and the youth press experienced increasing political pressure. The editorial board of the magazine of the students of Belgrade University, *Student*, was replaced and the Belgrade public prosecutor initiated a case against the magazine of the Maribor students (based in Slovenia) in front of the court in Belgrade for a regular supplement entitled 'Beograjska priloga' [Belgrade supplement]. This was without a precedent, since magazines were considered to be within the scope of regional legislature. But, as the

Maribor magazine was partially written in Serbo-Croatian and openly critical of the Serbian political elite, it was presented as a legitimate target.[33]

Eventually, it was the federal youth magazine *Mladost*[34] which also came under pressures from the Serbian Party. The pressures were channelled through by youth functionaries who were simultaneously active in the federal youth organisation and in the Serbian Party. In 1987 *Mladost* was voted 'youth magazine of the year' under the editorial leadership of Vlastimir Mijović (born 1956). Although officially the magazine of the federal youth organisation, it pursued a rather independent editorial policy and did not hesitate to encourage critical writing. For instance, in 1986 it published a 'dossier' on the initiatives for conscientious objection and the peace movement, while Mijović in his editorials openly targeted the SSOJ and its leadership, arguing that 'It is necessary, first of all, to say openly that the Yugoslav youth has an incompetent, sloppy, self-sufficient and in some cases foul leadership'.[35] Mijović was not granted a second two-year mandate and after the legally prescribed six-month period of 'acting editor' expired, the procedure for the appointment of a new editor was purposefully administratively delayed or hampered. 'In whose interest is it to obstruct the federal youth magazine?', asked the editorial staff of *Mladost*.[36] They pointed to the secretary of the presidency of the SSOJ – Zoran Anđelković, an active member of the Serbian League of Communists: 'In this case, it seems, what is decisive is pure political (ill) will of the organs of the SSOJ who, by the way, are often manipulated by their most senior political functionaries.'[37] This was a clear allusion to the top echelons of the Serbian Party and its leader Slobodan Milošević. The editorial staff and other youth magazines also raised the question of why the youth organisation through Anđelković (and some other functionaries such as Goran Milinović and Milan Janjić) sought an advisory opinion on the matter from the Serbian Committee for Information and not from the corresponding federal body.[38] It was Avdić who succeeded Mijović as editor. However, he also located the break-up of the common professional and socio-political space as having occurred during that period: 'I experienced [the break-up of Yugoslavia] two or three years before it actually happened. I experienced it in Belgrade ... As an editor of a federal magazine, I tried to reflect all type of interests – republican, provincial, so that no one had monopoly.' Thus, *Mladost* and *Student* were in a pool of media that came under pressures reflecting the new realignments on the volatile Yugoslav political scene, as Milošević 'simultaneously extended personal influence over the most influential media and shifted their supervision from the City to the Central Committee'.[39]

The narrative that Belgrade was changing beyond recognition in those years might have been reinforced by the subsequent events and the role of Serbia in the Yugoslav wars. Yet, individuals from different parts of the country and with very different biographies tend to share a similar sense of a major rupture and change. Indeed, 1988 features as the crucial year in Yugoslav late socialism, the 'point of no return', where a sense of personal disempowerment and disappointment was enhanced by novel, often shocking developments and claims made on behalf of individuals, groups and nations. The events of 1988 caused irreparable rifts at different levels within the SSOJ, including the youth press. This paved the way for the final debate on the future of the institutional youth sphere.

The demise of the SSOJ

By 1990, many different positions regarding the future of the SSOJ were put forward. As political debates on the future of the Yugoslav federation were intensifying, the youth organisation was not only preoccupied with its own future, but also with the future of the entire Yugoslav institutional and political set-up. The 'constitutional crisis'[40] of the late 1980s, as well as the first multi-party elections in 1990 led parts of the SSOJ to transform into political parties and effectively put an end to the organisation which was founded in 1919 as the youth wing of the Yugoslav Communist Party. This section explores the debates concerning the future of the SSOJ and Yugoslav federalism on the eve of the Yugoslav dissolution and seeks to shed light on the process of disintegration of the institutional youth sphere. This period saw both the growth not only of political and ethnic division within republican SSOs, but also a short-lived process of linking up across national lines – a development which was prematurely interrupted by the eruption of violence and the disintegration of the state.

In July 1989, the SSOJ took part in the international youth gathering in Paris organised as one of the events to commemorate the 200th anniversary of the French revolution. Each of the republican branches saw the international context of the event as an ideal space for promoting its programme or its (unofficial) agenda. The Greek youth from the New Democracy party, for instance, noted an increasing turn towards nationalism among some Yugoslav branches of the youth organisation, and found itself provoked by what they saw as 'aggressive Macedonian propaganda' of some of the publications placed on display by the Macedonian youth organisation. However, a report by the Bosnian SSO noted that 'The Yugoslav youth organisation […] was, after all, more united than it could be realistically expected, considering the actual and perhaps sometimes even dramatic differences which exist in the country.'[41] Indeed, the report reflected a wider sentiment that the changing nature of Yugoslav socialism might require a fundamental rethinking of the 'common umbrella' of the SSOJ. It stated:

> The concept, according to which the youth organisation of our country is once and for all ideologically determined, [seen] as a logical segment of a false conflict-free society, it seems that [such an organisation] definitely belongs to

the past ... a homogeneous society, compressed into one ideology in an unnatural way cannot be happier than an open and authentically pluralistic one.[42]

This quote captures the state of the youth institutional realm on the eve of the disintegration of the SKJ at its 14th extraordinary congress in January 1990 and the first multi-party elections.[43]

Branko Greganović, delegate of the ZSMS in Belgrade and the next-to-last president of the SSOJ was seen as an embodiment of a loosely defined 'Yugoslav option':

> I think there was a certain urban environment, an urban circle of people who felt Yugoslav not in the national sense, but saw it as an urban idea – 'why would I identify as anything else?' In my case my mixed origin is an additional reason, but I think no one saw the Yugoslav identification as problematic at the time ... After all, that is something we do not choose, you don't choose your place of birth, the place where you grow up [...]
>
> My Yugoslavism was not a political stance ... Those of us who felt Yugoslav in the urban, neutral sense, nationally neutral, although not in the sense of being nationally undeclared, but simply civically neutral, we did not realise that actually we are the instrument of a certain politics ... It was a genuine feeling, healthy vital feeling of belonging to a certain space. The rock 'n' roll and everything that was going on in the 1980s is an expression of that [...]
>
> My biggest support came from Bosnia-Herzegovina and Macedonia, while Croatia and Serbia were much more critical towards me personally ... What I argued for did not necessarily include the survival of the [Yugoslav] state. That should be clear ... At the time, I was perceived as a Yugoslav, as a representative of the Yugoslav option, although de facto that was never my fundamental goal. The fundamental goal was peace ... So, that perception was context-dependent, rather than a result of my own intimate goals and desires. In my own perceptions, I never argued that the state must survive, especially not if the price to pay for that survival is totalitarianism, war ... So, in that sense, I was not 'the Yugoslav option'. I was above all for democratic change and intimately for the preservation of peace. Objectively, in that context, it was what it was. One can't run away from what it objectively was.

The demise of the SKJ, however, did not result in an immediate institutional break up. A reformist, pro-Yugoslav and pro-European political platform most ardently represented by federal Prime Minister Ante Marković, was met with considerable approval in the youth realm, especially in the youth press. In December 1989, *Polet* organised a poll where it asked its readers to identify the most positive and negative events/individuals in Yugoslavia for 1989. Slobodan Milošević was voted the most negative, while Ante Marković the most positive. The editorial board of the Macedonian youth magazine *Mlad borec* was also asked to cast its vote – it pointed to Slobodan Milošević as the most negative and

Figure 10 Youth magazine *Naši dani* at a protest for media freedom, Sarajevo, 1991

to the program of Prime Minister Marković and his cabinet, the successes of the Yugoslav football and basketball national teams, the foundation of alternative political organisations, the opening of the first sex shop in Zagreb and the federal daily *Borba* as the most positive.[44] Similarly, the Bosnian student magazine *Valter* also maintained that

the promises given by the opposition fighting for power are not realistic and can hardly compare to [the prime minister's] achievements so far, which have caused – in a completely a-national manner – a level of support unseen before. We should not have any doubts that this is a period where we'll see a formal change of government, accompanied by strong disillusionment of manipulated voters. Because exclusive anti-communism does not imply automatic creativity; on the contrary, the motives are quite banal and easily recognisable – taking power.[45]

This reflected a wider appeal of the reformist (pro-Yugoslav and pro-European) option among the youth.[46] The youth press voiced the widespread opinion that the political vacuum is being filled by a new exclusivist, ethno-national doctrine. Even in Macedonia, where nationalism was rather tame, young journalists were warning of the impending dangers. In one of his editorials from 1990, the editor-in-chief of *Mlad borec*, Nikola Mladenov (1964–2013) targeted the rise of nationalism, both at Yugoslav and local level: 'As if it became a civic duty to propagate national tragedy and vulnerability. In place of one collectivity – the class, we are being offered another one – the nation, the easiest way of manipulation with the emotions of tomorrow's voters. The propagating of one's one history – always the most bloody and most difficult – hasn't bypassed us either.'[47]

The European future for Yugoslavia which was espoused by federal Prime Minister Ante Marković indeed struck a chord with the new youth leaderships at the end of the 1980s, although the Slovenian youth organisation was the most vocal on the matter. Zoran Thaler was responsible for the sector of foreign cooperation at the ZSMS in 1989 and initiated the drafting of a 'European declaration': 'In four points we determined what we are and what Europe means for us. Namely, that we are citizens of Europe and that we have had enough of the economic crisis and the inter-tribal conflicts and of the isolation of Yugoslavia from its natural historical surroundings and that we demand that Yugoslavia joins Europe.'[48] The fact that Thaler declared a 'liberal socialist'[49] could be partially explained by the argument that in the late stages of European state socialism, liberalism became synonomous with a political system responsive to pluralism, respect for human rights, equality before the law and rule of law, and 'for the majority of the people in East-Central Europe it was closer to what in the West has come to be called social liberalism'.[50] Azem Vllasi, who presided over the SSOJ between 1974 and 1978, emphasised in his testimony that even in the second half of the 1970s:

> We nurtured the seed of social democracy. At times we even ridiculed the rigid, communist idea and the way the generation of our parents or the members of the veterans' organisation defended the League of Communists as something eternal … One can say that the seed of the social-democratic idea almost everywhere in the former Yugoslavia was born within the youth organisation.

The platform of the federal prime minister also overlapped with that of the anti-regime pro-Yugoslav intellectuals who gathered around UJDI.[51] Sarajevo-based *Valter*, for instance, published lengthy interviews with almost all of the prominent members of UJDI: from Predrag Matvejević, Rudi Supek, and Branko Horvat, to Shkëlzen Maliqi and Zagorka Golubović.[52] UJDI had a trans-generational appeal and activist core and its civic-based, pro-democratic and pro-Yugoslav platform struck a chord with numerous young activists, be it from the media or the political realm. For instance, at the helm of the Kosovan branch of UJDI formed in December 1989 stood twenty-eight-year-old journalist Veton Surroi (born 1961), while another young journalist from the youth magazine *Zëri i rinisë* – Blerim Shala (born 1963) presided over the committee for a Youth Parliament which in 1991 became the 'Parliamentary Party of Kosovo'.[53] Considering the fact that the political space by 1990 had become

Figure 11 Youth celebrating Yugoslavia's football team victory at the 1990 World Cup, Sarajevo

considerably fragmented, even pan-Yugoslav initiatives such as UJDI had different local specificities which stemmed from the particular political context of the federal republics. Minutes from a meeting of the leadership of the Bosnian SSO, for instance, reveal that the meeting and cooperation with some of them was seen as problematic.[54] Senad Pećanin recalled this period of forming new political alliances:

> Of course we cooperated with UJDI – with Puhovski, Horvat, Žarko Korać, Vesna Pešić, Grebo … Crazy [Zdravko] Grebo had posters printed with the inscription 'People's Liberation Movement – we will die together' and him, Peđa and I were putting up these posters just before the war, at 2–3 a.m. HDZ and SDA had the slogan 'We will live together', so we went out that night and flooded the walls around the city with the posters – 'PLM-we will die together'.

Rasim Kadić credited the 'tolerant' and democratic character of UJDI's politics and brought up the 'non-partisan' character of the organisation:

> UJDI was one noble idea of noble, highly educated, tolerant, democratically oriented people, but numerically totally insignificant … Since we in the SSO had our own space and finances … we served as a kind of logistical base for UJDI in Bosnia-Herzegovina. I remember meetings taking place on our

premises, conferences … We once even invited [Serbian nationalist politician] Vuk Drašković … Why was UJDI important? Because it was a non-pretentious form [which allowed] for the hearing of a different opinion … It was the answer of smart people to the situation in which we found ourselves … We were somehow caught in between the non-partisan, non-political character of UJDI and our own ambitions to become a political party. That is why I could not really find my place, but I still think we were of some use for that idea … Of course it was clear that Yugoslavia can't exist without any of its parts. Let's be frank, that was one wicked game of the Slovenians and Milošević, where Milošević was acting as if he was trying to keep Slovenia in … while the Slovenes were playing the game eager to leave and pass the problems down south … No matter how liberal they were, they were nationalist.[55]

In the aftermath of the fall of the Berlin Wall and the demise of the Yugoslav Communist League, reforming the Yugoslav institutional and political framework became an imperative. A view which saw the Socialist Alliance of Working People as the initial framework where political reform should commence was shared across the youth sphere.[56] For instance, it was espoused by the Bosnian SSO, which maintained that a sudden shift from a mono-party to a multi-party system could be dangerous and even ruinous. Hence, it was argued that there should be a transitory period until the adoption of a new constitution: 'Potential solutions should be sought after in the independence of the existing socio-political organisations, their autonomy, the systemic reform of the SSRNJ which must become a modern pluralist organisation in the framework of which all the political interests of its existing and new members and parts could be articulated.'[57] Miha Kovač, as a member of UJDI, represented the moderate line which did not put Slovenian idependence from Yugoslavia over the priority of democratisation. Two decades later, he sees it as their attempt at the time to sideline the hard-liners:

You must understand that what I thought in those days was that the best solution is parliamentary democracy. But, in the Yugoslav context, we were thinking how to make this move slow enough in order to crush the hard-liners, who were much stronger in Belgrade and in the Yugoslav Army than in Slovenia or in Zagreb. So, the idea was to use the Socialist Alliance as a kind of a democratising movement …

On the other hand, I somehow liked Yugoslavia, because it was a crazy mess of very different cultures. And I actually felt very good when I was talking in Sarajevo or in Zagreb or in Belgrade with like-minded people. And I saw Yugoslavia as a kind of a small picture of Europe … So, I had this theory that if Yugoslavia is going to fail, then, at a certain point, Europe will fail too. So, I became close to some people in Zagreb and Belgrade [from UJDI] who thought about how to democratise and at the same time preserve Yugoslavia.

The loosely defined framework of Europeanisation and democratisation for Yugoslavia appeared acceptable to the majority who were active in the youth organisation and in the media at the end of the 1980s. Nowadays, however, in retrospective testimony one finds a high level of disapproval of Ante Marković's politics, mainly in light of his indecisiveness via-à-vis Milošević and the hard-liners within the army. Rasim Kadić's opinion evokes a particular Bosniak per-spective, reflective of a sense of disillusionment and betrayal:

> Ante Marković is a noble man, modern and very important in the history of Bosnia and he did what he did from the noblest and best of reasons. But, the consequences of what he did are catastrophic for Bosnia and Herzegovina, terrible, immeasurably terrible ... We trusted him like small children ... That's why Ante Marković is one of the biggest malefactors of Bosnia ... He totally neutralised us, pacified us, misled us, did nothing to help us ... and did not want to speak until they invited him at the [International Criminal Tribunal for Yugoslavia in] Hague. So, he didn't even want to speak against Milošević after [the genocide in] Srebrenica ... Regardless of the fact that he had noble, good intentions and ideas.

Zoran Thaler shared a similar type of critique:

> As far as Marković is concerned, he formed the wrong alliance in the key moments. He had a chance to form an anti-Milošević coalition with the support from Washington and Brussels, and he didn't ... [Foreign Secretary Budimir] Lončar and Marković were in the position to bring Yugoslavia into the EU in a very short time ... The old-fashioned ideological camp prevented them from undertaking radical reforms.

By the end of 1989 there was a consensus among the majority of the republi-can branches of the SSOJ that the organisation needed to undergo fundamental reforms, while the youth media did not shy away from portraying it as 'a sinking ship'.[58] Zoran Kostov, currently university professor of journalism and media, was editor-in-chief of the main student magazine in Macedonia and active member of the SSMM. As he put it:

> The big difference between the federal youth organisation and the other fed-eral bodies is that the former went through a controlled dissolution. It dissolved consensually ... 'Dissolution' perhaps is not even the right term. The federal Youth League went through a controlled process of transformation.

The widespread recognition that the SSOJ could not continue in its current framework was reflected in the fact that at the beginning of 1989 the federal level of the SSOJ initiated a 'public debate' [javna rasprava] about the main principles of its Statute.[59] That meant opening up a discussion which foreshadowed funda-mental changes to the mission and the aims of the organisation. In June 1989, the

SSOJ published an edited volume consisting of the summaries of the discussions and conclusions in the different branches of the League (for a more detailed overview, see Table 8). In addition to their views on the future of the organisation, the local youth organisations also outlined their visions of the future of the Yugoslav political system. Although nominally all of the republican branches of the SSOJ referred to the democratisation of the organisation and that of the state as the sine qua non of any future statute or constitutional change and a new political agreement, the views were diverging. The debate unfolded, sandwiched between two extremes: that the organisation should be immediately abolished because it had ceased to function at a local level (in particular after the abolishment of the Youth Day relay), on the one hand, and that it should keep its socialist orientation, on the other.[60] Whilst there was seemingly still a shared language around terms such as democracy, pluralism, rule of law, accountability and free elections, the implication of these terms meant very different things to different groups and individuals. One of the major points of contention was the 'generational' character of the SSOJ. Voices which questioned the generational principle of political organisation were most prominent in Slovenia, Croatia, as well as in Bosnia-Herzegovina. For instance, in 1989 Rasim Kadić was elected President of the Bosnian SSO with a programme which proposed the creation of a completely new youth organisation, rather than its reform: 'Do we need a political organisation on a generational principle at all? Political organisations of the generational type are very rare in the world.'[61] The Bosnian, Croatian and the Macedonian SSOs argued for 'an interest-based' organisation with voluntary membership, proposing an abandoning of the hierarchical model in favour of a network-based one, independence and abolishment of the 'paternalistic' role of the League of Communists. Within this camp there was a consensus that the SSOJ in its present conception (as a socio-political organisation and a mass, unitary and educational organisation) and form is obsolete. This view was not shared by the SSO in the JNA, the Serbian and the Montenegrin SSOs. Although the Serbian SSO maintained that the new youth organisation should be liberated from 'programatic dogmas', it also argued that it should preserve its socialist orientation and should not be organised on national/republican basis. The latter stood in stark contrast with the demand of the ZSMS that the youth organisation should not strive for 'unity', as it expressed its disapproval of the role of the SSOJ 'conference' as an arbiter and a 'supranational body'. The views of the different SSOJ branches on the future of Yugoslav socialist federalism similarly differed and could be said to reflect the views of the respective republican leaderships. For instance, the Serbian[62] and the Montenegrin SSOs argued for 'socialist political pluralism' and the JNA's Youth League for 'pluralism of self-managing interests'. The SSMM did not entirely abandon the socialist framework and advanced a vision of 'multi-programmatic political pluralism', while the ZSMS advocated 'complete affirmation of political pluralism' and parliamentary democracy.[63] The Macedonian Youth League maintained that

Table 8 Proposals for the reformation of SSOJ

League of Socialist Youth of Bosnia-Herzegovina	• Interest and project-based youth organisation • Independence and abolishment of the 'paternalistic' role of the League of Communists • Individual accountability and responsibility • Rule of law and democracy/direct elections
League of Socialist Youth of Montenegro	• For democratic socialism/socialist political pluralism • Against the inter-dependence among socio-political organisitons and the youth organisation as a transmission belt with regard to the Party • The Socialist Alliance of Working People as the main platform for political pluralism
League of Socialist Youth of Croatia	• Interest-based organisation /abolishment of the classical political forms of organisation and of the SSO as a socio-political organisation • Decentralisation of the decision-making process, instead of consensual/collective decision-making
League of Socialist Youth of Macedonia	• For a socialist rule of law (not party) state/against political monopoly/'multiprogramatic political pluralism' • The Socialist Alliance of Working People as the main platform, 'political parliament' • An interest-based youth organisation, instead of exclusively territory-based • Abandoning of the hierarchical model in favour of a network-based one • Voluntary membership • The definition of the SSO as mass, unitary and educational organisation no longer tenable
League of Socialist Youth of Slovenia	• The League of Communists should become one of many political parties/parliamentary democracy • 'Complete affirmation of political pluralism' • Nationalism as a consequence of the inadequate political system • Depoliticisation of all state organs/decentralisation of federal institutions • Optional political convergence at federal level • European accession • The youth organisation should not strive for 'unity' and its 'conference' should give up on the role of ultimate arbiter and a 'supranational body'

(cont.)

Table 8 (*cont.*)

League of Socialist Youth of Vojvodina	• The SSO lacks legitimacy • For democratic socialism/rule of law/federative union of equals citizens • The new Youth League as an independent political organisation
League of Socialist Youth of Serbia	• The SSO as a pale copy of the other socio-political organisations • The new youth organisation should be liberated from 'programatic dogmas' • For 'socialist political pluralism'/one citizen-one vote • The new Youth League should preserve its 'socialist' orientation/abolish the 'congress' • It should not allow convergence on national basis • Socialist, federative, non-aligned Yugoslavia
League of Socialist Youth in the JNA	• The main principles outlined in the Statute should not be changed, only supplemented • 'Pluralism of self-managing interests' • The Youth League should remain a unitary organisation, 'open and democratic' • Differences and divisions should not be 'glorified or absolutised'

Source: Igor Lavš (ed.), *Prilozi iz javne rasprave o opštim načelima Statuta SSOJ* (Belgrade: Predsedništvo Konferencije SSOJ, 1989).

'political pluralism' is the opposite of the existence of a political monopoly, i.e. a one-party system. However, the concept also 'transcends the narrow framework of party pluralism'. In the 'spirit' of the time, they foresaw the SSRNJ as a 'political parliament' and demanded a new type of socialism 'that guarantees material and spiritual progress, socialism that encompasses all the progressive achievements of modern civilization, socialism of rich people, motivated for work and creation, where individual innovation, creativity, initiative and ability would be affirmed and stimulated ... where all human rights and liberties would be respected'.[64]

Indeed, the debates about the new statute and role of the SSOJ became overshadowed by the more narrow republican debates on how to reorganise the youth organisation, particularly as the republican congresses used to precede the federal one in the Yugoslav political calendar. A sense of new beginning and enthusiasm was prevalent as the republican branches of the SSOJ embarked on the preparations for their last congresses in 1990. For example, the video clip for the last congress of the Macedonian Youth League had the slogan 'Let's make the world ours' [Да го направиме светот наш] and featured an egg on a naked actress – as a symbol of a new beginning, according to Risto Ivanov. He explained that in the Macedonian tradition the egg is also put on ill, wounded spots of the body and the intention was to symbolically convey the message of detecting the existing anomalies and exposing the 'naked', obvious truth. Moreover, the leadership of the SSMM repeatedly expressed sympathies and support for 'the Slovenian orientation', whilst also insisting on the significance of a vaguely civic, as opposed to an ethno-national concept of political organisation. Olivera Trajkovska, now a well-known journalist, was then presiding over the city of Kumanovo SSO branch. In an interview from 1990, she summarised this attitude:

> I still perceive Yugoslavia from Sežana to Gevgelija and I don't understand the Slovenian orientation as an attack on Yugoslavism. It might be an attack on our understanding of Yugoslavism, but, nevertheless, that is an absolutely legitimate option … The program of the RK SSMM is not burdened by the nation, it does not offer national salvation in any respect and reasons in a completely different way.[65]

In Croatia, related symbolism emerged as the youth organisation chose a stork for its pre-congress marketing materials and promoted 'pluralism, tolerance, compromise and creativity'.[66] The message reflected the 'liberal' values it stood for, as Dejan Jović pointed out:

> If you look at the posters for the last congress, you'll see a stork, which was the symbol of that congress … He [Srećko Pantović] made versions [of the poster] with four messages – tolerance, freedom, justice, something like that. And when you look at them, they are generally speaking liberal values. That was the direction. After all, that was a pluralistic organisation which was not nationalist, wasn't Yugoslav, wasn't an organisation which aspired to state-building … The organisation was really divided into two – the liberal camp and the 'etatist' one. Many people from that state apparatus camp later joined the national parties, the police, the intelligence services.

Some youth organisations used the congress to announce a more consolidated platform. At its congress in Portorož in 1989, the ZSMS put forward the slogan which followed its original acronym: ZSMS – *Za Svobodo Mislečega Sveta* [For freedom of the thinking world/For freedom-minded world]. At his opening speech, Jožef Školč – the president of the organisation – targeted 'the language of new Serbian communism', and announced the transformation of the ZSMS into a political party 'as a responsible and clearly articulated integral part of the Slovenian and Yugoslav political scene'.[67] The change was reflected in the amended Statute which described the Slovenian Youth League as an 'independent, open political and social organisation and part of the youth political movement'. In addition, the congress programme documents emphasised the demand for the end of 'political monism'.[68]

The new leadership of the Macedonian youth at the end of the 1980s also embraced a spectrum of liberal concepts and values. Like Rasim Kadić in Bosnia, Risto Ivanov, the last president of the SSMM from 1988 until 1991, represented 'a moderate liberal option', according to Kostov's testimony. He enjoyed considerable popularity for his support of change and what were considered at the time non-conventional values and political practices. Slobodan Najdovski (born 1961) worked at the SSOJ in Belgrade from 1986 until 1988 in the agro-industrial sector. He later joined the successor-party of the SSMM, which later became the Liberal Party. He located the germination of the processes of democratisation within the political elite of the youth organisation and in particular with the leadership of Ivanov. It is telling that, yet again, the 'Slovenian' demands became established as the model against which progressive politics was measured. For instance, the Macedonian Youth League also adopted a new acronym for the title of the organisation similar to the above-named Slovenian one: 'SSMM: Freedom for creation, thought and change' [ССММ – Слобода за создавање, мислење и менување]:

> Risto brought in new freshness and the Slovenian wave significantly impacted on the [Macedonian] youth organisation ... Risto gathered many professionals and he was more popular than [politician] Vasil Tupurkovski ... I think that the conception of democracy in Macedonia unfolded within that core of the youth organisation which demanded societal changes.

The Slovenian Youth League was renamed 'ZSMS-Liberal Party' and at the first multi-party elections in 1990 it won twelve mandates in the new Slovenian Parliament, but remained in opposition against the government led by the DEMOS coalition. While in 1989 the idea of Yugoslavia still figured prominently in the congress documents, at the 14th congress of the ZSMS-LP in 1990, it was Slovenia which was the focus and the principal frame of reference. Yugoslavia at that point was perceived and portrayed as a problem that requires a solution, albeit in a constructive manner: 'We believe that it is possible to solve the inter-ethnic problems in the Balkans through negotiation; because it is in our core interest that those problems are solved, as Slovenia can't exist peacefully with a civil war on its borders, we will cooperate with all those political forces in Yugoslavia which would advocate dialogue, tolerance and compromise, irrespective of their political orientations.'[69] Zoran Thaler reiterated the mission of the Slovenian youth organisation intially as one of democratisation, where the 'national question' did not figure prominently, to one of 'exit from socialism' as things began to deteriorate at federal level after 1989:

The national question initially was none of our concern, us – students and youth, that was the story of DEMOS and *Nova revija 57*. What we were interested in was democratisation, civil rights, the question of the verbal crime, civil service, new social movements, the greens, gay, lesbians, death penalty ... When I came back from Belgrade in 1988, the atmosphere, the tension was much worse compared to 1986 ... When we simplified our program (from 1990) it boiled down to – we no longer need the reform of socialism – Gorbachev was popular at the time, perestroika and glasnost – we need an exit from socialism.

A somewhat different type of path of institutional transformation was pursued by the Macedonian youth organisation. It eventually had three legal successors: the 'Young democratic progressive party' [*Млада демократска прогресивна странка*], the Macedonian Youth Council [*Младински совет на Македонија*] and the Student Union [*Сојуз на студенти*]. After the Slovenian Youth Council [*Mladinski svet*] joined the Council of European National Youth Committees (later 'European youth forum') in 1991, it was assisting the Macedonian Youth Council until it was admitted in 1993. The political successor of the SSMM, which later merged with the Liberal Party, went to the first multi-party elections as part of Ante Marković's Alliance of Reform Forces [*Savez reformskih snaga/ Сојуз на реформските сили*]. They won five MPs, in addition to the nine from the Alliance of Reform Forces, which eventually obtained fourteen seats. Ivanov pointed to the importance of the economic platform of the federal prime minister's electoral agenda:

> L.S.: *Why did you decide to go with Marković?*
> Because everything here boiled down to political frustrations. From the very beginning of my political engagement my only goal was the improvement of the condition of the individual in Macedonia. It could only improve through economic measures, not politics. Marković was the one who focused the most on that problem ... Secondly, I feared the severing of all ties and communication with the rest of the Yugoslav space, because in that case it was clear who would dominate here.

New political platforms which echoed the broad demands for democratisation and Europeanisation of Yugoslavia similarly marked the formation of the Liberal Party (later Liberal-Democratic Party) of Bosnia-Herzegovina. Stemming from the Bosnian SSO, it was originally established in 1989 as a party under the name SSO-DS (Socialist Youth League – Democratic League). During the electoral campaign for the first multi-party elections, they went ahead with the slogan 'liberty, democracy, harmony'.[70] In the highly fragmented political space in 1990, this platform did not find great support among the electorate. Nevertheless, they were aware of the fact that a platform based on the sovereignty of the citizen (as opposed to the nation), would not attract much support when

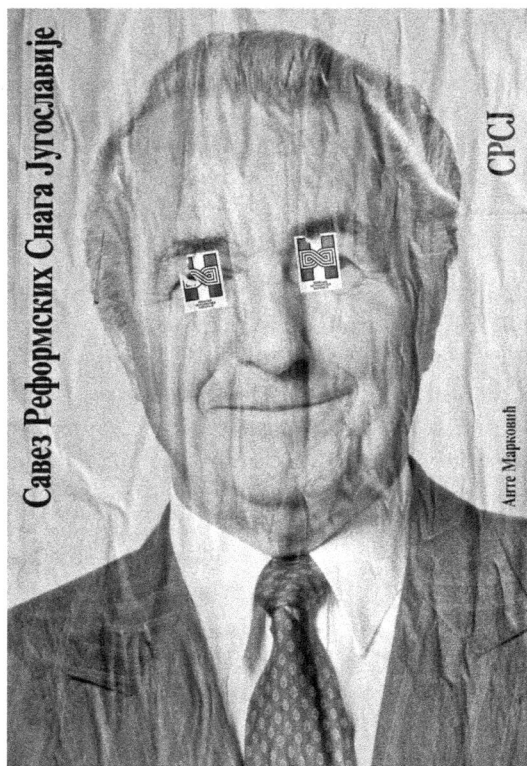

Figure 12 Federal Prime Minister Ante Marković on election poster, Sarajevo, 1990

they rebranded themselves as liberals in 1991. Kadić argued that the 'salvation' of Bosnia-Herzegovina lies in 'the beginning of the demise of the nation-based political parties'.[71] Martin Raguž (born 1958) was also one of the leaders of the young Bosnian liberals. He reiterated the generational, the trans-national and the civic dimension of their liberal platform:

> This attitude of ours has a biological-generational aspect, the fact that we were born and brought up without, with very little or at least with an insufficient amount of communist indoctrination; also taking into account the communi-cation aspect – CNN and MTV. Today we don't want to compare ourselves only with what is happenning in this country, but also with developments at global level, in any sphere – music, culture, politics, sports … Of course, we know that our Liberal Party won't become a major power in society, as is the case everywhere in the world … But, we hope that it will be an influential political option … which would attract those who don't perceive their national belonging as their profession.[72]

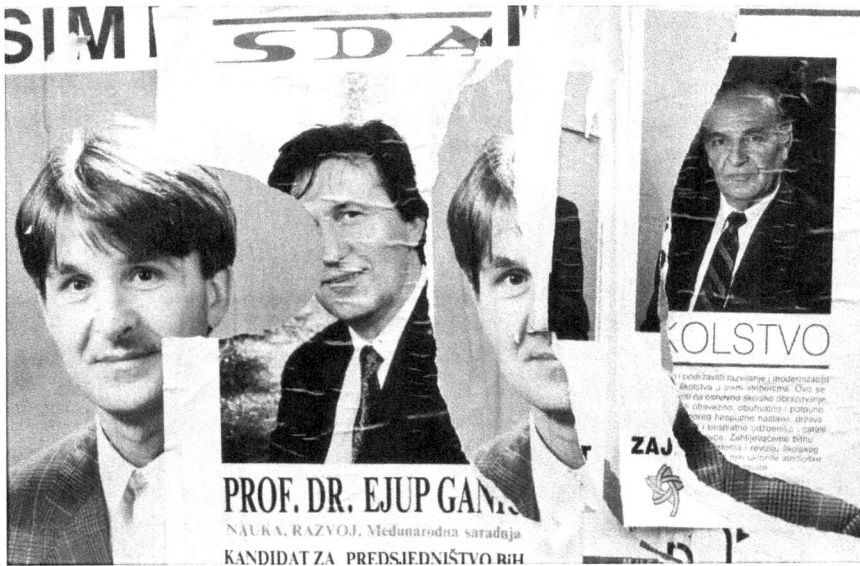

Figure 13 Rasim Kadić on election poster, Sarajevo, 1990

As late as September 1990, certain individuals and circles within what used to be the SSOJ still worked on the creation of a new youth body for the envisioned democratic, multi-party Yugoslav (con)federation, even after the SSOJ self-abolished itself at its last federal congress in Ljubljana in 1990.[73] Namely, the Coordination Committee for the establishment of the Yugoslav New Forum [*Jugoslovenski Novi Forum – JNF*], on an old letterhead bearing the logo of the SSOJ invited all newly established organisations and parties – successors of the old youth organisation to attend the meeting of the Committee and deliver an opinion on the 'draft codex'.[74] The letter also included an invitation for a round-table discussion entitled 'The Yugoslav Community (working title)' [*Jugoslovenska zajednica (radni naslov)*]. The Yugoslav New Forum was envisioned to act as an umbrella organisation, i.e. a 'programmatic coalition of political parties stemming from the former League of Socialist Youth organisations'. Among other things, it stated 'a reaffirmation of the civic status of the individual in politics', 'preservation of the Yugoslav state as a parliamentary republic'; 'for a realistic and tolerant debate about a confederal arrangement as a legitimate proposal during the constituent process'; and 'a state founded upon the sovereignty of the citizen'.[75] The majority of the platforms articulated within the broad network of the SSOJ on the eve of its demise overlapped with the ideas and visions put forward by the intellectual and political front of the UJDI and the above-mentioned party led by federal Prime Minister Ante Marković. This polyphonic reformist, pro-democratisation, liberal, pro-European camp envisioned Yugoslavia as a democratic (con)federation, part of the European Community.

Nevertheless, the question remains as to why this generation's new sense of layered citizenship failed to materialise into a viable, pan-Yugoslav political alternative at the end of the decade. Indeed, why their political, cultural and media activism did not translate into a more coherent and politically artic-ulated 'Yugoslav option' with the advent of multi-partism at the end of the 1980s? The answer is threefold. The first aspect relates to the general context and the role of the older generation in the events of the late 1980s, while the other two relate more specifically to the generation under scrutiny here. First, the answer to the question about the reasons for the Yugoslav *Sonderweg*[76] could be partially found in the argument about the multi-level crisis. To paraphrase the question about why Germany – unlike comparable countries in the West and North – turned to fascist and totalitarian perversion: 'why did Yugosla-via – unlike comparable countries such as Czechoslovakia – turn to violent conflict and nationalist perversion?' The thesis that 'three basic developmental problems of modern societies came to the fore at about the same time' and 'the temporal overlap of and interaction among these three crises [formation of a nation-state, constitutional decision on parliamentarisation and the social question]' which led to their incomplete resolution and National Socialism, seems equally plausible if transposed to the Yugoslav context. The fact that an international and a domestic economic crisis coincided with a political/ constitutional one at home and a major post-Cold War reconfiguration in international relations meant that several critical developments had to be han-dled at the same time by elites belonging to different biological and politi-cal generations which held very different views on the future. Moreover, the individuals who held the real positions and bastions of power and in the sec-ond half of the 1980s fought hard to bring the 'republicanisation of Yugoslav politics'[77] to a definite conclusion, generally belonged to the older, what was described as the second dominant Yugoslav generation – the 'post-war gener-ation', which 'to a large extent managed to build its own egoism/self-interest into the social and political system'.[78] Andrew Wachtel similarly argued that the conflicts and wars throughout the 1990s 'were led, not by the generation that grew up on "soft" Yugoslavism from the mid-1950s to the 1970s, but by a group who had come of age during or just after the ethnic slaughter that had riven the country during World War II'.[79] Zoran Thaler echoed this view in his testimony by blaming the older generation for the tragic outcome: 'Yugoslavia was destroyed by the generation which was 50 at the time, or rather, between 40 and 60 … None of us was in a position of power so that one could seriously do or prevent something.'

Second, the layered sense of citizenship where the ethno-national and the Yugoslav dimensions coexisted harmoniously and complemented each other was contingent upon the inherited political consensus and the existing social context, where this sense of layered Yugoslavism was encouraged and provided with the space to develop and exist as such. Towards the end of the 1980s, as the prominence of the ethno-national grew in every sphere, the tension between these different identities grew as well to the point that the multi-layered citizenship began to fracture. As I have argued elsewhere, the notion of 'fractured citizenship' relates to a 'segmented political life and cemented ethno-national identities', where the fractures could be either healed, so to say, or they could deepen and produce a 'fragmented citizenship with more neatly delineated and segregated identities, institutions and forms of political and cultural belonging'.[80] As it has been shown in this chapter, with the pronounced polarisations in the public sphere in the second half of the decade, and as the existing Yugoslav political/ideological consensus was being destabilised, individuals were compelled to make political choices in a political space which was being predominantly realigned along ethno-national lines. Moreover, with the disappearance of the League of Communists and the abolishement of the League of Socialist Youth at the end of the decade, the common political institutional platforms which provided the space for supra-ethnic convergence and pan-Yugoslav debate, were irretrievably lost.

Finally, the role the young Slovenes had played throughout the decade in pioneering new models of cultural, media and political youth activism proved to be critical at the end of the decade as well. As has been underlined on several occasions, activists in the other Yugoslav republics took inspiration from and often modelled their own activism upon what was unfolding in the Slovenian youth realm. However, as it was shown above with regard to the congress materials of the Slovenian Youth League in 1989–90, there was a dramatic shift in priorities and frames of reference, to the extent that there was an evident sense of distancing from the rest of the Yugoslav space. Hence, the consolidation of a 'Yugoslav' political option at the end of the decade failed mainly because at the critical juncture of 1988–90 it was not pursued by those who had been at the forefront of this generation's political organisation. Instead, subsumed by the developments on the Slovenian political scene and the growing internal divisions in the youth realm among leftist/liberals and conservative nationalists, they shifted their focus on Slovenia and abandoned any attempts at forging a pan-Yugoslav alternative. This explains the sense of betrayal and disappointment present among the interviewees from Bosnia-Herzegovina. Rasim Kadić's testimony is particularly illustrative of a common narrative which faults the Slovenian elites for abandoning the project of democratisation for the whole of Yugoslavia, for embracing nationalism and choosing to step out of the federation without carefully considering all the consequences it would entail:

> ZSMS for me were genuine democrats who spoke in a completely new manner. I was supporter of that ... Few years later, when Yugoslavia really began to disintegrate, I actually realised that all of them generally acted primarily as Slovenes and only secondly as liberals, social democrats, conservatives ... At the beginning maybe they were for democratisation of Yugoslavia, but since that was impossible with Milošević, they quickly transformed their demands into demands for independence ... They are my friends, democrats, but nevertheless they were nationalist ... Now, Branko Mamula was saying this about them from day one. Who was right? [laughs] But, you can't halt the flow of history with force. I was the only politician from Bosnia who, when the conflict in Slovenia started, wrote a letter that the Slovenian journey to independence can't be stopped forcefully, that the JNA lost its credibility because it acts as a Serb and not as a Yugoslav army and that I absolutely oppose the use of force for political aims.

The period from 1986 until 1990 saw a radical change in the way the SSOJ articulated its politics and defined its role. From a relatively strong consensus on the need for change and reform within the framework of socialist self-management in 1986, after 1987 it was caught in the prevailing political debates which worked to polarise Yugoslav public opinion. The fragmentation along republican lines simultaneously engendered internal de-homogenisation, as the political upheavals in 1988 forced everyone to take a stand. When the wide anti-regime, anti-bureaucratic frame which initially united overlapping demands from industrial workers, students and ordinary citizens shrank to the point of accommodating demands which were perceived as particular to Serbia and the Kosovan Serbs, the youth infrastructure and the shared programmatic goals of the SSOJ began to lose their cohesiveness. A sense of shock in front of the drastic change in the publicly acceptable discourse, imagery and the forging of a new ethnocentric consensus were present in the majority of the personal memories of those who happened to be in Belgrade and Serbia during the last years of the decade. The proposed statute changes which came out of the public debate organised by the SSOJ in 1989 reflected both the gap between the Slovenian, on the one hand, and the Serbian, the Montengrin and the JNA youth organisation, on the other, but also shed light on a spectrum of shared visions and values which existed among the other branches. The particular blend of Serbian nationalism, socialism and Yugoslavism espoused by Slobodan Milošević dealt a decisive blow to any viable socialist vision. By the end of the decade the 'pluralism of self-managing interests' was almost entirely replaced by a new discourse which experimented with a range of social democratic and

Figure 14 *Mladina* front cover, 1991

liberal concepts and values and which foresaw 'an exit from socialism', without necessarily envisioning an outright exit from Yugoslavia. Democratic, pro-European Yugoslavism remained a credible and desirable political framework for most of the activist youth in the SSOJ and in the youth media who chose not to side with the politics of the new ethno-nationally defined parties.

Writing in July 1991, in the midst of the 'Ten-Day War' in Slovenia, Miljenko Jergović (born 1966), a renowned novelist and one of the protagonists at the Sarajevo 'Nazi party', recalled a slap in the face from a policeman on a Sarajevo street in 1987 because of a badge he was wearing – 'Slovenija moja dežela'[81] [Slovenia, my country]:

> Few months before that, I was questioned and harassed by the State Security Service because of the so-called fascist birthday ... These days a war has passed through Slovenia. The generals sent my peers to defend Yugoslavia's

borders. [Janez] Janša sent my peers to defend Slovenia's borders. Those two defenses are no longer the same, like they were in Tito's time … I feel warmth and I will always feel this way whenever I put my hand on the map of Slovenia. My opinion of sergeant Janša is the same one I have of the [JNA] generals. I will neither love Slovenia less because of him, nor will I regard Serbia with hatred because of them.[82]

Notes

1 'The socialism of the sons cannot be in its concrete vision and embodiement the socialism of the fathers.' As cited in: Siniša Dimitrijević, 'Socijalizam sinova ili socijalizam očeva', *Polet* 347 (11 April 1986), p. 4.

2 Igor Mekina and Silvo Zapečnik, 'Somrak štafete', in *Kompendij za bivše in bodoče politike* (Ljubljana: ZSMS, 1989), p. 116.

3 The preliminary documents for the 12th congress of the League of Socialist Youth of Slovenia in the section entitled 'For democratisation of political culture' underlined that the struggle for the withering away of the state is not a struggle directed against the consolidation of the state apparatus, but it is a struggle for the democratisation of socialist self-management, for a tolerant treatment of the independent initiatives which although are not established within the system are in their essence democratic and self-managing.' Archive of Slovenia, Ljubljana (hereafter AS), AS 538, *RK ZSMS 1974–1990*, technical unit 383, 'Dokumenti 12. Kongresa Zveze socialistične mladine Slovenije, Ljubljana', 15 November 1985.

4 Dejan Jović, *Yugoslavia: A State That Withered Away* (West Lafayette: Purdue University Press, 2009), p. 3.

5 George Schopflin, 'Political decay in one-party systems in Eastern Europe: Yugoslav patterns', in Pedro Ramet (ed.), *Yugoslavia in the 1980s* (Boulder: Westview Press, 1985), p. 316.

6 The second half of the 1980s, especially in the aftermath of the economic reforms of the federal government, saw the emergence of a new 'managerial/entrepreneurial' youth elite within the SSOJ, which was essentially part of the liberal camp. They upheld the abolishment of the organisation and ushered in the new era of market economy, many of whom went on to becoming successful businessmen.

7 Siniša Dimitrijević, 'Socijalizam sinova ili socijalizam očeva', *Polet* 347 (11 April 1986), p. 4.

8 *Ibid.*

9 *Predlog dokumenti dvanaestog kongresa Saveza socijalističke omladine Jugoslavije, Beograd 12–14 juna 1986* (Belgrade: Konferencija SSOJ/Službeni list SFRJ, 1986), p. 71.

10 *Ibid.*, p. 7.

11 *Ibid.*, pp. 13–14.

12 *Ibid.*, p. 69.

13 *XII конгрес на Сојузот на социјалистичка младина на Македонија* (Скопје/Кочани: Републичка конференција на ССММ/Младост, 1986).

14 *Омладина, чинилац друштвених промена: реферат Зорана Анђелковића, председника РК ССОС* (Београд: Републичка конференција ССО Србије, 1986), p. 16.

15 *Ibid.*, p. 6.
    Zoran Anđelković (born 1958) remained influential within the SSOJ after 1986 and
    joined the camp of Slobodan Milošević in the Serbian Party. He remained in pol-
    itics when the League of Communists of Serbia rebranded itself into the Socialist
    Party of Serbia and was appointed in different political roles.

16 AS 538, *RK ZSMS 1974–1990*, technical unit 383, '12. Kongres ZSMS: predlog
    gradiva za kongres. Izhodišča za ključne usmeritve'.

17 AS 538, *RK ZSMS 1974–1990*, technical unit 383, 'Referat Predsednika RK ZSMS
    R. Černeta dan SJO ob 12. Kongresu ZSMS'.

18 '"The Slovene spring": An interview with Miha Kovač', *New Left Review* 177 (1988),
    115–123, p. 121.

19 AS 538, *RK ZSMS 1974–1990*, technical unit 391, 'Predsedništvo konferencije SSOJ,
    Komisija za politički system: Ljudska prava i slobode', Belgrade, March 1989.

20 *Ibid.*

21 Svilanović worked as a teaching assistant at the Faculty of Law in Belgrade and
    was dismissed in 1998 for publicly opposing a controversial university law. He
    presided over the 'Civic Alliance of Serbia' that later merged with the Liberal
    Democratic Party. He served as Minister of Foreign Affairs from 2000 to 2004.

22 In 1987, the Committee for the Defence of Human Rights was created in Serbia,
    alongside a similar committee in the Writers' Association. The following year
    saw the creation of the Yugoslav Forum for Human Rights and the Slovenian
    Committee for the Defence of Human Rights on the occasion of the 'trial of the
    four'. See: Jasna Dragović-Soso, *Saviours of the Nation: Serbia's Intellectual Opposition
    and the Revival of Nationalism* (London: Hurst & Company, 2002).

23 Lenard Cohen, *The Socialist Pyramid: Elites and Power in Yugoslavia* (Oakville, New York
    and London: Mosaic Press, 1989), p. 444.
    For a detailed account of the 'antibureaucratic revolution' and the role of indus-
    trial workers and other non-state actors in the events of 1988, see: Nebojša
    Vladisavljević, *Serbia's Antibureaucratic Revolution: Milošević, the Fall of Communism and
    Nationalist Mobilization* (London: Palgrave Macmillan, 2008).

24 See, for instance, Raif Dizdarević, *From the Death of Tito to the Death of Yugoslavia*
    (Sarajevo and Zagreb: Šahinspahić, 2009). In his memoir, Dizdarević observes that
    'Realistically speaking, the process of orchestrated destabilisation of the country
    began during that "hot summer" of 1988' (Chapter 5, 'The months of Yugoslavia's
    destabilization', pp. 185–247).

25 Tihomir Ladišić, 'Avanti popolo: ova zemlja je ipak dom', *Polet* 396 (14 October
    1988), p. 12.

26 *Izveštaj o radu SSO Srbije između 11. i 12. Kongresa* (Belgrade: RK SSO Serbije, 1990),
    p. 9. The 'exodus' of Serbs from the province of Kosovo came to occupy a cen-
    tral place in political debates after the 1981 riots. The high birthrate of Kosovan
    Albanians was often portrayed as a 'conscious decision on the part of Albanians
    to reproduce rapidly in order to change the demographic picture of Kosovo'. By
    the end of the decade, the migration of the Kosovan Serbs and the birth rate
    of Albanians became some of the issues that featured prominently in Serbian
    nationalist discourse and in the debates on the constitutional amendments of
    the status of the two autonomous provinces on Serbia's territory. See: Momčilo

Pavlović, 'Kosovo under autonomy, 1974–1990', in Charles W. Ingrao and Thomas Allan Emmert (eds), *Confronting the Yugoslav Controversies: A Scholars' Initiative* (West Lafayette: Purdue University Press, 2009), pp. 48–82.

27 Momir Bulatović (born 1956) held various positions within the SSOJ. He became leader of the League of Communists of Montenegro after the old republican leadership was overthrown. He served as the President of Montenegro from 1990 until 1998. Milo Đukanović (born 1962) was a youth functionary at republican and at federal level. He was the Montenegrin Party's secretary after 1988 and in 1991, aged twenty-nine, he was elected Prime Minister of Montenegro.

28 Ladišić, 'Avanti popolo', p. 12.

29 Sabrina Ramet, *Nationalism and Federalism in Yugoslavia 1962–1991* (Bloomington: Indiana University Press, 1992), p. 16.

30 Cohen, *The Socialist Pyramid*, p. 445.

31 On the role of the media in inciting ethnic antagonism, see: Kemal Kurspahić, *Prime Time Crime: Balkan Media in War and Peace* (Washington, DC: US Institute of Peace Press, 2003).

32 'Otvoreno pismo Stipi Šuvaru', *Naši dani* 949 (2 September 1988), p. 8.

33 Svetlana Vasović, 'Katedrine satelitske zabrane', *Studentski list* 8:971 (9 March 1988), p. 9.

34 *Mladost* had assumed the role of a vocal critic as early as the 1960s. During the 1969 elections it openly criticised the elitist nature of the candidate lists: 'Stories for good and obedient children – it can now safely be said that this is what all those convincing promises made by the Socialist Alliance in January have amounted to: promises that a new chapter would open and room be found for more workers, youth and women.' See the subchapters on the 'Youth Federation' and the 'Student Union' in April Carter, *Democratic Reform in Yugoslavia: The Changing Role of the Party* (London: Frances Pinter, 1982), pp. 161–84.

35 Vlastimir Mijović, 'Riba smrdi od glave', *Mladost* 21 (13 June 1986), p. 1.

36 Redakcija, 'NJ.V.V.D. Kome treba gužva oko Mladosti?', *Mladost* 58 (18–31 January 1988), p. 7.

37 *Ibid.*

38 Miroslav Višić, 'Dokle seže ruka Slobodana Miloševića: Lov na vještice', *Studentski list* 3 (27 January 1988).

39 Vladisavljević, *Serbia's Antibureaucratic Revolution*, p. 72.

40 The wider public and political debates on the constitutional reform at federal and at republican level were on the agenda of the youth organisation and significantly animated its leaderships after 1987. For instance, the Slovenian youth organisation was actively involved in the constitutional debates in Slovenia and was part of the so-called 'Zbor za ustavo' [Assembly for the constitution], initially led by the president of the youth organisation Jožef Školč (born 1960). The Slovenian Youth League, however, did not endorse or sign the 'Slovenian declaration 89' of the Slovenian Democratic Union (later the Slovenian Democratic Party) led by Dimitrij Rupel and later by Janez Janša. The entire spectrum of visions between the demand of the non-institutional opposition groups in Slovenia for a confederation and market economy and the proposals of the communist leadership for an asymmetric federation and party pluralism within the framework of the SSRN

reverberated throughout the youth institutional realm. For an overview of the political debates within Slovenia, see: Božo Repe, 'Slovenci v osemdesetih letih (drugi del)', *Zgodovinski časopis* 3 (2000), 413–48.

41 Archive of Bosnia and Herzegovina, Sarajevo (hereafter ABH), *Republička konferencija SSOBIH*, 'Materijali sa sjednica predsjedništva SSOBIH, 1990', box 82, 'Izvještaj o učešću delegacije SSOJ na skupu Pariz 89'.

42 *Ibid.*

43 The title of the declaration of the 14th congress was 'New project for democratic socialism in Yugoslavia'. On the debates within the republican/provincial branches of the SKJ and within the political realm in general in advance of and during the 14th extraordinary congress, see: Davor Pauković, 'Poslednji kongres Saveza Komunista Jugoslavije: uzroci, tijek i posljedice raspada', *Suvremene teme* 1:1 (2008), 21–33.

44 Vesna Jurić Vurušić and Vlado Rukavina, 'Poletov izbor' 89, *Polet* 419–420 (22 December 1989), p. 3.

45 Goran Todorović, 'Sveti Ante', *Valter* 28 (17 April 1990), p. 2.

46 Srećko Mihailović *et al.*, *Deca krize Omladina Jugoslavije krajem osamdesetih* (Beograd: Institut društvenih nauka/Centar za politikološka istraživanja i javno mnenje, 1990).

47 Nikola Mladenov, 'Народе македонски', *Mlad borec* 1971 (7 March 1990), p. 11. Mladenov died in a car accident in March 2013. He was the founder and editor-in-chief of the Macedonian weekly *Fokus* and an ardent critic of the Macedonian political elites, their involvement in various corruption affairs and the curbing of media freedom by political influence. The weekly was sued for slander in 2006 in a major legal battle it eventually lost.

48 Vladimir Spasić, 'Zoran Thaler: želimo politički pluralizam', *Polet* 403 (24 February 1989), p. 6.

49 *Ibid.*

50 See: Sabrina P. Ramet and Danica Fink-Hafner, 'Values, norms, and education', in Sabrina P. Ramet and Danica Fink-Hafner (eds), *Democratic Transition in Slovenia: Value Transformation, Education, and Media* (College Station: Texas A&M University Press, 2006), p. 20.

51 See: Ljubica Spaskovska, 'Landscapes of resistance, hope and loss: Yugoslav supranationalism and anti-nationalism', in Bojan Bilić and Vesna Janković (eds), *Resisting the Evil: [Post] Yugoslav Anti-War Contention (Baden Baden: NOMOS, 2012)*, pp. 37–61.

52 *Valter* 23 (interview special), 26 January 1990.

53 Gëzim Krasniqi, ' "For democracy – against violence": A Kosovar alternative', in Bilić and Janković, *Resisting the Evil*, pp. 83–103; Branka Magaš, 'Kosovo and the struggle for democracy in Yugoslavia: Interview with Veton Surroi', *The Destruction of Yugoslavia: Tracing the Break-Up 1980–92* (London and New York: Verso, 1993), pp. 243–53; Miljenko Buhač, 'Interview: Veton Suroi, čelni čovjek kosovske alternative', *Valter* (9 March 1990).

54 Đorđe Latinović: 'The fact that we are secretly or on the margins meeting with Abdulah Sidran, Gajo Sekulić, Zdravko Grebo is also [seen as] problematic...' ABH, *Republička konferencija SSOBIH*, box 82, 'Magnetofonski snimak sa 37. sjednice Predsjedništva RK SSOBIH', 7 February 1990.

55 This observation echoes certain scholarly arguments which similarly emphasise the fact that the violent conflicts essentially stemmed from Slovenia's unilateral

exit from the federation. Shoup, for instance, argued that 'Slovenia's move to assert her independence, as subsequent events proved, played the role of the first falling domino from which the wars in Croatia, Bosnia-Herzegovina, and finally Kosovo, were to follow'. See: Paul Shoup, 'The disintegration of Yugoslavia and Western foreign policy in the 1980s', in Jasna Dragović-Soso and Lenard J. Cohen (eds), *State Collapse in South-Eastern Europe: New Perspectives on Yugoslavia's Disintegration* (West Lafayette: Purdue University Press, 2007), p. 348.

56 Igor Lavš (ed.), *Prilozi iz javne rasprave o opštim načelima Statuta SSOJ* (Beograd: Predsedništvo Konferencije SSOJ, 1989).

57 *Ibid.*, p. 11.

58 Hajrudin Redžović, 'Rasim Kadić: Neću da mi netko puca iznad glave', *Polet* 413 (29 September 1989), p. 15.

59 Lavš, *Prilozi iz javne rasprave o opštim načelima Statuta SSOJ.*

60 Dejan Jović, 'Kad bi SSOJ postojao, trebalo bi ga ukinuti (1)' *Polet* 402 (10 February 1989), pp. 28–9; Aca Cvetković, 'Dali SSOJ treba ukinuti?', Okrugli sto *Mladosti*, *Mladost* 74 (7 November 1988), pp. 30–3.

61 Redžović, 'Rasim Kadić', *Polet* 413, p. 15.

62 The Serbian Youth League was not uniform either. The camp that did not want to join the Socialist Party of Serbia under Milošević's leadership established the 'Social-democratic alliance of youth of Serbia' which in July 1990 was registered as the 'New Democracy' party, whose program was 'based on liberal ideas in the field of economy and on the social-democrat ideas in the social sphere'. Its leader was Dušan Mihajlović (born 1948), a former youth functionary from the older generation. The party was in opposition during the first half of the 1990s, but later joined a coalition led by the Socialist Party. In 2003 the party changed its name into 'Liberals of Serbia' [*Liberali Srbije*]. It ceased to exist in 2010.

63 Lavš, *Prilozi iz javne rasprave o opštim načelima Statuta SSOJ.*

64 Archive of Macedonia, Skopje (hereafter AM), Републичка конференција на ССММ, box number 1/1989, 'Сојузот на социјалистичката младина на Македонија и реформата на политичкиот систем', March 1989.

65 Antonio Dimitrievski, 'Оливера Трајковска-првиот човек на кумановската младина: Не сме „бижутерија,,!', *Mlad borec* (20 April 1990), p. 13.

66 The congress was scheduled for 30 March to 1 April 1990. However, at the seventh session of the 'Republican Conference' of the SSOH in February 1990, there was a friction over the future re-organisation of the youth organisation. One group formed '*Autonomni demokratski savez Hrvatske*' [The autonomous democratic league of Croatia – ADSH] and its delegates left the session in protest, leading some journalists to compare them to the Slovenian Party delegates at the last congress of the Yugoslav League of Communists the previous month. The ADSH later joined the Social-Democratic Party of Croatia (SDSH) which in 1994 merged with the Social-Democratic Party (SDP) which came out of the League of Communists of Croatia. Snežana Dragojević Harapin, 'Burevjesnik u našim redovima', *Polet* 424 (23 February 1990), p. 8.

67 AS 538, *RK ZSMS 1974–1990*, technical unit 387, 'Uvodni govor Predsednika RK ZSMS Jožeta Školča'.

68 AS 538, *RK ZSMS 1974–1990*, technical unit 387, 'Predlog dokumentov XIII. kongresa ZSMS, Portorož, 3–5 novembra 1989'.

69 AS 538, *RK ZSMS 1974–1990*, technical unit 391, 'Programski dokumenti za 14. Kongres ZSMS-LS. Predlog. Manifest liberalizma'.

70 Neven Andjelić, *Bosnia-Herzegovina: The End of a Legacy* (London: Frank Cass Publishers, 2003), p. 183. The non-political successor of the Bosnian SSO was the Alliance of Youth Organisations [*Savez omladinskih organizacija-SOO*]. It was meant to unite the former interest-based units of the SSO.

71 Senad Pećanin, 'Intervju: Rasim Kadić, predsjednik Liberalne stranke BiH', *Naši dani* 1017 (7 June 1991), p. 9.

72 Predrag Kojović, 'Dobro došli, liberali', *Naši dani* 1016 (24 May 1991), p. 15.

73 Azem Vllasi was invited to the last congress in Ljubljana as a former president of the SSOJ and also as a symbolic political gesture, since he had just left prison after his conflict with the Serbian political leadership and the abolishment of Kosovo's autonomy. He described the way the SSOJ put up with the dissolution of the socialist institutions as 'civilised': 'It was unbelievable. If only everyone else followed the example of the Youth League … In a nice, peaceful way they announced the end of the SSO … very civilised.'

74 AS 538, *RK ZSMS 1974–1990*, technical unit 391, 'Koordinacioni odbor za osnivanje Jugoslovenskog Novog Foruma', Belgrade, 4 September 1990.

75 AS 538, *RK ZSMS 1974–1990*, technical unit 391, 'Prednacrt Kodeksa Jugoslovenskog Novog Foruma'.

76 Jürgen Kocka, 'Asymmetrical historical comparison: The case of the German *Sonderweg*', *History and Theory* 38:1 (1999), 40–50.

77 Schopflin, 'Political decay in one-party systems', p. 316.

78 Djordjije Uskoković, 'Neke najčešće teorijsko-metodološke teškoće i jednostranosti empirijskih istraživanja društvenog položaja i svesti mladih u Jugoslaviji', in *Mlada generacija, danas: društveni položaj, uloga i perspektive mlade generacije Jugoslavije* (Belgrade: NIRO Mladost/Predsedništvo Konferencije SSOJ, 1982), p. 162.

79 Andrew B. Wachtel, *Making a Nation, Breaking a Nation: Literature and Cultural Politics in Yugoslavia* (Stanford: Stanford University Press, 1998), p. 197.

80 Ljubica Spaskovska, 'The fractured "we" and the ethno-national "I": The Macedonian citizenship framework', *Citizenship Studies* 16:3–4 (2012), 383–96.

81 'Slovenija, moja dežela' was the title of a marketing campaign for Slovenian tourism in 1985–86 sponsored by the Slovenian Chamber of Commerce. For more on the campaign and its role in the 'national homogenisation' in the 1980s, see: Božo Repe, 'Vloga akcije "Slovenija, moja dežela" pri nacionalni homogenizaciji osemdesetih let', in Mitja Ferenc, Jurij Hadalin and Blaž Babič (eds), *Osamosvojitev 1991: država in demokracija na Slovenskem v zgodovinskih razsežnostih* (Ljubljana: Univerza v Ljubljani, 2011), pp. 225–40.

82 Miljenko Jergović, 'Slovenia on my mind', *Naši dani* 1019 (12 July 1991), p. 1.

Conclusion: rethinking youth politics and culture in late socialist Yugoslavia

Moja prva i najveća želja bi bila da se probudim
i da ustanovim da je 1990 godina i da kažem
'Uh, al' sam nešto ružno sanjao ...'

Milan Mladenović, EKV

Amidst a major rethinking of the economic and political status quo, the 1980s saw the revival of a generational challenge to Yugoslav socialism, in which socialist self-management was not necessarily rejected, but rather seen as capable of reform within the existing Yugoslav federal framework. The book showed how an urban trans-republican network developed that expressed novel ideas in politics and culture and engendered issue-oriented activism, in addition to a new 'sense of citizenship', where the Yugoslav and the ethno-national line of identification were seen as complementary and not mutually exclusive. Although significantly conditioned by the republican contexts, debates, exchanges and interactions took place across republican borders. This realm of youth politics and culture which had the wide decentralised network of the SSOJ as its institutional umbrella broke down only very late in the decade once the physical dissolution of the country began to materialise. The book analysed a range of public 'acts' the youth actively engaged at different levels of the institutional youth realm undertook during the 1980s, against the background of Yugoslav late socialist research that dealt with 'the crisis generation'. It also addressed the ways in which the actors themselves mobilised the rhetoric of youth/generation to challenge the mainstream, establishing new political languages through cultural acts, journalistic writing or issue-oriented activism.

The book focused on the reinvention of the institutional youth sphere and the new concepts of freedom members of this generation put forward through the youth media and through their various 'acts of citizenship'. The first chapter elaborated on the notion of space – both in physical terms and as a form of public platform where the boundaries of permitted critique and 'tolerated freedom' could be challenged and tested. In addition, it addressed the subtle border between negotiation and dissent in the rapport these youngsters had with their youth organisation and with the state. The League of Socialist Youth was perceived as capable of reforming and acting as a conduit for new forms of politics and culture, whether derived from internal sources or taken from new developments, particularly in Western European countries. In this sense, representatives of this generation – for the most part – still believed in a 'Yugoslav way'. A more daring style of journalistic writing, new forms of music and art and new forms of political expression and activism found shelter within the institutional youth sphere. As a state 'socio-political' institution that was nevertheless decentralised in form, relatively distanced from the realm of high politics, and full of 'experimental' peripheral spaces, the SSOJ was perfectly positioned to channel and support new ideas and forms of cultural and political activism with its considerable material resources and infrastructure. At the same time, it had to maintain a balance between 'the new' and 'the old'. In addition, the federal level of the youth organisation often faced the challenge of reconciling the disparate attitudes and views coming from its diverse 'base' all over the country. Moreover, being part of the political system, it had to frame the new demands and aspirations in the politically acceptable vocabulary, although internal debates about 'the democratisation' of the SSOJ began soon after the death of Josip Broz Tito in 1980. Hence, a closer look at the internal dynamics, internal debates and changes over time within socialist institutions provides a venue for studying socialist societies beyond the often taken-for-granted paradigm of 'binary socialism'.

The concept of 'freedom' was central to this generation's cause: it was primarily associated with freedom of thought, speech and expression, which became particularly prominent during the banning of particular issues of youth magazines, the contestations of the 'verbal offense' Article 133 and the elusive definition of the crime of 'enemy propaganda', as well as during the rise of the new issue-oriented campaigns around peace, environmentalism and sexual freedom. However, freedom for many of these activists did not mean the end of Yugoslavia and socialist self-management, at least until the very late 1980s: for most, Yugoslav socialism was still capable of reforming itself and accommodating these demands. The second chapter reflected on the debates concerning the future of the inherited socialist framework of values and commemorative practices and the ways Tito's legacy was going to be carried forward following his death. Although frequently reproached for an alleged appropriation of far right ideologies, the different cultural acts (punk music, the controversial Youth Day poster) essentially challenged the norms and discourse of an older generation and sought to rethink the performative dimension through which the various levels of the Yugoslav post-war consensus were manifested.

Until the late 1980s, the young activists involved in the different issue-oriented campaigns that used the institutional youth realm as a platform to gain visibility in the public space, still operated within the discourse of socialist self-management, social justice and solidarity, seeking to put under scrutiny the malfunctions of the system and the corrupt elites. As it was demonstrated in Chapter 3, new areas for political expression opened up around issues of peace, anti-militarism, environmentalism/nuclear disarmament and sexuality, and it was the League of Socialist Youth that brought these issues to public attention. What was unique to this generation's understanding of the socio-political context was an acceptance of the Yugoslav institutional framework and an identification with Yugoslavia in a cultural, or civic sense, as they essentially sought to correct, criticise or ridicule the regime, thus drawing a rather clear line between their anti-regime activism and the overt anti-Yugoslavism which began to dominate in the late 1980s, in particular among the intellectual circles in Serbia and Slovenia. The way they framed their 'acts of citizenship' and articulated their demands conflated their particular identity as stemming from the Yugoslav context, possessing Yugoslav-specific contestations of the socio-political framework with challenges resulting from developments at international level, as the latter served both as a personal inspiration and a platform for meaningful exchange and interaction.

One of the prevalent debates both within the political realm and the sphere of institutional youth culture up until 1987 was how to maintain but rethink and reform Yugoslav socialist federalism. After 1987 the clashes intensified, the envisioned responses to the crisis further diversified and the ideological gaps widened to the extent that one could observe more conflicting approaches rather than constructive debate. This was particularly visible during the debates for the amendment of the Serbian republican constitution in 1988 and the emerging anti-Albanian discourse which would eventually lead to Kosovo being stripped of its constitutional autonomy in 1989. In Chapter 4, the book provided new perspectives on this moment from the point of view of the young generation and the youth sphere. The period from 1986 until 1990 saw a radical change in the way the SSOJ articulated its politics and defined its role. In the late 1980s, the political debates and their framing in hostile and exclusivist terms started to migrate to the youth political and cultural realm, engendering conflicts, statements or observations which did away with the previously established codes of public debate and political communication. At the same time, however, an intra-republican diversification among the young political and media elite occurred, accompanied by a convergence on individual or group basis across national lines and mainly around reformist and liberal values.

Like the majority of the anti-nationalist liberal and leftist intellectuals in the second half of the 1980s, some of the vocal representatives of this generation advanced a vision of Yugoslavism/Yugoslav citizenship that could stand apart from dogmatic socialism and ethnic nationalism. Born and raised in socialist Yugoslavia, these youngsters had internalised to a certain extent the proclaimed notions of freedom and peace, social justice, equality and solidarity and thus openly campaigned through the youth media against public hypocrisy when it came to the proclaimed values and their actual implementation.[2] However, a prominent caesura detected by the absolute majority of my respondents was indeed the rise of Slobodan Milošević and Serbian nationalism after 1987. Hence, during the last three years of the decade there was an apparent discursive shift within the youth realm as hopes for amelioration of the system of socialist self-management and the federation in its current form were abandoned, debates which openly questioned accepted history were initiated and although generally speaking the youth press and the youth political elite preserved an anti-nationalist/reformist line, they embraced the 'liberal turn' and a relatively moderate discourse of national emancipation, eventually relegating Yugoslav socialist federalism to the past. Moreover, with the disappearance of the League of Communists in January 1990 and the abolishment of the SSOJ the same year, the common political institutional platforms which provided the space for supra-ethnic convergence and pan-Yugoslav debate were lost and the formation of the new supranational democratic institutions never took place. The multilayered sense of citizenship this generation was the embodiment of, where the ethno-national and the Yugoslav dimensions complemented each other, could only exist under the specific political consensus and the post-war social context. At the end of the 1980s, as the ethno-national became an omnipresent identity marker and frame of reference, the tension between these different identities insreased to the point that this multi-layered citizenship began to fragment irretrievably. Last but not least, the Slovene activists – those who stood at the helm of this generation's political, media and cultural activism, at the end of the decade decided to retreat, i.e. shift their focus away from the rest of the Yugoslav space and abandoned any attempts at forging a pan-Yugoslav alternative – which might explain why a viable Yugoslav political option failed to consolidate within the Yugoslav youth realm.

The book opens up new questions and hopes to suggest new ways of studying late socialism – from a critical rethinking of the concept of dissent, processes of domestication of Western social movements in a socialist context, to approaching the youth sphere more seriously and providing a history of alternatives. Moreover, since the book only analysed a limited group of individuals who have classified as an elite both in late socialism and today, other units of this generation remain unaccounted for in historical research, as well as many other groups who were ascribed similar importance and status within Yugoslav society – workers, miners, children/young pioneers, army officers, war veterans.

The last Yugoslav generation has been generally remembered through its achievements in culture and sport in the 1980s. It has been often represented as a generation which epitomises urbanity, cosmopolitanism, non-conformism and late Yugoslav culture. In reality, individuals who were actively involved in late socialist youth politics, media or culture followed diverse trajectories – some pursued their 'non-conformist' engagements in the realms of media and culture, some remained wholly or partially faithful to their liberal/progressive youthful ideals, while some chose to abandon/erase their socialist past and redefine their politics. Narratives of loss of 'geo-political dignity' and disillusionment with the post-Yugoslav reality and post-socialist politics were intertwined among my interviewees with wider reflections on the Yugoslav past, as well as with evocations of a sense of cosmopolitanism, a different way of engaging with both the Eastern and the Western world and a somewhat generational obsession with freedom. Twenty-five years after the break-up of Yugoslavia and the disappearance of European state socialism, individual professional trajectories and the different post-Yugoslav trajectories of the federation's successor states prove to be determining of the ways individuals reflect on their generational experience, on the 1980s and on the Yugoslav past in general. Nevertheless, there is a shared belief that some things could have been done differently to prevent the disastrous outcomes of the Yugoslav crisis of the 1980s. This is conveyed strongly in an interview with Aldo Ivančić, member of the Slovenian band Borghesia:

> I have always been inspired by artists who had the guts to talk about the injustices in this world, from the troubadours, protest singers, beatniks, hippies, punks ... Throughout the history of mankind the unnatural division between the elite (religious, political, and economic) and the others, manifests itself, that is the plebs on the one hand, and the quest for utopia on the other. With the fall of the Berlin Wall, many thought that we had come to the point that we have reached utopia. Twenty years and a lot of dead in this region were necessary for the mass to realize that war profiteers and nationalist dogs guide us thirsty through the water. They should listen to our album 'Resistance' from the end of the '80s ... With the establishment of the new nation states nothing was solved. These small states became an even easier prey for klepto[maniac] capitalism and local politicians and leaders have become the servants of capital, which charged a high price for their services. Cosmopolitanism is replaced with globalism and multiculturalism with cheap nationalism. Ethnic diversity is replaced by monocultures.[3]

Figure 15 *Mladina* front cover, 1995

As I have argued elsewhere, today, the notion of freedom has been taken to its other extreme semantic pole and has become synonymous with the freedom of travel and the social and economic rights – two features of the lives of the members of this generation under Yugoslav socialism which are now – to varying degrees – diminished. Interviewees often captured this idea by contrasting their sense of being free 'then' and being unfree 'now'.[4] Freedom, thus, becomes a thread which links the past and the present and to a certain degree continues to legitimise an oppositional subjectivity throughout the post-Yugoslav space.

Notes

1 'My first and biggest wish would be to wake up and realise that it is the year 1990 and say: "Uh, that was one bad dream!".'
2 From the list of twenty statements using the Thurstone scale in the 1986 federal youth survey, where respondents were asked to pick two, the highest ranked

were: 'The most important thing is to raise your children to become honest men' (32.2 per cent) and 'The most important is to fight against any type of injustice' (24.0 per cent). Ratko Dunđerović, 'Samoupravna orijentacija i (ne)zadovoljstvo pojavama u društvu', in Srđan Vrcan *et al.*, *Položaj, svest i ponašanje mlade generacije Jugoslavije* (Beograd: Centar za istraživačku, dokumentacionu i izdavačku delatnost Konferencije SSOJ/Zagreb: Institut za društvena istraživanja Sveučilišta, 1986), p. 85.

3 'Borghesia: "Budite samo svoji, ne kopirajte, ne imitirajte uzore!"', http://balkanrock.com/borghesiabudite-samo-svoji-ne-kopirajte-ne-imitirajte-uzore/ (last accessed 28 February 2014).

4 Ljubica Spaskovska, 'The "children of crisis": Making sense of (post) socialism and the end of Yugoslavia', *East European Politics and Societies* (forthcoming).

Select bibliography

Primary sources

Archives

Archive of Bosnia-Herzegovina, Sarajevo:

Collection 'Republička konferencija SSOBIH', 1982–90

Archive of Republic of Slovenia, Ljubljana:

Collection 'Republiška konferenca Zveze socialistične mladine Slovenije, 1974–1990'

Archive of Yugoslavia, Belgrade:

Collection 'Savez socijalističke omladine Jugoslavije', 1980–82

Open Society Archive (OSA), Budapest:

Radio Free Europe Background and Situation Reports (Yugoslavia), 1968–90

State Archive of Republic of Macedonia, Skopje:

Collection 'Сојуз на студенти на Македонија', 1968–74
Collection 'Републичка конференција на ССММ', 1989

Print media

Borba
Melody Maker
Mlad borec
Mladina

Mladost
Naši dani
New Musical Express
NON
Omladinski pokret
Polet
Republika
Student
Studentski list
Studentski zbor
Valter

Surveys and youth-related publications

Bošković, Blaž (ed.). *Bliska perspektiva Jugoslavije s posebnim osvrtom na društveni položaj omladine* (Beograd: Predsedništvo Konferencije SSOJ, 1985).

Davidović, Dušan (ed.), *Mladi Jugoslavije: opšti pregled* (Beograd: Centar za istraživačku i dokumentaciono-izdavaćku delatnost Predsedništva Konferencije SSOJ, 1982).

Izveštaj o radu SSO Srbije između 11. i 12. Kongresa (Beograd: RK SSO Serbije, 1990).

Jedanaesti kongres SSOJ (Beograd: NIRO Mladost, 1983).

Klasno-Socijalna Struktura Saveza Komunista Jugoslavije (Beograd: Izdavački centar Komunist, 1984).

Kompendij za bivše in bodoče politike (Ljubljana: ZSMS, 1989).

Lavš, Igor (ed.). *Prilozi iz javne rasprave o opštim načelima Statuta SSOJ* (Beograd: Predsedništvo Konferencije SSOJ, 1989).

Lolić, Marko. *Revolucionarni omladinski pokret u Jugoslaviji (SKOJ-SSOJ, 1919–1984)* (Beograd: Radnička štampa, 1984).

Mihailović, Srećko *et al. Deca krize: Omladina Jugoslavije krajem osamdesetih* (Beograd: Institut društvenih nauka/Centar za politikološka istraživanja i javno mnenje, 1990).

Mlada generacija, danas: društveni položaj, uloga i perspektive mlade generacije Jugoslavije [Zbornik radova sa naučnog skupa 'Društveni položaj, uloga i perspektive mlade generacije Jugoslavije', održanog 22–24.IX.1982 u Kumrovcu] (Beograd: NIRO Mladost/Predsedništvo Konferencije SSOJ, 1982).

Omladina i politika: jugoslavenska omladina između političke apatije i autonomnog političkog subjektiviteta (Split: Marksistički centar Međuopćinske konferencije SKH za Dalmaciju, 1988).

Омладина, чинилац друштвених промена: реферат Зорана Анђелковића, председника РК ССОС (Београд: Републичка конференција ССО Србије, 1986).

Posavec, Stanko *et al. Omladina i socijalizam – ostvarenja i mogučnosti* (Zagreb: Centar za društvene djelatnosti omladine, 1971).

Predlog dokumenti dvanaestog kongresa Saveza socijalističke omladine Jugoslavije, Beograd 12–14 juna 1986 (Belgrade: Konferencija SSOJ/Službeni list SFRJ, 1986).

Punk pod Slovenci (Ljubljana: Univerzitetna konferenca ZSMS/Republiška konferenca ZSMS, 1985).

Ule, Mirjana. *Mladina in ideologija* (Ljubljana: Delavska enotnost, 1988).

Vrcan, Srđan *et al. Položaj, svest i ponašanje mlade generacije Jugoslavije* (Beograd: Centar za istraživačku, dokumentacionu i izdavačku delatnost Konferencije SSOJ/ Zagreb: Institut za društvena istraživanja Sveučilišta, 1986).

'Yugoslavia', in *From Below: Independent Peace and Environmental Movements in Eastern Europe and the USSR* (New York: Helsinki Watch Report, 1987), pp. 179–206.

Youth Prospects in the 1980s: Synthesis Report Presented to the General Conference of UNESCO at its Twenty-First Session (Paris: UNESCO, 1980).

XII конгрес на Сојузот на социалистичка младина на Македонија (Скопје/ Кочани: Републичка конференција на ССММ/Младост, 1986).

Interviews

Culture:

1. Zemira Alajbegović (Slovenia). 19 March 2012, Ljubljana.
2. Aleš Debeljak (Slovenia). 15 March 2012, Ljubljana.
3. Toše Filipovski (Macedonia). 12 October 2011, Skopje.
4. Srđan Gojković (Gile) (Serbia). 30 October 2011, Belgrade.
5. Bojan Hadžihalilović (Bosnia-Herzegovina). 9 March 2012, Sarajevo.
6. Nikolai Jeffs (Slovenia). 16 March 2012, Ljubljana.
7. Neven Korda (Slovenia). 4 May 2012, Ljubljana.
8. Milčo Mančevski (Macedonia). 6 September 2012, Skopje.
9. Zoran Predin (Slovenia). 16 November 2011, Ljubljana.
10. Vlatko Stefanovski (Macedonia). 19 December 2011, Skopje.
11. Goran Tanevski (Macedonia). 24 August 2012, Skopje.
12. Gregor Tomc (Slovenia). 17 November 2011, Ljubljana.
13. Igor Vidmar (Slovenia). 13 November 2011, Ljubljana.

Media:

14. Senad Avdić (Bosnia-Herzegovina). 24 February 2012, Sarajevo.
15. Robert Botteri (Slovenia). 16 March 2012, Ljubljana.
16. Velimir Ćurguz-Kazimir (Serbia). 10 April 2012, Belgrade.
17. Petar Janjatović (Serbia). 27 October 2011, Belgrade.
18. Ljupčo Jolevski (Macedonia). 6 October 2011, Skopje.
19. Predrag Kojović (Bosnia-Herzegovina). 2 March 2012, Sarajevo.
20. Boro Kontić (Bosnia-Herzegovina). 7 March 2012, Sarajevo.
21. Miha Kovač (Slovenia). 4 May 2012, Ljubljana.
22. Milomir Kovačević-Strašni (Bosnia-Herzegovina). 20 June 2012, Paris.
23. Zoran Kostov (Macedonia). 30 April 2012, Skopje.
24. Dragan Kremer (Serbia). 1 November 2011, Belgrade.

25. Sašo Ordanovski (Macedonia). 7 October 2011, Skopje.
26. Senad Pećanin (Bosnia-Herzegovina). 7 March 2012, Sarajevo.

New social movements:

27. Danica Fink Hafner (Slovenia). 15 March 2012, Ljubljana.
28. Marko Hren (Slovenia). 19 March 2012, Ljubljana.
29. Nataša Sukič (Slovenia). 16 March 2012, Ljubljana.

Politics:

30. Branko Greganović (Slovenia). 26 September 2012, via Skype.
31. Dr Risto Ivanov (Macedonia). 30 April 2012, Skopje.
32. Dejan Jović (Croatia). 11 June 2012, Zagreb.
33. Rasim Kadić (Bosnia-Herzegovina). 22/24 February 2012, Sarajevo.
34. Slobodan Najdovski (Macedonia). 26 April 2012, Skopje.
35. Martin Raguž (Bosnia-Herzegovina). 1 March 2012, Sarajevo.
36. Hasib Salkić (Bosnia-Herzegovina). 29 February 2012, Sarajevo.
37. Zoran Thaler (Slovenia). 18 March 2012, Ljubljana.
38. Azem Vllasi (Kosovo). 4 September 2012, Prishtina.

Military:

39. Milan Lišanin (Serbia). 25 August 2012, via Skype.
40. Vladimir Rajtar (Croatia). 13 June 2012, Zagreb.
41. Simo Spaskovski (Macedonia). 22 November 2011, Skopje.

Other

'Указ за прогласување на законот за измени и дополненија за законот за военната обврска', *Службен лист на Социјалистичка Федеративна Република Југославија* 26/1989 (21 април 1989).
'Pravilnik o vršenju vojne obaveze', *Službeni vojni list* 21/1991 (25 septembar 1991).
Statistički godišnjak Jugoslavije 1985 (Beograd: Savezni zavod za statistiku, 1985).

Secondary sources

Books

Abrams, Lynn. *Oral History Theory* (London: Routledge, 2010).
Allcock, Paul B. *Explaining Yugoslavia* (London: C. Hurst, 2000).

Anderson, Kathryn and Dana C. Jack, 'Learning to listen: Interview techniques and analyses', in Robert Perks and Alistair Thomson (eds), *The Oral History Reader* (London/New York: Routledge, 1998), pp. 129–43.

Andjelić, Neven. *Bosnia-Herzegovina: The End of a Legacy* (London: Frank Cass Publishers, 2003).

Badovinac, Zdenka Eda Čufer and Anthony Gardner (eds), *NSK from Kapital to Capital: An Event of the Final Decade of Yugoslavia* (Cambridge, MA: MIT Press, 2015).

Bakhtin, Mikhail. 'Forms of time and of the chronotope in the novel', in Michael Holquist (ed.), *The Dialogic Imagination: Four Essays* (Austin: University of Texas Press, 1981), pp. 84–258.

Benderly, Jill and Evan Kraft (eds), *Independent Slovenia: Origins, Movements, Prospects* (London: Macmillan, 1994).

Bertsch, Gary K. *Values and Community in Multi-National Yugoslavia* (Boulder: East European Quarterly, 1976).

Betts, Paul. *Within Walls: Private Life in the German Democratic Republic* (Oxford and New York: Oxford University Press, 2010).

Bilandžić, Dušan. *Historija Socijalističke Federativne Republike Jugoslavije: glavni procesi 1918–1985* (Zagreb: Školska knjiga, 1985).

Bilić, Bojan. *We Were Gasping for Air: [Post-]Yugoslav Anti-War Activism and Its Legacy* (Baden-Baden: Nomos, 2012).

Bunce, Valerie. *Subversive Institutions: The Design and the Destruction of Socialism and the State* (Cambridge: Cambridge University Press, 1999).

Burg, Steven L. *Conflict and Cohesion in Socialist Yugoslavia: Political Decision Making since 1966* (Princeton: Princeton University Press, 1983).

Carter, April. *Democratic Reform in Yugoslavia: The Changing Role of the Party* (London: Frances Pinter, 1982).

Cohen, Lenard. *The Socialist Pyramid: Elites and Power in Yugoslavia* (Oakville, New York and London: Mosaic Press, 1989).

Ćorić, Tomislav. *Pola stoljeća Studentskoga centra u zagrebu (1957. – 2007.)* (Zagreb: Sveučilište u Zagrebu/Studentski centar u Zagrebu, 2007).

Debeljak, Aleš. *Twilight of the Idols: Recollections of a Lost Yugoslavia* (Buffalo: White Pine Press, 1994).

Denitch, Bogdan Denis. *Limits and Possibilities: The Crisis of Yugoslav Socialism and State Socialist Systems* (Minneapolis: University of Minnesota Press, 1990).

Dizdarević, Raif. *From the Death of Tito to the Death of Yugoslavia* (Sarajevo and Zagreb: Šahinspahić, 2009).

Djokic, Dejan (ed.). *Yugoslavism: Histories of a Failed Idea, 1918–1992* (Madison: University of Wisconsin Press, 2003).

Dragović-Soso, Jasna and Lenard J. Cohen (eds), *State Collapse in South-Eastern Europe: New Perspectives on Yugoslavia's Disintegration* (West Lafayette: Purdue University Press, 2007).

Dugandžija, Nikola. *Jugoslavenstvo* (Beograd: NIRO Mladost, 1985).

Eakin, Paul John. *How Our Lives Become Stories: Making Selves* (Ithaca: Cornell University Press, 1999).

Erjavec, Aleš (ed.). *Postmodernism and the Postsocialist Condition: Politicized Art under Late Socialism* (Berkeley, Los Angeles and London: University of California Press, 2003).

Fink Hafner, Danica. *Nova družbena gibanja: subjekti politične inovacije* (Ljubljana: FDV, 1992).

Fulbrook, Mary. *Dissonant Lives: Generations and Violence through the German Dictatorships* (Oxford: Oxford University Press, 2011).

Fürst, Juliane. *Stalin's Last Generation: Soviet Post-War Youth and the Emergence of Mature Socialism* (Oxford: Oxford University Press, 2010).

Gillis, John R. *Youth and History: Tradition and Change in European Age Relations, 1770–Present* (San Diego: Academic Press, 1981).

Gorsuch, Anne E. and Diane P. Koenker (eds). *Turizm: The Russian and East European Tourist under Capitalism and Socialism* (Ithaca: Cornell University Press, 2006).

Goulding, Daniel J. *Liberated Cinema: The Yugoslav Experience 1945–2001* (Bloomington: Indiana University Press, 2003).

Grandits, Hannes and Karin Taylor (eds). *Yugoslavia's Sunny Side: A History of Tourism in Socialism (1950s–1980s)* (Budapest and New York: Central European University Press, 2010).

Hann, Chris (ed.). *Postsocialism: Ideals, Ideologies and Practices in Eurasia* (London and New York: Routledge, 2001).

Haug, Hilde Katrine. *Creating a Socialist Yugoslavia: Tito, Communist Leadership and the National Question* (London: I. B. Tauris, 2012).

Ingrao, Charles W. and Thomas Allan Emmert (eds). *Confronting the Yugoslav Controversies: A Scholars' Initiative* (West Lafayette: Purdue University Press, 2009).

Isin, Engin and Greg Nielsen (eds). *Acts of Citizenship* (London: Palgrave Macmillan, 2008).

Jeffs, Nikolai. 'FV and the "Third Scene", 1980–1990', in *FV – Alternative Scene of the Eighties* (Ljubljana: International Center for Graphic Arts, 2008), pp. 345–94.

Jović, Dejan. *Yugoslavia: A State That Withered Away* (West Lafayette: Purdue University Press, 2009).

Kenny, Padraic. *A Carnival of Revolution: Central Europe 1989* (Princeton: Princeton University Press, 2003).

Klasić, Hrvoje. *Jugoslavija i svijet 1968* (Zagreb: Ljevak, 2012).

Knopp, Karen *et al.* (eds). *Rethinking Federalism: Citizens, Markets, and Governments in a Changing World* (Vancouver: University of British Columbia Press, 1995).

Krasniqi, Gëzim. '"For democracy – against violence": A Kosovar alternative', in Bojan Bilić and Vesna Janković (eds), *Resisting the Evil: [Post] Yugoslav Anti-War Contention* (Baden Baden: NOMOS, 2012), pp. 83–103.

Kršić, Dejan. *Mirko Ilić: Fist to Face* (New York: F+V Media, 2012).

Kurti, Laszlo. *Youth and the State in Hungary: Capitalism, Communism and Class* (London: Pluto Press, 2002).

Laing, Dave. *One Chord Wonders: Power and Meaning in Punk Rock* (Milton Keynes and Philadelphia: Open University Press, 1985).

Levi, Pavle. *Disintegration in Frames: Aesthetics and Ideology in the Yugoslav and Post-Yugoslav Cinema* (Stanford: Stanford University Press, 2007).

Lydall, Harold. *Yugoslavia in Crisis* (Oxford: Clarendon Press, 1989).

Mannheim, Karl. 'The problem of generations', in Paul Kecskemeti (ed.), *Essays on the Sociology of Knowledge* (London: Routledge, 1964), pp. 276–320.

Mastnak, Tomaž (ed.). *Zbornik Socialistična civilna družba* (Ljubljana: RK ZSMS/UK ZSMS, 1986).

Matvejević, Predrag. *Jugoslavenstvo danas: pitanja kulture* (reprint) (Belgrade: MVTC, 2003).

Milivojević, Marko, John B. Allcock and Pierre Maurer (eds). *Yugoslavia's Security Dilemmas: Armed Forces, National Defence and Foreign Policy* (Oxford and New York: Berg Publishers, 1988).

Monroe, Alexei. *Interrogation Machine: Laibach and NSK* (Cambridge, MA and London: MIT Press, 2005).

Monroe, Alexei. 'Laibach: *Made in* Iugoslávia', in Fernando Oliva and Marcelo Rezende (eds), *Comunismo da forma* (São Paulo: Alameda Casa Editorial, 2007), pp. 135–43.

Muršič, Rajko. 'Punk anthropology: From a study of a local Slovene alternative rock scene towards partisan scholarship', in Laszlo Kűrti and Peter Skalnik (eds), *Postsocialist Europe: Anthropological Perspectives from Home* (New York and Oxford: Berghahn Books, 2009), pp. 188–206.

Patterson, Patrick Hyder. *Bought and Sold: Living and Losing the Good Life in Socialist Yugoslavia* (Ithaca: Cornell University Press, 2011).

Petrović, Momčilo. *Pitao sam Albance šta žele, a oni su rekli: republiku … ako može* (Beograd: Radio B92, 1996).

Pilcher, Jane. *Age & Generation in Modern Britain* (Oxford: Oxford University Press, 1995).

Popov, Nebojša (ed.). *The Road to War in Serbia: Trauma and Catharsis* (Budapest: Central European University Press, 2000).

Portelli, Alessandro. *The Death of Luigi Trastulli, and Other Stories: Form and Meaning in Oral History* (Albany: SUNY Press, 1990).

Ramet, Pedro (ed.). *Yugoslavia in the 1980s* (Boulder: Westview Press, 1985).

Ramet, Sabrina. *Nationalism and Federalism in Yugoslavia 1962–1991* (Bloomington: Indiana University Press, 1992).

Ramet, Sabrina P. and Danica Fink-Hafner (eds). *Democratic Transition in Slovenia: Value Transformation, Education, and Media* (College Station: Texas A&M University Press, 2006).

Robinson, Gertrude J. *Tito's Maverick Media: Politics of Mass Communication in Yugoslavia* (Urbana, Chicago and London: University of Illinois Press, 1977).

Rusinow, Dennison. *Yugoslavia: Oblique Insights and Observations* (Pittsburgh: University of Pittsburgh Press, 2008).

Saunders, Anna. *Honecker's Children: Youth and Patriotism in East Germany, 1979–2002* (Manchester: Manchester University Press, 2011).

Savage, Jon. *England's Dreaming* (London: Faber & Faber, 2005).

Savic, Obrad. 'Concepts of civil society in former Yugoslavia', in Dane R. Gordon and David C. Durst (eds), *Civil Society in Southeast Europe* (Amsterdam and New York: Rodopi, 2004), pp. 75–83.

Šešić, Milena Dragićević. *Umetnost i alternativa* (Beograd: Fakultet dramskih umetnosti, 1992).

Spaskovska, Ljubica. 'Landscapes of resistance, hope and loss: Yugoslav supranationalism and anti-nationalism', in Bojan Bilić and Vesna Janković (eds), *Resisting the Evil: [Post] Yugoslav Anti-War Contention* (Baden Baden: Nomos, 2012), pp. 37–61.

Spaskovska, Ljubica. 'The Yugoslav chronotope: Histories, memories and the future of Yugoslav studies', in Rory Archer, Armina Galijas and Florian Bieber (eds), *Debating the Dissolution of Yugoslavia* (London: Ashgate, 2014), pp. 241–53.

Stanković, Slobodan. *The End of the Tito Era: Yugoslavia's Dilemmas* (Stanford: Hoover Institution Press, 1981).

Thomson, Alistair. 'Unreliable memories: The use and abuse of oral history', in William Lamont (ed.), *Historical Controversies and Historians* (London and New York: Routledge, 1998), pp. 23–35.

Thomson, Paul. 'The voice of the past: Oral history', in Robert Perks and Alistair Thomson (eds), *The Oral History Reader* (London and New York: Routledge, 1998), pp. 25–32.

Timotijević, Slavko *et al. Ovo je Studentski kulturni centar/This is the Students Cultural Center: prvih 25 godina: 1971–1996* (Beograd: BMG, 1996).

Tomanović, Smiljka *et al. Mladi – naša sadašnjost. Istraživanje socijalnih biografija mladih u Srbiji* (Beograd: Čigoja/Institut za sociološka istraživanja Filozofskog fakulteta, 2012).

Tomc, Gregor. 'Spori in spopadi druge Slovenije', in *Punk pod Slovenci* (Ljubljana: Univerzitetna konferenca ZSMS/Republiška konferenca ZSMS, 1985), pp. 9–27.

Tomc, Gregor. 'Škandal v rdečem baru', in *Punk je bil prej: 25 let punka pod Slovenci* (Ljubljana: Cankarjeva založba, 2002), pp. 86–90.

Tomić, Đorđe and Petar Atanacković (eds). *Društvo u pokretu: novi društveni pokreti u Jugoslaviji od 1968 do danas* (Novi Sad: Cenzura, 2009).

Tratnik, Suzana and Nataša S. Segan (eds). *Zbornik o lezbičnem gibanju na Slovenskem 1984–1995* (Ljubljana: ŠKUC, 1995).

Turner, Victor. *From Ritual to Theatre: The Human Seriousness of Play* (New York: PAJ Publications, 1982).

Vladisavljević, Nebojša. *Serbia's Antibureaucratic Revolution: Milošević, the Fall of Communism and Nationalist Mobilization* (Basingstoke and New York: Palgrave Macmillan, 2008).

Von der Goltz, Anna (ed.). *'Talkin' 'bout My Generation': Conflicts of Generation Building and Europe's '1968'* (Göttingen: Wallstein Verlag, 2011).

Vučetić, Radina. *Coca Cola Socialism: The Americanization of Yugoslav Popular Culture in the 1960s* (Belgrade: Službeni glasnik, 2012).

Vurnik, Blaž. *Med Marksom in Punkom: Vloga Zveze socialistične mladine Slovenije pri demokratizaciji Slovenije (1980–1990)* (Ljubljana: Modrijan, 2005).

Wachtel, Andrew B. *Making a Nation, Breaking a Nation: Literature and Cultural Politics in Yugoslavia* (Stanford: Stanford University Press, 1998).

Woodward, Susan L. *Balkan Tragedy – Chaos and Dissolution after the Cold War* (Washington, DC: The Brookings Institution, 1995).

Woodward, Susan L. *Socialist Unemployment: The Political Economy of Yugoslavia 1945–1990* (Princeton: Princeton University Press, 1995).

Yugoslavia: Prisoners of Conscience (London: Amnesty International Publications, 1985).

Yurchak, Alexei. *Everything Was Forever Until It Was No More: The Last Soviet Generation* (Princeton: Princeton University Press, 2006).

Zimmerman, William. *Open Borders, Nonalignment, and the Political Evolution of Yugoslavia* (Princeton: Princeton University Press, 1987).

Journal articles

Abrams, Philip. 'The conflict of generations in industrial society', *Journal of Contemporary History* 5:1 (1970), 175–90.

Clissold, Stephen. 'Review: *Novi prilozi za biografiju Josipa Broza Tita* by Vladimir Dedijer', *The Slavonic and East European Review* 60:4 (1982), 632–4.

Conover, Pamela J. 'Citizen identities and conceptions of the self', *Journal of Political Philosophy* 3 (1995), 133–65.

Dević, Ana. 'Anti-war initiative and the un-making of civic identities in the former Yugoslav republics', *Journal of Historical Sociology* 10:2 (1997), 127–56.

Flere, Sergej. 'Vojvođanska omladina, jugoslovenstvo i stavovi prema etnosu', *Ideje – časopis za teoriju suvremenog društva* 2:3 (1987), 150–65.

Gagnon, V.P. 'Yugoslavia in 1989 and after', *Nationalities Papers* 38:1 (2010), 23–39.

Isin, Engin. 'Citizenship in flux: The figure of the activist citizen', *Subjectivity* 29 (2009), 367–88.

Jansen, Stef. 'After the red passport: Towards an anthropology of the everyday geopolitics of entrapment in the EU's "immediate outside"', *Journal of the Royal Anthropological Institute* 15:4 (2009), 815–32.

Joppke, Christian. 'Transformation of citizenship: Status, rights, identity', *Citizenship Studies* 11:1 (2007), 37–48.

Kocka, Jürgen. 'Asymmetrical historical comparison: The case of the German *Sonderweg*', *History and Theory* 38:1 (1999), 40–50.

Kodrnja, Jasenka and Katarina Vidović. 'SOS telefon za žene i djecu žrtve nasilja', *Žena* 46 (1988), 68–77.

Krasniqi, Gëzim. 'Socialism, national utopia, and rock music: Inside the Albanian rock scene of Yugoslavia, 1970–1989', *East Central Europe* 38 (2011), 336–54.

Kumar, Krishan. 'Civil society: An inquiry into the usefulness of an historical term', *The British Journal of Sociology* 44:3 (1993), 375–95.

Massey, Garth, Randy Hodson and Dusko Sekulic. 'Nationalism, liberalism and liberal nationalism in post-war Croatia', *Nations and Nationalism* 9:1 (2003), 55–82.

Mulej, Oskar. '"We are drowning in red beet, patching up the holes in the Iron Curtain": The punk subculture in Ljubljana in the late 1970s and early 1980s', *East Central Europe* 38 (2011), 373–89.

Parsons, Talcott. 'Age and sex in the social structure of the United States', *American Sociological Review* 7:5 (1942), 604–16.

Pauković, Davor. 'Poslednji kongres Saveza Komunista Jugoslavije: uzroci, tijek i posljedice raspada', *Suvremene teme* 1:1 (2008), 21–33.

Polletta, Francesca. '"Free spaces" in collective action', *Theory and Society* 28 (1999), 1–38.

Pottie, David. 'The politics of meaning in punk rock', *Problématique* 3 (1993), 1–21.

Repe, Božo. 'Slovenci v osemdesetih letih (drugi del)', *Zgodovinski časopis* 3 (2000), 413–48.

Roberts, Adam. 'Yugoslavia: The constitution and the succession', *The World Today* 34:4 (1978), 136–46.

Sagasta, Sanja. 'State of the art: Lesbian movements in former Yugoslavia', *The European Journal of Women's Studies* 8:3 (2001), 357–72.

Sekulic, Dusko, Garth Massey and Randy Hodson. 'Who were the Yugoslavs? Failed sources of a common identity in the former Yugoslavia', *American Sociological Review* 59 (1994), 83–97.

Šiber, Ivan. 'Konformizam i političko ponašanje', *Naše teme* 2 (1977).

'"The Slovene Spring": An interview with Miha Kovač, *New Left Review* 177 (1988): 115–28.

Spaskovska, Ljubica. 'The fractured "we" and the ethno-national "I": The Macedonian citizenship framework', *Citizenship Studies* 16:3–4 (2012), 383–96.

Spitzer, Alan B. 'The historical problem of generations', *The American Historical Review* 78:5 (1973), 1353–85.

Tomc, Gregor. 'Civilna družba pod slovenskim socializmom', *Nova revija* 57 (1987), 144–50.

Vladisavljević, Nebojša. 'Institutional power and the rise of Milošević', *Nationalities Papers* 32:1 (2004), 183–205.

Vuletić, Dean. 'Gay i lezbijska povijest Hrvatske od Drugog svjetskog rata do 1990', *Gordogan* 1:45 (2003), 104–23.

Wimmer, Andreas and Nina Glick Schiller. 'Methodological nationalism and beyond: Nation-state building, migration and the social sciences', *Global Networks* 2:4 (2002), 301–34.

Wyn, Johanna and Dan Woodman. 'Generation, youth and social change in Australia', *Journal of Youth Studies* 9:5 (2006), 495–514.

Zaharijević, Adrijana. 'Being an activist: Feminist citizenship through transformations of Yugoslav and post-Yugoslav citizenship regimes', *CITSEE Working Paper Series 2013/28.*

Zarkov, Dubravka. 'Feminism and the disintegration of Yugoslavia: On the politics of gender and ethnicity', *Social Development Issues* 24 (2002), 59–68.

Internet files

Barbara Borčić 1982–85, www.galerija.skuc-drustvo.si/textborcic2.html (last accessed 27 February 2014).

'Festival Magnus', http://slovenska-pomlad.si/1?id=168 (last accessed 28 February 2014).

Pavlović, Pavle. 'Otrovni dim Zabranjenog pušenja', www.media.ba/mcsonline/files/shared/Pavle_P.pdf (last accessed 27 February 2014).

'Pioneering as a lifestyle: A conversation with Dunja Blažević', www.bifc-hub.eu/interview/pioneering-as-a-life-style-a-conversation-with-dunja-blazevic (last accessed 9 December 2015).

'Plakatna afera', http://slovenska-pomlad.si/1?id=199&aofs=3 (last accessed 28 April 2016).

'Socialism' (video by Borghesia), www.e-arhiv.org/diva/index.php?opt=work&id=385 (last accessed 25 February 2014).

UN Commission on Human Rights, *Conscientious Objection to Military Service*, 10 March 1987, E/CN.4/RES/1987/46, www.refworld.org/docid/3b00f0ce50.html (last accessed 6 May 2013).

Velikonja, Nataša, '20 festivalskih let', www.ljudmila.org/siqrd/fglf/20/20let.php (last accessed 2 January 2014).

Virtual Museum of Avantgarde, www.avantgarde-museum.com/en/museum/collection/authors/sven-stilinovic~pe4572/ (last accessed 7 May 2014).

'Yugoslavia: Criminal Code of the Socialist Federal Republic of Yugoslavia', www.refworld.org/docid/3ae6b5fe0.html (last accessed 1 March 2014).

'Yugoslavia nuclear chronology', *Nuclear Threat Initiative*, www.nti.org/media/pdfs/yugoslavia_nuclear.pdf?_=1316466791 (last accessed 25 February 2014).

Yurchak, Alexei, 'Mimetic critique of ideology: Laibach and Avia', http://chtodelat.org/b8-newspapers/12–51/mimetic-critique-of-ideology-laibach-and-avia/ (last accessed 28 April 2016).

Other sources

'Poruka Štafete mladosti '87', Museum of the History of Yugoslavija, Belgrade.

Vurnik, Blaž. *Plakatna Afera, 20 Let Potem*. Ljubljana: National Museum of Contemporary History, 2007.

Index

EU authorised representative for GPSR:
Easy Access System Europe, Mustamäe tee 50,
10621 Tallinn, Estonia
gpsr.requests@easproject.com

www.ingramcontent.com/pod-product-compliance
Lightning Source LLC
Chambersburg PA
CBHW052002270326
41929CB00015B/2759